INVESTING IN CAPACITY BUILDING

A Guide to High-Impact Approaches

INVESTING IN CAPACITY BUILDING

A Guide to High-Impact Approaches

by Barbara Blumenthal

THE FOUNDATION CENTER

Printed and bound in the United States of America.

Library of Congress Cataloging-in-Publication Data

Blumenthal, Barbara.
Investigating capacity building : a guide to high-impact approaches / Barbara Blumenthal.
p. cm.
Includes bibliographical references and index.
ISBN 1-931923-65-5 (pbk.)
1. Proposal writing for grants. 2. Nonprofit organizations—Management. I. Title.
HG177.B58 2003
658.15'224—dc22

2003022975

TABLE OF CONTENTS

PREFACE

At the Grantmakers for Effective Organizations conference in March 2000, I met dozens of grantmakers who were enthusiastic about the need for capacity building. Many, however, were disappointed with their initial experiences with grantees and were searching for guidance about how to improve the effectiveness of their capacity building dollars. These discussions led me to investigate the evaluation research on capacity building, delve deeper into the lessons learned from long-standing programs and to identify factors that may explain capacity building effectiveness.

Much of this book describes the work of others who have dedicated themselves to improving nonprofit capacity, many for twenty years and longer. This book would not be possible without the early efforts of grantmakers who sponsored capacity building programs and the consultants and MSOs that delivered support to grantees. I am grateful for the willingness of those profiled in this book to contribute their time, providing background information on their programs and reviewing initial drafts.

Fran Barrett, *Executive Director*
Valyrie Laedlein, *Director of Research, Planning & Evaluation*
Community Resource Exchange

Barbara Kibbe, *former Director, Organizational Effectiveness and Philanthropy*
David and Lucile Packard Foundation

Nancy Roob, *Vice President, Youth Development/Institution and Field Building*
Michael Bailin, *President*
Bruce Trachtenberg, *Director of Communications*
Edna McConnell Clark Foundation

Rachel Liel, *Director*
Shatil New Israel Fund

Madeline Lee, *Executive Director*
New York Foundation

Barbara Lippman, *Culture Program Officer*
The Pew Charitable Trusts

Martin Cohen, *Director*
Philadelphia Cultural Management Initiative

Susan Gross, *Executive Director*
Management Assistance Group

Gail Crider, *Vice President, Community Programs*
National Arts Strategies

Rudeen Monte, *Director*
Community Impact Consulting

Clara Miller, *President*
Daniel Berrett, *Senior Program Associate*
Nonprofit Finance Fund

Acknowledgments

In addition, other grantmakers, consultants, and researchers shared their insights and experiences, and reacted to early drafts of the ideas developed in this book. Although more than a hundred people contributed to the study, I would like thank several who influenced this work: Annemarie Riemer, Carol Lukas, Don Crocker, Mike Allison, Kathleen Fletcher, Deborah Linnell, MaryAnn Holohean, and Mary MacIntyre Hamilton.

Finally, a special thanks to three people who offered detailed and thoughtful comments as this work evolved over two years and greatly influenced the ideas presented here. Valyrie Laedlein, Director of Research, Planning and Evaluation, Community Resource Exchange, offered a detailed view of the needs of community-based organizations and the challenges of consulting. Brenda Bodenheimer Zlatin, independent consultant in philanthropy and former Assistant Director of the New Israel Fund, provided the perspective of a funder with a long-standing, deep commitment to building the capacity of its grantees. Finally, Thomas B. Harris is a national consultant with considerable experience helping organizations recognize the need for change, often using a strong financial reality check. His comments and musings always made me think.

Finally, I am grateful to Patricia Taylor, who provided valuable editing assistance, and Rick Schoff of the Foundation Center, who added his own valuable perspective.

PART I

CHAPTER 1

The Need for Capacity Building

The quality of nonprofit management is a widespread and growing concern among the philanthropic community. According to Lester Salamon, "In addition to the fiscal and economic challenges confronting the nonprofit sector at the present time is a third challenge, a veritable crisis of effectiveness. Because they do not meet a 'market test,' nonprofits are always vulnerable to charges of inefficiency and ineffectiveness. However, the scope and severity of these charges have grown massively in recent years."[1]

This concern has led grantmakers to invest substantial sums in nonprofit efforts to build management capacity. Technical assistance grants pay for outside consulting, while general operating support and management development grants can fund internal management costs. In addition, grantmakers have supported the development of a growing community of management support organizations (MSOs) around the country that provide management support to local nonprofits.

These investments in capacity building have shown a marked increase in recent years, not only in absolute dollars, but as a percentage of total grant dollars. According to information reported to the Foundation Center, from 1997 to 2001, a period when total grants grew steadily, technical assistance grants increased from $62 million to $218 million and from 0.8 percent to 1.3 percent of total grant dollars. Similarly, management development grants increased from $60 million to $260 million, and from 0.8 percent to 1.6 percent of all grant dollars. In addition, general operating support increased steadily during this period, reaching 13.6 percent of total grant dollars in 2001.[2]

For some grantmakers, capacity building is simply a new name for what they have been doing for years through technical assistance grants and support for MSOs. For others, capacity building means stepping back from such practices, and making a concerted effort to learn about the impact of prior work, compare approaches, and make adjustments. There seems to be a growing recognition that nonprofit improvement is difficult, and that grantmakers need not only to understand the challenges but to learn from each other. This interest in learning led to the formation of Grantmakers for Effective Organizations (GEO), an affinity group of the Council on Foundations. Founded in 1988, GEO consisted of 360 organizational members in 2003. The purpose of GEO is described in its bylaws:

> . . . to promote learning and dialogue about the effectiveness of nonprofit organizations among funders, about the effectiveness of nonprofit organizations working to build a more just and sustainable society. The organization does this by exploring the wide range of strategies for accomplishing organization-building; and the constructive and catalytic roles funders can play in encouraging and supporting organizational effectiveness among nonprofits.
>
> GEO seeks to support grantmaking nonprofit organizations in increasing their effectiveness, to strengthen the overall practice of organizational effectiveness grantmaking, and to increase attention to organizational effectiveness within the broader foundation and nonprofit communities.

Today, there is much at stake as the interest in helping nonprofit effectiveness has outpaced the field's knowledge of what does and does not work. Despite the growing interest, there are lingering questions about the impact of investments in capacity building. Studies show that results are mixed, and some grantmakers are disappointed in their results, as grantees remain unstable despite years of investments.

It is tempting to attribute the lack of real improvement to the fact that organization change is difficult, and has an inherently low rate of success. Perhaps grantmakers have undertaken this work with unrealistically high expectations. Barbara Kibbe cautions that, "We could easily have a chilling effect on what is a constructive, holistic approach to supporting organizations as well as programs if we set unrealistic expectations by seeming to imply that modest efforts at capacity building should have impacts far beyond their depth or intensity."[3]

It is also tempting to blame external conditions that explain why, despite successful assistance, an organization floundered. In other words, the treatment was effective, but the patient died anyway. A competing explanation, one that should not be ignored, is that some capacity building programs have simply not been very effective. Leaders of GEO express concern that weak results from poorly designed or implemented programs will cast doubt on the value of such investments.

Rather than accepting a modest impact, the field needs to understand the reasons for lack of improvement and develop better approaches. This book offers guidance to improve the impact of capacity building programs. Specifically, grantmakers can design more effective approaches and consultants can provide more effective assistance. While additional funding will improve impact for some, for others more effective programs and consulting can be achieved within the same budget. High-quality capacity building programs are within the reach of all grantmakers, at varying levels of investments.

What is Capacity Building?

Capacity building is defined as actions that improve nonprofit effectiveness. Nonprofit managers are responsible for building capacity, although they may get assistance from consultants or others. Grantmakers get involved by developing *capacity building programs* that provide resources to support nonprofits as they work to improve their effectiveness. Capacity building programs are often designed with a specific type of grantee in mind, a particular set of issues to address, or a goal of improving one area of nonprofit performance. Others are more loosely constructed and offer support to any type of nonprofit to address whatever issues will improve performance.

A *sponsor* designs and delivers a capacity building program but does not necessarily fund it. Capacity building programs can be sponsored and funded by a single grantmaker, such as the Organization Effectiveness Grants made by the Packard Foundation. Programs can also be sponsored by an independent consultant, consulting firm, or management support organization, who also solicit funding for the program.

Management support organizations (MSOs) are nonprofits, often supported by a large number of funders, who assist other nonprofits to improve their effectiveness. They provide a range of services from reference materials, training, or opportunities for networking to on-site consulting. Many MSOs provide regional support to nonprofits, such as CompassPoint in San Francisco, Community Resource Exchange (CRE) in New York City, and the Support Center for Nonprofit Management in New York City. Other MSOs, such as National Arts Strategies and the Environmental Support Center, generally confine their assistance to one program area and support nonprofits across the country.

Capacity building support can address management practices, provide financial resources, or both. For some nonprofits, additional resources are all that is needed to become more effective. While many nonprofits *seem* to suffer from "poor management"—tasks not getting done, poor planning or poor communication—the cause may be lack of staff, equipment, or even office space. An effective capacity building intervention may be as simple as funding an assistant director position or providing additional overhead funds. Grantmakers can provide extra resources in a variety of ways: providing loans, grants for capital projects, funds for administrative staff, or funds for technology.

While additional resources can be valuable, or even critical, to a nonprofit's effectiveness, they are not particularly difficult to implement. If a nonprofit needs an assistant director, providing funds for the position solves the problem (at least until this funding runs out). A far greater challenge comes from trying to improve a grantee's management practices. This type of capacity building relies heavily on outside consultants who can help in a variety of ways, such as building the staff's knowledge and capabilities in specific management areas, helping design systems and procedures, improving decision processes, facilitating discussions, coaching leaders, and resolving conflicts.

This book focuses specifically on capacity building programs that seek to improve nonprofit performance by improving management practices. Such programs are widespread, but they present very difficult challenges. For nonprofit leaders, organization change can prove a daunting undertaking, even for highly skilled leaders. For consultants, the challenge is to bring their expertise to bear on issues that have to be solved by others. And for grantmakers, the challenge is to entice grantees to undertake capacity building work, which is only successful if grantees are motivated. Overall, improving management practices can be quite a challenge for all involved.

In general, having a goal of management improvement is not a sign of weakness, but a sign of organizational strength. All organizations, commercial as well as nonprofit, need to make adjustments to their structures and systems, acquire new skills and capabilities, and adjust their strategies in order to be effective. Excellent organizations constantly seek to improve program implementation, develop new resources or address unmet needs in the community.

At the same time, it should not be surprising that the nonprofit world includes many organizations that lack important management capabilities, largely because some nonprofit leaders come into these positions without much experience or training in management. A lack of management experience is not a fatal shortcoming, however, as there are far more important skills and talents that nonprofit leaders bring to their organizations: expertise in a program area, knowledge of the community, respect of community leaders, access to a network of resources, strong interpersonal and negotiation skills, a compelling vision, and the ability to persuade others to join in their effort. Management skills and capabilities can be learned, particularly if capacity building support is available.

Defining Nonprofit Effectiveness

The goal of capacity building is to help nonprofits become more effective, but there are different views about what constitutes an effective nonprofit. For some, effectiveness is viewed as a set of organization capabilities, practices, and behaviors. The David and Lucile Packard Foundation describes its view of effectiveness:

> Organizational effectiveness is difficult to define precisely and impossible to reduce to a set of attributes or activities. It is a rich blend of strong management and sound governance that enables an organization to move steadily toward its goals, to adapt to change, and to innovate. The pursuit of organizational effectiveness means continuous learning and improvement in the management of resources and the coordination and leadership of people. It assumes clarity of vision and alignment of goals and activities with that vision. It embraces the importance of defining hoped-for outcomes and the need to measure progress toward achieving those outcomes. And, it implies periodic reflection and critical self-assessment to reevaluate the organization's role in the context of an increasingly complex and ever-changing society.[4]

GEO has developed a working definition of organizational effectiveness: the ability of an organization to fulfill its mission through a blend of sound management, strong governance, and a persistent rededication to achieving results. This definition focuses on fulfilling mission as an outcome and a set of capabilities to achieve it, although the capabilities are a bit vague ("sound management," "strong governance").

For this book, improved effectiveness is defined in terms of organization performance, *not* as a set of management capabilities or practices. Thus, an organization is not more effective because it has a strategic plan; it is only more effective if the planning process leads to specific outcomes such as better program outcomes, expanded programs, or a more stable organization. Similarly, a board is not more effective just because it has a higher attendance rate at meetings. A board is more effective if the organization's performance improves as a result of the board's actions.

There is also considerable debate over how to assess nonprofit performance. For this analysis, four aspects of performance are defined. Acknowledging that capacity building programs may be designed with very different goals in mind, "improved performance" may describe improvements in one or more of the following aspects of performance.

Organization stability. At the very least, an effective organization must consistently *deliver* its programs and services and *survive* over the longer run. Delivery requires management systems to attract and retain staff and organize the work. A stable organization is able to adapt to changes in funding or community needs. It also attracts sufficient resources, both financial and volunteer, to continue to operate. If financial support for the organization's mission has declined, the organization must be able to adjust the level of programs and services accordingly. The most basic measure of organization stability is whether an organization survives, and whether programs and services have consistently been delivered.

Financial stability. Financial stability protects organizations from going out of business due to unexpected short-term events. Financial stability refers to short-term survival, while organizational stability is concerned with attracting resources for long-term survival. Organizations can be considered financially stable if they have sufficient working capital to meet normal fluctuations in cash flow and sufficient reserves to meet capital needs, such as building maintenance and replacement. One measure of financial stability is working capital as a percentage of the total budget. Capacity building work often ignores this area of performance.

Program quality. The consistent delivery of programs and services does not guarantee that programs will be of high quality. Particularly for social services, quality can only be determined by assessing a program's long-term impact. But very few programs have such information, so surrogate indicators of program quality are needed, such as whether: 1) a program design is based on research about effective programs; 2) a system for outcome measurement is in place that provides management with short- and intermediate-term measures of performance; 3) management uses such data to make improvements to program implementation and design. An organization using all three management practices is much *more likely* to have high-quality programs. Here again, program quality is a neglected goal of much capacity work.

There is also a connection between organization stability and program quality, as it is unlikely that a program will have a long-term impact unless it has been consistently implemented for three years or longer. Thus, a stable organization is a prerequisite to high-quality programs.

Organization growth. Attracting additional resources and providing more programs and services can be an indicator of an effective organization. Too often, however, organizations suffer from unhealthy growth that leaves them financially unstable and hurts program quality. Growth alone, then, is not a useful indicator without taking into account financial stability and program quality. At the same time, an organization need not grow to be considered effective. Both stable and growing organizations can be considered effective, whereas decline may indicate ineffective performance.

Research Background

Much of the data and conclusions in this book are derived from two sources of information: 1) an analysis of existing research on capacity building and related topics, and 2) interviews with experienced capacity builders. The author's review of research included over 100 articles on organization effectiveness and organization change, many from the field of Organization Development. In addition, more than thirty evaluations of capacity building were reviewed. Evaluations provide important information about programs, challenges, and outcomes. Many programs report that change is disappointing based on short-term evidence, and describe plans to improve impact. From this analysis, the author developed preliminary hypotheses about factors that influence capacity building impact, and incorporated them into interviews with capacity builders about their experiences.

Interviews with Capacity Builders

The second source of information for this analysis is interviews and background discussions with more than a hundred individuals experienced in capacity building work—primarily foundation staff, intermediaries who design programs, and consultants who provide assistance to nonprofits. An initial round of interviews, conducted from October 1999 through December 2000, provided an important "view from the field" that helped shape the rest of the research and the structure of this book. Additional interviews were conducted between mid-2001 and January 2003.

In general, questions were asked about the details of program implementation, program effectiveness, evaluation methods, lessons learned, program improvements, and continuing challenges. Experienced capacity builders were asked about their successes and failures—grantees that achieved significant improvement, and those that failed to make progress. A variety of possible explanations were examined: the impact of external conditions, grantee conditions and capabilities, actions of the consultant, actions of the sponsor, and consulting skills and experience.

Thirty capacity building programs were studied in greater depth, many with long histories and approaches that have evolved over time. From these programs, a typology was developed of three general approaches to capacity building, designated as Capacity Grants, Development Partners, and Structured Programs. Nine programs were selected to illustrate these general approaches.

The initial round of interviews revealed strong views about what works, and significant disagreement among experienced capacity builders about program design and impact.

- Some sponsors designed alternative approaches because they view popular approaches as largely ineffective. These sponsors are skeptical of the claims offered by some grantmakers about their impact with grantees. Either evidence from these programs has not been offered, or they find it unconvincing.
- Many considered the quality of consulting to be uneven, and responsible for poor results.
- Some believe that the consulting approach has a strong impact on client progress, apart from the consultant's skills and knowledge. Several sponsors were using a consulting approach that they believe differs from traditional consulting, and is more effective.
- Interviews also revealed two opposing views of organization change: that change is a simple process, and that change is complex. This perspective on change influenced not only the design of capacity building programs, but views about effective consulting.

Through these interviews, it became clear that to understand a capacity building program, it is most important to uncover the assumptions and beliefs about organization change, organization effectiveness, and consulting effectiveness that underlie the design and implementation of any program. Chapter 2 lays the groundwork for this by summarizing relevant research on characteristics of effective organizations, the dynamics of organization change and improvement, and research on consulting. Chapters 3 through 5 present rich descriptions of nine capacity building programs, with an emphasis on the logic that underlies each approach, and describes challenges, improvements, lessons learned, and evidence of impact.

Chapter 6 describes an approach—called Developmental Consulting—that the author believes is better suited to capacity building. This approach arises from research on organization change, and is consistent with the consulting approach used by several programs highlighted in Chapters 4 and 5. Chapter 7 describes important issues for grantmakers or sponsors to consider when designing an approach to capacity building, and goes beyond capacity building programs per se, to describe other grantmaker practices that promote grantee capacity. Finally, Chapter 8 presents conclusions for the philanthropic field to consider.

What the Book Promises

- Help grantmakers and sponsors develop more effective capacity building programs;
- Help consultants learn techniques that promise to improve their impact with clients;
- Help nonprofit managers obtain more effective assistance;
- Improve the impact of the limited dollars available for capacity building.

Notes

1. Lester M. Salamon, 1999, p. 173.
2. Foundation Center, *Foundation Giving Trends: Update on Funding Priorities*, 2003 edition.
3. Correspondence with Barbara Kibbe, December 17, 2002.
4. David and Lucile Packard Foundation, Organizational Effectiveness and Philanthropy Program Guidelines.

CHAPTER 2

Research on Nonprofit Effectiveness and Improvement

To truly understand an organization, try to change it. —Kurt Lewin

Capacity building presumes that someone—grantmaker, consultant, or nonprofit leader—has a point of view about how to improve a nonprofit's performance. But what is the basis for this view? It seems that much capacity building assistance is based largely on common-sense notions about good management, popular management books, and assessment tools. Proponents of capacity building recognize this gap in knowledge and have called for additional research. While research specifically on the special management challenges of nonprofits is certainly needed, more than fifty years of research and thousands of empirical studies about organization effectiveness and organization change already exist. This chapter reviews research on two questions central to capacity building.

1. What management practices are common to high-performing organizations?
2. How do organizations improve performance?

It is important for grantmakers, nonprofit leaders, and consultants to understand the strengths and limitations of different types of research so that they can interpret and make use of findings. Thus it may be useful to first discuss what organization research is and how it is carried out.

Organization Research: A Brief Primer

Theories about organizations are tested using either quantitative or qualitative techniques. Quantitative research evaluates data from a large sample of organizations, focuses on a limited number of organization characteristics, and tests whether a particular characteristic (such as the extent of centralization) is related to other factors. Quantitative research is particularly useful for testing which characteristics are associated with organization performance. A strong sample should include both high-performing and low-performing organizations, based on an independent measure of performance or multiple measures of performance. Many management practices are not found to be "significant" predictors of organization success because they are present in both high- and low-performing organizations. For example, if both high- and low-performing organizations have strategic plans, then plans per se will not be a distinguishing characteristic of high-performing organizations.

Researchers are careful not to overstate findings because, even if statistically significant, associations between organizational practices and performance are usually far from perfect. Organizations that exhibit important characteristics do not always demonstrate high performance, and some that deviate greatly from these characteristics attain high levels of performance. While empirical studies provide support that some practices are likely to produce better results, they also remind us that there are many paths to successful performance.

In applying findings from empirical research, practitioners should also be aware that just because a particular practice is associated with higher performance does not mean that it *caused* the improvement. For example, it has always been unclear whether organizations with strong balance sheets spend more on staff training because they can afford to do so, or whether spending additional money on training brings about higher performance. There are relatively few empirical studies that can test for causality. Only studies that include longitudinal data—a snapshot of organization capabilities taken at more than one point in time—can test for a causal relationship.

Most quantitative studies show an association but do not explain how or why a particular factor impacts performance. To be useful to managers, findings should be explained by a well-developed theory or by qualitative, field-based research. Single case studies are most common, but often generate few insights. A study that compares several organizations is better able to highlight factors that can be overlooked with a single case. Would the actions taken by managers be equally effective if the organization had different leadership, strategy, or culture? Would an untried tactic have been even more effective?

The combination of large sample empirical studies and rigorously designed comparative case studies, of both high- and low-performing organizations, provides a solid foundation to draw conclusions about what works. While well-designed empirical research reveals important insights about high performance, less rigorous research is all too common and often misleading. As a result, Karl Weick, a leading organization scholar, observes that "learning is superstitious and misleading, and what appears to be knowledge creation in fact becomes the enlargement of ignorance."[1]

For example, some studies describe the management practices of high-performing organizations based only on a sample of high performers. Many popular books on management are based on such "research." The most famous example is *In Search of Excellence*, a best seller in the mid-1980s written by two very experienced management consultants. They identified a number of factors that were common across a sample of excellent organizations, and held them up as "best practices" to be imitated. The excellent companies, however, did not fare very well after the publication of the book. A follow-up study by academics showed that this sample of firms in fact performed less well than the average firm in the Standard & Poors 500.

High-Performance Organizations

Hundreds of empirical studies have examined the relationship between organization characteristics and performance. Characteristics commonly used in research include: Environment; Mission, Goals, and Strategy; Strategic Planning; Decision Process and Communication; Culture; Control Systems; Structure; Leadership; Human Resource Management; Performance Measurement; and Board of Directors (Figure 1). Research tries to capture important dimensions of each characteristic, such as whether the environment is stable or turbulent; structure is centralized or decentralized; and reward systems are tied to performance. From this body of research, a few central conclusions are important for capacity building.

FIGURE 1. Factors Critical to Organization Performance

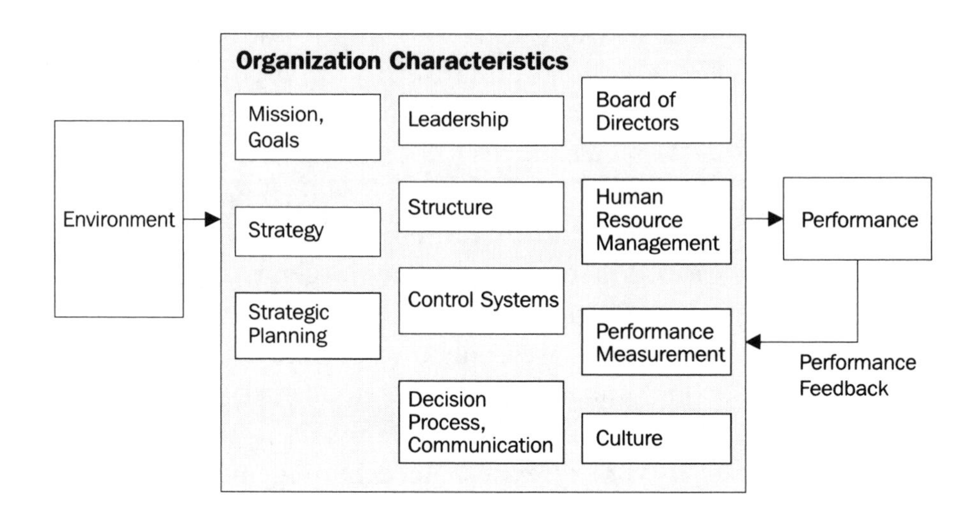

Internal consistency is important. A common finding is that consistency between components of an organization leads to higher performance. For example, a decentralized structure within which frontline staff make decisions is more effective if supported by recruitment and training. Similarly, a fundraising strategy that calls for expanding the pool of individual donors will depend on how actively the board is involved in fundraising.

Many studies show that the consistency, or fit, between components is more important than the choice of any particular component.

The implication for capacity building is that change should be holistic, rather than piecemeal, as any major issue facing the organization may require changes in a number of areas. For example, to improve the financial management of a nonprofit requires more than a new computer system and staff training on how to use it. The senior staff and board should incorporate financial information into their decision process, and leaders must be willing to make difficult decisions based on better financial information. Financial management will not improve unless behaviors and attitudes support the use of new systems.

Culture is central to performance. A consistent finding in organization research is the importance of organization culture. "All areas of the literature: theoretical, anecdotal and empirical suggest that organizational culture is central in determining organizational outcomes, including performance."[2] Organization culture refers to commonly held values, beliefs, and attitudes that shape the behavior of organization members, and is often overlooked by nonprofit managers as an explanation for high performance. There is a strong consensus among researchers that the following practices, behaviors, and attitudes are important to the effectiveness of *any* organization:[3]

Performance matters. High performance begins with the belief that nonprofits *should be* effective at producing outcomes and efficient in the use of resources, and that improvement efforts are worthwhile. Capacity building work often runs into trouble when staff are not enthusiastic about improving performance.

Management by fact. Staff believe that it is important to set goals, collect data, and track progress toward goals. Problem solving is based on valid data.

Open discussions. Staff is comfortable identifying problems and raising issues, even when they might prove embarrassing to the organization, particularly its leaders. Honesty and candor are highly valued. Conflict is managed, not suppressed or avoided. Efforts are made to uncover disconfirming data and contrary opinions. The use of power has a powerful impact on openness.

The autocratic use of power can create risk-averse behaviors and ineffective problem solving.

Problem solving. Effective problem solving has several steps: identify problems; analyze root causes; develop solutions to address the most important causes; implement solutions; and evaluate progress. It relies heavily on the use of data to identify problems and evaluate solutions. Nonprofits that do not collect data engage in problem solving based on intuition, and are often less effective.

Learning. Learning is more proactive than problem solving, as the organization does not wait to be confronted with a problem. Organization learning requires an investment of time to evaluate failures and even to question how successful efforts could be improved. Groups that value learning set aside time to reflect on how well they are performing.

Demonstrate effectiveness. Not all nonprofit managers consider it important to demonstrate the effectiveness of their work, and believe it is enough to undertake enormously difficult and challenging work, such as fighting the causes of poverty and racism. They do "good work," but should not be held accountable for proving it. Managers who believe it is important may well be more effective because the process of asking questions about effectiveness leads to learning and improvement.

Focus on the future. Efforts to improve financial stability and organization stability are based on the belief that it is important to have sustainable organizations. While all managers face time constraints, managers choose to take time away from the demands of daily operations to focus on the future.

The choice of how to allocate current funds pits the desire to help people today against the desire to have a sustainable program or organization. An organization's financial situation provides important evidence of management's future orientation. Managers focused only on the present may find it acceptable to devote every available penny to delivering the current program, without putting funds aside for working capital, building maintenance, or emergency purposes.

Willingness to make tough decisions. To improve performance, nonprofit leaders may be faced with unpleasant decisions, such as reducing or closing a program, providing candid feedback to staff on job performance, or even terminating an under-performing employee. Some leaders simply do not believe that these steps should be necessary in a nonprofit organization.

There is no simple recipe for management success. Much has been learned about the role of structure, decision processes, and other characteristics—how they relate to environmental conditions, how they relate to each other, and their effect on performance. The most important conclusion about which factors are associated with high performance is that *it all depends*. Studies frequently show that the impact of a particular organization component is contingent on some aspect of the organization's context—the environment, strategy, size of the organization, or type of work. For example, the most effective organization structure depends on the rate of change in the environment or the size of the organization, and may differ by industry or sector. No particular strategy, structure, or control system is correlated with high performance in every situation, across all studies, which means there are no hard and fast rules. This body of research suggests that designing and managing organizations is complex.

While research has generated a great deal of knowledge and insights about individual components of organizations and how they relate to performance, it is difficult to summarize succinctly, and beyond the scope of this book. To learn more about organization design, consultants and nonprofit managers can consult review articles summarizing research on a particular topic,[4] or refer to a general organization theory textbook that reviews research in the field.[5]

There are multiple patterns of effective management. Another general conclusion from research is that there is no single best way to manage, even for similar organizations. While research identifies management practices that are ineffective in a given situation, there is often more than one pattern of effective management.

One reason that multiple patterns of effectiveness are possible is that organizations present managers with paradoxes. As managers take actions to improve effectiveness—such as introducing more rules and procedures to achieve greater coordination—they solve one organizational issue while creating new ones. For example, an increase in rules may well lead to better coordination, but can also lead to lower levels of innovation and adaptability. An alternative is to use frequent face-to-face meetings, strong cultural norms, and a common understanding of goals, but such practices require significant time of leaders and staff. Rules and procedures may well be more expedient.

Bob Quinn describes two important dimensions of organizations that present competing demands on managers: internal versus external focus; flexibility versus control. Using these two dimensions, Quinn describes the competing values framework, which highlights four different views of effectiveness.

FIGURE 2. Competing Values Framework: Effectiveness

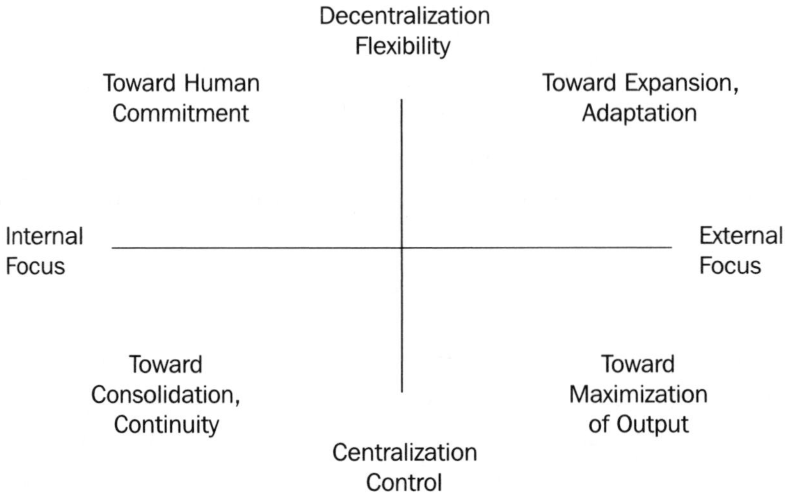

Decentralization
Flexibility

Toward Human
Commitment

Toward Expansion,
Adaptation

Internal
Focus

External
Focus

Toward
Consolidation,
Continuity

Toward
Maximization
of Output

Centralization
Control

These views of effectiveness seem to conflict:

> We want our organizations to be adaptable and flexible, but we also want them to be stable and controlled. We want growth, resource acquisition, and external support, but we also want tight information management and formal communication. We want an emphasis on the value of human resources, but we also want an emphasis on planning and goal setting. The model does

> not suggest that these oppositions cannot mutually exist in a real system. It suggests, rather, that these criteria, values, and assumptions are oppositions in our minds. We tend to think that they are very different from one another, and we sometimes assume them to be mutually exclusive.[6]

An organization that neglects any one of these quadrants is unlikely to succeed over the longer run. Empirical research using this model shows many patterns of effective organizations, each with different strengths. While each dimension is helpful to performance, too much of any dimension can lead to "ineffective" patterns. Rather than thinking of organization design choices as "solutions" or "best practices," this research emphasizes that managers have to resolve competing pressures in order to achieve high performance.

In a comprehensive review of management research, Andrew Pettigrew reaches a similar conclusion:

> Overall, a general message emerging from the literature in this chapter is that there are no universal solutions; no 'magic bullets'. The way forward lies in customization. This is manifest in the move away from a search for a universal blueprint for leadership, a retreat from the idea of 'optimal' organizational structures for delivering high performance, a de-emphasis of 'best-practice' in organizations in favour of good alignment and 'fit' between different configurational parts of the organization (and indeed, between the organization and its environment).[7]

Implications for Nonprofit Management

As yet, relatively few empirical studies have focused on nonprofits. A number of studies have examined one aspect of management—such as the board of directors or strategic planning—and have drawn conclusions about effective practices. Much more work is needed to identify patterns of effective nonprofit management that will offer managers insights for organizations of different size, stage of development, and type of services. At this point, the best guidance for managers comes from the small body of research on nonprofits, and the much larger body of work on organizations in general.

Even without strong empirical evidence, nonprofit managers are offered advice—in books, articles, assessment tools, and from consultants—about steps to improve performance. Much of the advice focuses on formal planning processes, formal procedures, and documentation as the keys to better management. Organization research suggests that organization culture may be far more important to effective performance than this advice would suggest. Two separate research studies have found that some of the conventional wisdom is, in fact, not helpful to improving performance.

Thomas Holland has conducted considerable research on nonprofit boards, and describes the origin of advice on managing boards:

> On closer inspection, however, it is apparent that most of this literature is based almost entirely upon individual experience and opinion, tends to be exhortative rather than empirical, is more anecdotal than systematic, and provides a limited basis for understanding the problems or improving the practices of governance. The advice of a few observers of boards tends to stress idealized, even romanticized, versions of what boards should be (for example, Carver, 1990), while others include important details about budgets, planning, or other functions, but offer little help on how the board can assess its performance or take purposive action to become more effective as a group.[8]

Holland developed an instrument for assessing board effectiveness and tested whether the questions were useful in discriminating between boards with high and low performance. After considerable effort and revisions, he developed a set of questions that *are* associated with performance. Other than Holland's Board Self-Assessment Questionnaire (BSAQ) instrument for assessing board effectiveness, few self-assessment tools have been validated in this manner.[9] With other assessment tools, managers should note that there is often no empirical evidence that the factors selected (which are often very prescriptive) will lead to higher performance.

Another study demonstrated that for a cross section of health and welfare organizations, the conventional wisdom about "correct practices" does *not* relate to performance. A group of nonprofit practitioners (executives, technical assistance providers, and funders) were asked to identify the criteria they actually use in evaluating the performance of nonprofit organizations.[10] The initial list was reduced to eleven "objective" indicators of effectiveness, which reflect the general view about good management practices in the field.

- Mission statement
- Use of form or instrument to measure client satisfaction
- Planning document
- List of calendar of board development activities
- Description of or form used in CEO performance appraisal
- Description of or form used in other employees' performance appraisal
- Report on most recent needs assessment
- By-laws containing a statement of purpose
- Independent financial audit
- Statement of organizational effectiveness criteria, goals, or objectives
- Board manual

In a sample of 64 nonprofits, the study found that "correct procedures" are not related to organization effectiveness. It seems that indicators commonly considered important by nonprofit practitioners are not robust. If there are factors that predict organization effectiveness, they are missing from the list.

Culture may help to explain why functional capabilities viewed by many as important are not linked to performance. Holland's research reached the same conclusion, as he found that board practices and behaviors were key to understanding board effectiveness, rather than formal procedures and systems. Strategic planning provides a useful example of the importance of practices and behaviors. Research has found that whether a nonprofit has engaged in strategic planning is often not correlated with performance.[11] A possible explanation is that organizations develop plans that are not of high quality, or are never implemented.

Conclusions about High Performance

- In effective organizations, internal components are consistent.
- Organization culture—specific behaviors, practices, and attitudes—contributes to effectiveness.
- Research findings offer important insights, but not a simple recipe for management success.
- For a given organization, there are often several patterns of effective management.
- Much of the advice offered to nonprofit managers has not been tested empirically.

Rather than simply encouraging nonprofit managers to undertake strategic planning, it might be more useful to focus on the factors that make a strategic planning process effective: Did the organization candidly assess its own program outcomes? Do organization managers and staff ask whether the programs are effective and how they might be improved? Do managers and staff learn from research on program impact and model programs that have demonstrated long-term impact? Are organization leaders actively assessing external trends related to the program? Is feedback from clients solicited?

Similarly, the key to useful strategies and adaptability is not the yearly (or twice a decade) planning process, but whether the organization thinks and acts strategically on a daily basis. Do staff seek out model programs? Collect and use data about program impact? Constantly question what factors are critical to impact and how to increase those factors? Question whether limited resources are being used most productively? Such "strategic behaviors" may be better indicators of effectiveness than simply asking about "management artifacts" such as strategic plans.

Improving Organization Performance

Knowledge about effective management practices is not easy to put into practice. To improve performance, organization leaders begin with an image of how the organization should function—which structures, decision processes, systems, or cultural norms will make the organization more effective. But even with a clear idea of what to change, leaders often find that building new capabilities is a daunting challenge.

Researchers have long recognized that it is easier to describe a high-performing organization than to create one. After extensive research on effective organization structures, Nohria and Ghoshal caution managers that putting these important findings into practice promises to be difficult:

> None of the foregoing analysis should be interpreted to imply that adopting the optimal organization form for a company is a simple or seamless process. . . . Managers must possess a profound understanding of the business environment in which they are operating to decide which organization form is most appropriate for addressing the challenges of the particular environment. Even if a manager successfully identifies the ideal type of structure the firm needs, achieving the institutional change necessary to implement it presents an additional obstacle. Selecting the appropriate structure is not an easy task; learning to manage it may be just as difficult.[12]

Research on organization change has generated important insights for both managers and consultants. Five conclusions are particularly relevant to the work of building the capacity of nonprofits: 1) underlying issues must be recognized; 2) the difficulty of change needs to be understood; 3) client readiness should be evaluated; 4) the change process should be managed; and 5) active leadership is crucial.

1. Underlying Issues Must Be Recognized

When nonprofit leaders seek help, the issue that they identify to the consultant (the presenting issue) is often a symptom of deeper, underlying issues. Projects that fail to address important underlying issues either never get off the ground, or don't improve performance.

Common presenting issues include fundraising, strategic planning, information systems, personnel policies, or supervisor training. Yet consultants often discover other problems—the mission is unclear, the board is not engaged, leaders avoid discussing external threats or assessing program impact. Some issues become obvious to the consultant, but are embarrassing and threatening to nonprofit leaders. Leaders may not want to bring up political conflicts, ineffective management skills or style, or poor interpersonal relationships among the leaders. Even if raised by the consultant, leaders may be unwilling to address such issues.

Improvements often fail because of underlying political and cultural conflicts. Organization leaders and consultants can be more effective if they anticipate political and cultural issues and learn how to manage resistance.

Political conflicts. If a power struggle is already present, an improvement project can easily become a lightning rod for the conflict. In other situations, the improvement effort itself triggers political conflicts. In either case, political issues need to be resolved before improvement work can begin.

Political conflict can transform a "rational" intervention like strategic planning into a useless exercise. One nonprofit engaged in a lengthy (and expensive) strategic planning process that did not resolve conflicting views or lead to program changes. The disagreement between two senior leaders was less about strategic direction than who had greater power and influence. Power struggles cannot be addressed by planning, hence this strategic planning exercise was doomed before it got started.

External power relationships also impact performance. Many nonprofit organizations are at the center of a diverse community of grassroots volunteers, clients, staff, board members, and grantmakers who bring to bear different skills, interests, and perspectives on issues of common interest. Not only are there differences of opinion on important issues, but many of these diverse groups bring differing types of power to the relationship. Volunteers can withdraw their labor if they don't like the nonprofit's direction or policies; supporters can withhold contributions. While political conflicts occur in all organizations, the diffused nature of power may make nonprofit actors less willing to defer to central authority and more willing to assert their positions. Any disaffected group—community members, advocacy groups, and even staff—can appeal to board members, grantmakers, political figures, and even the press to influence decisions.

Political resistance can, and often does, thwart changes intended to improve performance. At a private boarding school, for example, a headmaster was named to improve the academic standing of the school. When he tried to hire new teachers in the weakest department and force the early retirement of several longtime faculty, there was an outpouring of resistance from other faculty, parents, and alumni directed at members of the board of trustees. An important cultural value of the school—personal relationships and loyalty—was at the heart of the resistance, and turned out to be more important than academic excellence. In trying to change the culture of the school, the headmaster had not counted on the power of the faculty and alumni to stop specific changes. Eventually, he was replaced.

An improvement project can result in a shift of power that enhances the organization's effectiveness, but the process is rarely smooth. In one national nonprofit, leaders of a local chapter refused to implement a rather benign technical improvement to the accounting system. At the heart of the dispute was an effort by field units to increase their influence over headquarters strategy. The organization reassessed the respective roles and authority of the headquarters and field units and decided on a new relationship that provided adequate central coordination while encouraging local initiative.

Cultural change. Improvement programs often call for the introduction of new practices and behaviors throughout the organization. New practices may conflict with existing values, beliefs and attitudes in the organization, resulting in anything from lukewarm enthusiasm to outright hostility. Managers and staff may be uncomfortable comparing their program to others and questioning how it could be better; setting measurable goals, tracking progress, and using data to make decisions; or thinking about the long-term implications of decisions and developing multiyear financial plans.

Research on large-scale change programs undertaken in the private sector, such as total quality management and reengineering, not only document that such programs often fail, but cite culture as a major reason. A survey conducted by CSC Index, the consulting firm that introduced the reengineering concept, found that 69 percent of the firms surveyed in the U.S. and 75 percent of the European firms had engaged in at least one reengineering project.[13] Yet, 85 percent of those firms found little or no gain from the change program. The authors concluded that failed programs were treated as a technique or change program, while successful programs integrated reengineering with an overall program that addressed the organization's direction, values, and culture.

Other studies confirm that long-term change and performance improvement depend on cultural change. According to organization scholars Cameron and Quinn, "Although tools and techniques may be present and the change strategy implemented with vigor, many efforts to improve organization performance fail because the fundamental culture of the organization remains the same; i.e., the values, the ways of thinking, the managerial styles, the paradigms and approaches to problem solving."[14] They go on to explain why culture is so critical:

> This dependence of organizational improvement on culture change is due to the fact that when the values, orientations, definitions, and goals stay constant—even when procedures and strategies are altered—organizations return quickly to the status quo. . . . Without an alteration of the fundamental goals, values, and expectations of organizations or individuals, change remains superficial and short term in duration.

An organization's existing culture is often implicit, and the cause of resistance may be unclear to all concerned. When faced with uncomfortable change, members will identify a number of "rational" objections that hide what is largely an emotional response. By facing and working through these conflicts, staff can often figure out how to remain true to their values while increasing performance. By ignoring cultural resistance, leaders find that planned improvements are never fully implemented, or don't lead to improved performance.

Capacity building is based on the notion that effectiveness, efficiency, and performance improvement are important goals. In contrast, some board members, staff, and volunteers view planning, priorities, and the collection of data as "business practices" that are not to be trusted.[15] Conflict often arises when leaders decide to invest in programs that have the greatest impact and eliminate less effective programs. Few issues are more gut wrenching for nonprofit staff than a decision to stop programs that benefit some or perhaps all of their clients. Less effective programs may be the only ones available to a "difficult to serve" population. One women's shelter developed a transition program to provide job skills and education to women likely to reenter the workforce. Eligibility criteria were based on a careful study of successful participants. Some longtime members of the staff were deeply troubled that some of the neediest women thereby became ineligible, and did not agree with the new focus on effectiveness. As a result, several staff left the program.

2. The Difficulty of Change Needs to Be Understood

The overwhelming conclusion from studies of organization change is that most planned change efforts fail. More worrisome is the finding that interventions can be successful in the short term, but not produce lasting change. Thus, successful projects and satisfied consulting clients are not good indicators of capacity building success. Fortunately, not all projects are difficult, and the success rate can be quite high for simple, technical projects.

The following issues indicate a higher degree of difficulty:

Power. Involve a shift of priorities and resources; change in responsibilities and reporting.

Management style. Require a change in the way key managers (the founder, board chair, or executive director) perform their jobs.

Behaviors, practices. Require a change in the way groups of managers and staff perform their jobs; require new behaviors and/or new skills.

Culture. Challenge widely shared beliefs and assumptions.

Values. Changes are based on values that appear to conflict with other organizational values.

Difficult conditions require a more sophisticated understanding of the change process by both consultants and managers. An important question for capacity builders is whether a particular project is difficult and calls for a consultant with more sophisticated skills. Experienced consultants report, however, that cultural and political issues can be lurking below the surface even in seemingly simple technical projects.

3. Client Readiness Should Be Evaluated

A motivated client can tackle even the most difficult change conditions and succeed. Equally important, when the client lacks internal motivation, there are few techniques or interventions an outsider can use to help. According to Marvin Weisbord, a leading scholar and consultant, "I also believe we can consult only under relatively narrow circumstances: where a client leader is willing to stick his or her neck out, where there is a pressing organizational dilemma, where some people are already searching for a way out."[16] Weisbord goes on to use the model of a "four-room apartment" developed by Swedish social psychologist Claes Janssen that describes how individuals deal with change.

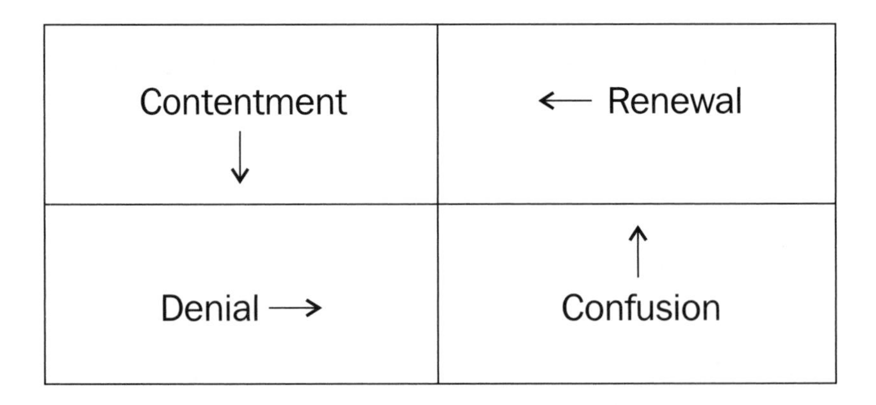

> In Contentment we like things the way they are. If somebody 'helps' us we may start with good-natured acceptance and soon turn our backs on the helper if pushed to do something new. We may even be thrown by the helper into denying that the offer of help is a problem. In Denial we repress feelings of anger, fear, anxiety brought on by change, pretending everything's okay. If we become aware of and own our feelings, then we move into Confusion. In that room we admit openly that we don't know what to do, are worried, upset, unsure. We are helpable. In Renewal we become aware of more opportunities than we can actualize. Working through that (good) dilemma puts us back in Contentment.

> Janssen's concept struck me as a useful diagnostic tool, the simple way of assessing 'readiness.' We can't consult to people in Contentment or Denial. We should not even try. The best we can do is validate people's right to be there. The room hospitable to flip charts, models, and rational problem solving is Confusion. And we might be helpful in Renewal if we're fast enough with new ideas and can keep up with the clients.[17]

Readiness is a dynamic concept that begins with a willingness to seek help, engage in a joint diagnosis, and learn about underlying issues; work on issues; and persist in the face of difficult challenges. If changes are not difficult, then clients are more likely to persevere and be successful. If, however, difficult underlying issues are present, then the client's readiness to tackle difficult issues is critical.

In assessing readiness it is important to take into account whether the client is informed and realistic about the challenges facing the organization. Many clients are motivated to improve fundraising, expand programs and services, or improve program impact, but are not well informed about underlying issues, or the work required to achieve their goals. They may be in "confusion" about how to raise more money, but in "denial" about the board's role in fundraising. With a realistic sense of the challenges ahead, the question turns to whether organization leaders are willing to devote sufficient time and are prepared to deal with barriers to change. Painful choices may be required. Despite a strong desire to increase fundraising, leaders may be reluctant to recruit new board members, shift power from the board to staff, or challenge the founder's autocratic management style. Clients may be motivated to seek help, but not enough to do what it takes to improve performance.

A common view of capacity builders is that comprehensive organization assessment is an effective tool to promote readiness and improvement. Some capacity builders rely on formal assessments to stimulate clients to tackle areas where they lack "correct practices." Using formal tools, consultants conduct a thorough analysis of the organization's issues, explain their findings to the client, and offer advice on how to address the issues that emerge. In contrast, organization researchers and many experienced consultants are skeptical about the value of presenting an outsider's diagnosis of organization issues. Instead, they believe that a diagnosis does not deal with the more important question of motivation. Weisbord concludes, "There is no direct connection between the accuracy of a diagnosis and people's willingness to act on it."[18]

4. The Change Process Should Be Managed

Research shows that improvement projects undertaken in similar organizations, for similar reasons, can produce very different outcomes. The difference is the way that leaders manage the change process. Three specific actions can lead to more successful change initiatives: building support, monitoring progress, and learning.

Build Support. If change has a direct effect on large numbers of managers and staff, then it is important to take steps to build support from the outset and to reinforce that support as changes unfold. When improvement is first discussed, it is important for leaders to construct a compelling case for why the change is necessary and how performance will be affected. Building support requires much more than announcing changes and answering a few questions. In some cases it is useful for leaders to engage the organization in developing a future vision that spells out not only long-term goals but specific organization capabilities that will be required to achieve them.

Initial enthusiasm can wane, however, as change becomes personal. Resistance can develop when individuals are asked to report to a new boss or change the way they perform their job. Leaders may need to negotiate with key players, using a combination of logic, persuasion, incentives, and even the threat of sanctions.

Monitor Progress. Research reveals that the greatest challenges lie in implementation, rather than in planning change. Scholars agree that while planning provides an opportunity to build consensus, discuss and anticipate many of the challenges ahead, organization change rarely unfolds according to plan. They conclude that constant monitoring and adjustment are essential to success. Rather than following an elaborate blueprint for change, leaders define a few concrete steps to get the process moving and engage in regular assessment of progress toward goals.

Many changes are inherently difficult and take time. Building new capabilities often requires changes to everyday management practices, group behaviors, and personal management style. An executive director who has been effective at managing fifteen direct reports faces a new challenge when another layer of management is added and he/she now has to learn to manage through five senior staff. While some managers find the transition easy, others do not. Similarly, while it is easy to acknowledge that the board needs to function more effectively and play a greater role in fundraising, it may take several years to reshape the board. Developing new leadership, recruiting new board members, rotating longtime members off the board, and introducing new practices to make meetings more effective all take time and require personal learning and change from each and every board member.

Emphasize Learning. Learning new behaviors and practices requires the active involvement of organization leaders. The key is to make the connection between new behaviors and improved performance, and to point out old behaviors when they occur. Consistent feedback from managers and peers is useful because individuals do not always notice when they revert to old behaviors. One practice is allowing time for reflection so that staff can discuss whether practices are being used effectively, and whether they are working.

Researchers promote "action learning" as a powerful technique not only to change individual behaviors but to develop lasting organization capabilities and improve performance. Action learning is based on the notion that practices and behaviors are best learned when applied to solve real problems. New practices may seem straightforward in a training session, but challenges and complexities become apparent when they are applied to real issues. At first, participants are often unsuccessful and need coaching from managers or consultants to make adjustments. When new practices are effective, participants make a strong connection between practices and results, which eventually changes their underlying beliefs as well. Leaders can create opportunities for action learning by asking staff to identify an important issue and set goals for improvement.

Increasingly researchers find that learning is critical to organization success. "The process of change relies on the development and utilization of less visible organizational capabilities (particularly those concerning learning and change) called intangible assets. [They] . . . believe that an organization's ability to learn and change is the most fundamental of its intangible assets."[19]

Conclusions About Improving Performance

- Change can be difficult, particularly if cultural and political issues are present.
- Client readiness is required for change.
- An accurate diagnosis does not motivate change.
- The change process requires monitoring and adjustment.
- Learning is central to long-term change.
- Active leadership is required.

5. Active Leadership Is Crucial

Research shows that active leadership of the change process is crucial to success. Leaders play a crucial role in building a case for change, diagnosing underlying issues, and anticipating and handling resistance. Only leaders have the power to negotiate political conflicts. Cultural change will not occur without consistent support from the top. Rewards, promotions, and hiring reinforce the new culture, and are only available to those at the top. A study of nonprofit change found that change is more successful when leaders are actively involved.[20]

Internal leadership is crucial to change, yet nonprofit managers may have little training or experience relevant to the challenge. Outside assistance—through leadership development workshops, coaching, or on-site assistance—can be helpful to coach leaders on managing change and improve the odds of success.

The Use of Consulting to Improve Performance

Because consultants have played a major role in capacity building to date, it is useful to examine the record of consulting as a vehicle for producing lasting change. The federal government has provided extensive technical assistance as part of major policy reforms in agriculture, community development, youth development, and education, hoping to change local practice by providing expert knowledge to the front lines. Some government initiatives were subjected to extensive research on long-term impact. The history of government-sponsored technical assistance is particularly relevant to capacity building programs, in which a three-party relationship develops between local providers, consultants, and funders.

A recent review of more than fifty years of history with technical assistance strategies reveals that technical assistance often fails to achieve sought-for change. Rand conducted one of the most thorough studies of educational innovation, examining data on 293 local projects funded by four federal education programs.

> The study found that while the federal programs stimulated local education agencies to undertake innovative projects, that participation did not insure successful implementation and successful implementation did not insure continuation of the project over time. . . . The Rand study deemed most of the technical assistance strategies ineffective, especially those that did not respond to the needs and motivations of teachers or the basic conditions of school districts. . . .[21]

The Rand report describes that, "Outside experts were typically ignored because their advice was too abstract, or their awareness of local problems was inadequate. . . . In short, federally supported assistance efforts often were ineffective because they did not deal in an adaptive way with the concrete problems facing local staff."[22]

While the government can insist on evaluations of technical assistance programs, there is no such pressure on private sector consulting. A small band of scholars and independent consultants have raised fundamental questions about the impact of traditional consulting. Yet, private sector consulting is a profitable and growing industry with over $50 billion in revenues. Consultant Jack Phillips describes an all-too-common consulting engagement that fails to bring about any change:

> When the senior staff of the firm objected to the consultants' report, the CEO, who had hired the consultants previously, praised the work of the consultants and suggested their recommendations be adopted. The staff resisted in every way and ultimately did nothing with what was originally planned. The recommendations were never implemented by the senior staff.

> In a reference check by another organization seeking consulting advice, the CEO praised the report and gave the consulting firm very high marks for its efforts. Privately, he said, "Although we did not implement all the recommendations and some were already in planning, it was a good exercise for the organization."[23]

Robert Schaffer, the author of *High Impact Consulting*, agrees that much consulting is ineffective and offers one explanation:

> Throughout our lives, we are trained to depend on the experts to give us the answers. . . . Conventional consulting methodologies reinforce this perception by putting consultants in the lofty role of diagnosticians and solution providers. This mystical faith in what the consultant's magic potions can accomplish often motivates otherwise hardheaded business executives to spend huge sums and considerable time and energy on consulting projects that have no demonstrable connection to bottom-line achievements.[24]

Evidence from both the private and public sectors raises questions about consulting approaches for nonprofits. At the very least, nonprofit consultants and grantmakers should be very careful before adopting practices from private sector consulting or large-scale technical assistance programs. It is clearly *not* safe to assume that if techniques or practices are commonly used, they must be effective. Chapter 6 analyzes why traditional consulting is often ineffective, and suggests an alternative consulting approach that promises to be more effective at improving nonprofit performance.

Notes

1. Weick, 1996, p. 309.
2. Pettigrew, et al., 1999, p. 50.
3. Baldridge National Quality Program, Criteria for Performance Excellence.
4. Forbes, 1998; Stone, et al., 1999; Pettigrew, et al, 1999.
5. Daft, 2001; Bolman and Deal, 1997.
6. Quinn, 1988, p. 49.
7. Pettigrew, et al., 1999, p.118.
8. Holland, 1991, p. 26.
9. Jackson and Holland, 1998.
10. Herman and Renz, 1988.
11. Stone, et al., 1999.
12. Nohria and Ghoshal, 1997, p. 190.
13. CSC Index, 1994.
14. Cameron and Quinn, 1999, p. 9–10.
15. "Technical Assistance & Progressive Organizations for Social Change in Communities of Color," A Report to the Saguaro Grantmaking Board, The Funding Exchange, 1999.
16. Weisbord, 1988, p. 63.
17. Weisbord, 1988, p. 70.
18. Weisbord, 1988, p. 66.
19. Pettigrew, et al., 1999, p. 71.
20. Nutt, 1989.
21. Wahl, et al., 1988, p. 14.
22. Berman and McLaughlin, 1974, p. 38.
23. Phillips, 1999, p. 4.
24. Schaffer, 1997, p. 133.

PART II

Capacity Building Models

Capacity building programs vary greatly in their design and delivery, and undoubtedly in their effectiveness. In Part II, nine capacity building programs are described in some detail, including the sponsors' goals and assumptions about organization change, common challenges, lessons learned, and inherent weaknesses. These programs are used to illustrate three distinct models of capacity building: Capacity Grants, Development Partners, and Structured Programs. Each model is defined first by how it is funded, whether the capacity building assistance is provided through Capacity Grants to individual grantees; through General Contracts to a Development Partner, or through Structured Programs. A related question is whether assistance is delivered by consultants hired in the marketplace, a group of consultants referred to as a "Development Partner," or an intermediary.

Programs using the same approach—similar funding and delivery models—face similar challenges, and often share a common philosophy about how organizations improve.

FIGURE 1. Funding and Delivery Options

Funding Options	Description
Capacity Grant	Funding is provided for a specific capacity building project, often paid directly to the grantee from the grantmaker.
Development Partner	One or more funders purchase a block of consulting time for a designated group of grantees from a consulting group (referred to as the Development Partner), who then provides assistance to the funders' grantees. Typically, grantees seek help from the Development Partner when ready.
Structured Program	One or more funders provide long-term and sometimes comprehensive support to a group of selected grantees. The program often imposes a structured process on grantees, and may include significant financial incentives linked to performance goals.
Delivery Options	
Independent Consultant	A consultant is hired, typically by the grantee, to deliver assistance. Independent consultants, consulting firms, and MSOs compete in the marketplace for consulting contracts.
Development Partner or Intermediary	The sponsor has chosen a group of consultants to provide assistance to grantees. This group is often an MSO. Grantees are often able to exercise some degree of choice in selecting a consultant from the group.

While Capacity Grants delivered by independent consultants are by far the most common capacity building model used, two other combinations are highlighted in the coming chapters—Development Partners and Structured Projects, often delivered by an intermediary. The following table categorizes several well-known capacity building programs, and other specific programs that are described in Chapters 3 through 5.

FIGURE 2. Featured Capacity Building Programs

Capacity Building Approach	Featured Programs	Delivery Method
Capacity Grants	Packard	Consultants
	PCMI	
Development Partner	Shatil/New Israel Fund	Development Partners
	Community Resource Exchange/New York Foundation	
	Management Assistance Group/Ford Foundation	
Structured Program	National Arts Strategies	Intermediary
	Build for the Future℠ (BFF)	Intermediary
	Matrix	Intermediary
	Edna McConnell Clark Foundation	Assistance from funder and consultants

FIGURE 3. Comparison of Nine Capacity Building Programs

	Key Features of Capacity Building Programs				
Capacity Building Examples	**Sponsor**	**Primary Funder**	**Type of Grantee**	**Geography of Grantees**	**Costs per Grantee**
Packard OE Grants	Grantmaker	Packard only	Several sectors, sizes	National	Average $40,000
PCMI OD Grants	MSO	Pew Charitable Trusts	Arts organizations	Philadelphia region	Up to $80,000 for OD grants
Community Resource Exchange	MSO	Several	Community-based	New York City	$10,000 per year
SHATIL	MSO	New Israel Fund	Community-based	Israel	$10,000 per year
Management Assistance Group	MSO	Ford Foundation	Peace and social justice	National	$6,000 per year
National Arts Strategies	MSO	Many Funders	Arts organizations	National	$12,000 to $20,000 per year Plus grants
Build For the Future	MSO	Hayden Foundation	Boys & Girls Clubs	East Coast	$3,000 for support Grants average $194,000
Matrix	Consulting Firm—Community Impact Consulting	Stuart Foundation	Social service organizations	National	$10,000 to $17,500 total cost
Edna McConnell Clark Foundation	Grantmaker	EMC only	Youth development	East Coast	$1–$4 million $250,000 for planning consultants

CHAPTER 3

Capacity Grants

For many grantmakers, a major commitment to building the capacity of grantees begins with offering a new source of funding—Capacity Grants—to pay for improvement projects undertaken with the help of outside consultants. These grants enable motivated grantees to identify an important need and hire consultants for on-site work that would otherwise be beyond their reach. Capacity Grants have been an important capacity building strategy for close to twenty years, and have undoubtedly helped many nonprofits address important issues and improve their performance.

In a conventional approach to Capacity Grants, implemented by many local and regional grantmakers, regular program officers review applications from current grantees for capacity building assistance. Approval is based on information contained in written applications and occasional phone conversations. Program officers look for well thought-out proposals with project workplans, time frames, and budgets, and Capacity Grants are generally considered successful if the project deliverables are met, within budget and on time. Program officers often assume that grantees know what they need and will identify useful projects.

In practice, grantmakers find that it can be difficult to fund projects that will have a lasting impact. An important reason is that grantees are unlikely to reveal important issues that reflect poorly on the organization. Requests tend to stick to safe subjects like strategic planning, fund development, or information technology. Program officers have considerable power over funding for grantees, a fact that cannot be erased by a philosophy of "partnership" or the best of intentions. Grantees have good reason to be cautious. Stories abound of grantmakers who learned of organization issues through capacity building work and decided to eliminate or reduce further program grants. Thus, grantees remain cautious about revealing internal issues, despite pleas for candor.

In addition, program officers often oversee a large number of grants, rarely have time to make site visits, and consequently have few insights about an applicant's internal issues. Some lack training or experience in management topics. It is all too easy for well-intentioned program officers to dispense simplistic advice, steer organizations to adopt "best practices" that are not relevant or important, or offer suggestions in a way that does not lead to real commitment by grantees.

Modified Capacity Grants

While Capacity Grants provide critical support for motivated grantees and have enabled thousands of nonprofits to improve their performance, they have not been uniformly effective. As a result, many grantmakers have adjusted their approach to overcome inherent limitations in these grants, and these are referred to in this book as Modified Capacity Grants. While similar in structure, these grants feature important differences in the way projects are defined, selected for funding, and monitored.

Improve grantee candor and reflection. To improve candor a number of foundations have introduced the position of capacity program officer (CPO), someone who is more involved in the grantee's management issues but does not reveal confidential information to the primary program officers. The degree of confidentiality varies, with some capacity building program officers promising complete confidentiality to grantees, while others share only general information with program officers.

The primary role of CPOs is to review applications for capacity building grants, investigate issues, approve work plans, and monitor progress as grantees receive assistance. CPOs are often selected because of their extensive management knowledge and experience, and may have consulting experience as well. Depending on the workload, some CPOs are able to conduct an assessment of each grantee, including site visits, while others have little information about the grantee other than what they glean from a written application and a couple of phone conversations.

CPOs work hard to improve each grantee's understanding of its own situation and add considerable value to the capacity building process through frank and challenging discussions with grantees. To give the CPO a chance to intervene early and help to shape a more effective project, some ask for a simple letter of inquiry rather than a full-blown project proposal.

CPOs can offer grantees a relationship with a trusted advisor over a long time period. The CPO often keeps in touch with grantees as long as they receive program grants, regardless of whether there is a current consulting project underway. Some executive directors develop a high degree of trust in the CPO and view them as a valuable coach on a wide range of issues.

Provide project flexibility. Funders can reduce the need for project flexibility by requiring every grantee to go through a comprehensive review, and selecting projects that demonstrate a high level of self-awareness. Other grantmakers use two-part Capacity Grants. In the first phase, a consultant is engaged to conduct a complete diagnosis with the client and decide upon a useful project. The nonprofit then applies for the second phase, by presenting a workplan, budget, and timeline. Often the same consultant conducts the assessment and works on the project.

When a project deviates from the workplan, it can be difficult for funders to tell whether the consultant is inept, the client is dragging their feet, or the workplan was naïve. Some grantmakers are more comfortable making adjustments because they know the grantee well and can make an informed decision about whether a change is warranted, or they know the consultants well and trust their judgment. Funders who know neither their grantees nor local consultants face a difficult problem.

Research on Capacity Grants

Some funders view projects as quite effective, while others are disappointed, complaining that grantees are no more stable than before despite having completed several projects. Unfortunately, these conflicting views are based largely on impressions and anecdotal evidence, as few studies have been conducted on the long-term impact of Capacity Grants. Research is needed to answer important questions about the impact of Capacity Grants, such as:

- How often do projects lead to lasting improvements in capabilities and improved performance?
- Under what conditions are projects most effective? What are the characteristics of grantee organizations that benefit the most from assistance?
- What type of projects lead to lasting change? What type of consulting is effective at creating lasting change?

Two exploratory studies shed light on these questions. The Packard Foundation commissioned a study of eleven strategic planning grants, averaging around $40,000,[1] to learn why organizations pursued strategic planning, how planning is carried out, and the plan's impact. Eight of the grantees produced a strategic plan and identified specific improvements arising from the process. The study relied on interviews and observation of six grantees that had completed their strategic planning work about a year before the interviews. Although there is some evidence of immediate changes, it is difficult to draw conclusions about the extent of organization change, or the impact of planning on performance. Also studied were five additional grantees in the midst of a planning process.

Some projects failed to achieve even their short-term goals. Of eleven strategic planning projects, three did not result in a plan, and a fourth plan was judged no longer relevant within a year. In seven of eleven cases, grantees moved forward to implement their plans. A range of short-term changes resulted from the planning process. In a few instances, planning led to a shift in priorities or changes in mission. One nonprofit decided to merge two programs, while another dropped a program area. In most instances, however, the changes were more operational—a decision to hire a full-time director, hire additional staff, upgrade computers, and secure additional resources. Some planning projects also triggered behavioral changes—more productive board meetings and better relations between the board and staff.

The second study, by Kathleen Fletcher,[2] is the only one that looks at long-term changes and performance improvements linked to a specific fundraising Capacity Grant. Fletcher's primary conclusion is that most grantees achieve a great deal for a small amount of money. Fletcher studied 21 projects that were funded by grants from the San Francisco Foundation from 1985 to 1989. Interviews were conducted with both the grantee and the consultant in 1992, three to seven years after the projects were completed. The grants were relatively modest, averaging $4,000 to $5,000, enough to purchase only about ten days of consulting at that time.

While each of 21 nonprofits actually completed a plan, and was judged a success in the short-term, meaningful long-term change was far more difficult. Twenty organizations (involved in 21 projects) developed plans, but only twelve moved ahead with implementation after they were completed. In three additional cases, unanticipated events distracted the organizations for a few years, but leaders eventually began to make progress on the plans. In the six remaining cases, either the leaders never implemented the plan or the plan failed. Of the fifteen plans that were eventually implemented, some led to a dramatic increase in funding and greater diversification of funding sources, while others had a more modest impact. Overall, about half the grantees achieved significant gains, and many of these leaders pointed to the Capacity Grant as the turning point in their organization's development.

FIGURE 1. Studies that Evaluate Capacity Building Impact

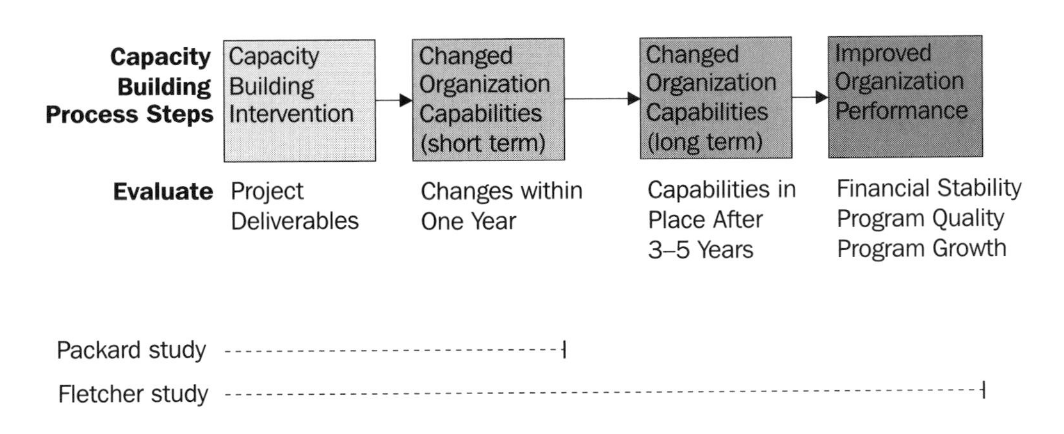

Explanations for Effective Projects

The major conclusion suggested by these studies is that *effective consulting* is critical to long-term change. While each study identified conditions in the grantee organization that make change difficult and projects less likely to succeed, effective consulting was able to recognize and deal with many of these conditions. Effective consulting is less important if grantee conditions are favorable for change, at least in the short term. Finally, other factors can either inhibit or facilitate further change.

FIGURE 2. Factors Affecting Long-Term Improvements in Capabilities and Performance

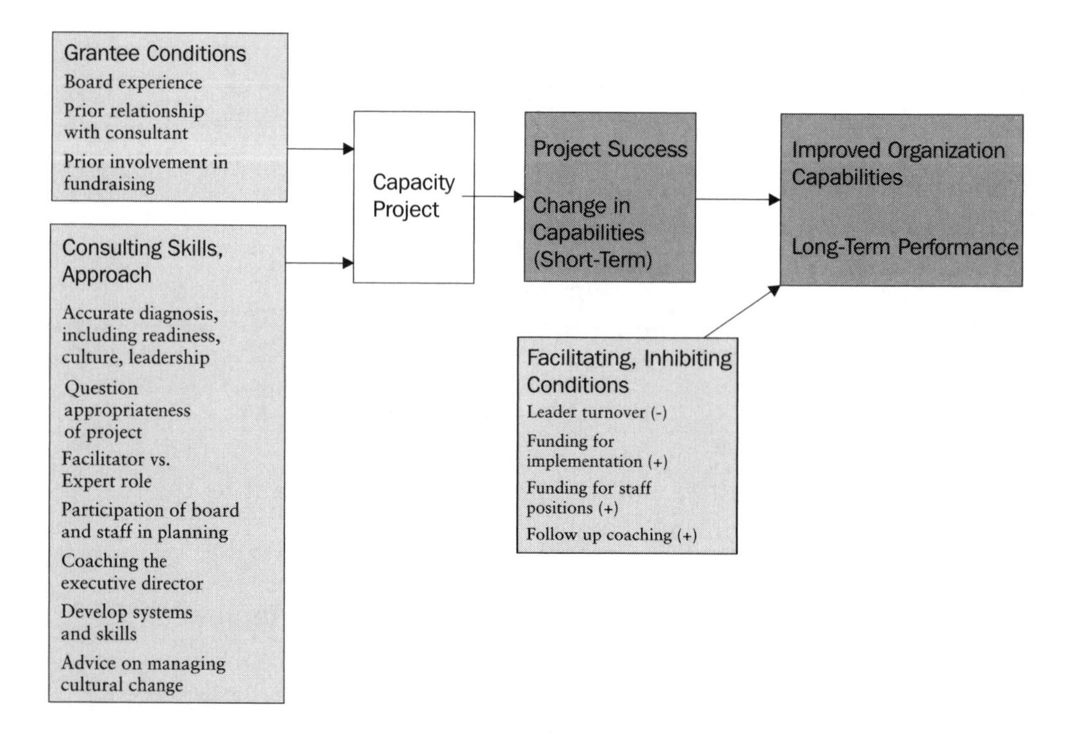

The studies identified six hurdles that prevent projects from achieving long-term success, but also can be overcome by specific consulting practices. These practices help to define important elements of "effective consulting." Two additional hurdles are not influenced by consultants, but also help to explain project success.

1. A weak initial diagnosis often leads to ineffective projects. Consultants that rely on the client to correctly diagnose issues can easily run into trouble once the project begins. Nonprofit leaders often ask for assistance with pressing issues such as fundraising and board development. The project, however, may only deal with symptoms and not root causes. Either the program officer or the consultant can help the client gain a better understanding of the organization's fundamental issues.

The strategic planning study found that less successful projects were primarily due to "weak diagnosis of the organization's needs and whether or not strategic planning was the appropriate tool for the situation." A weak diagnosis was also evident in more successful projects that got off to a shaky start, but were able to produce a plan.

A primary reason for a weak diagnosis was simply the minimal time devoted to it by consultants. The study reports that consultants learned more about the organization when they had effective interviewing skills and conducted multiple interviews. Yet, several consultants simply responded to the client's request and prepared a work plan based on one or two conversations with the executive director.

2. There is little financial incentive to conduct a thorough diagnosis. It appears that consultants have little financial incentive to conduct a thorough diagnosis or to question whether the project defined by the client is right for the organization. Consultants are asked to submit a detailed workplan, timeline, and budget to Packard, based on an initial assessment for which they are not compensated, without any guarantee that Packard will fund the project. If the consultant has doubts once the project is under way, there is little incentive to walk away from a project that the client wants and the funder has approved.

3. Consultants lack skills to conduct an effective diagnosis. Many consultants also lack skills or knowledge to conduct an effective diagnosis. It appears that few independent consultants assess readiness, organization culture, or stage of development in planning the project, assuming instead that an organization is ready to undertake the project as defined by the client. According to the strategic planning study, many consultants did not consider it part of their job to question an organization's motivation for planning or "determine whether the organization's board and staff were capable of and willing to carry out the diverse demands of strategic planning." Also, none of the consultants examined culture as part of their formal assessment, yet culture turned out to play "a vital role, aiding or impeding the planning process and affecting the impact of the plan on the organization." Similarly, in the fundraising study a lack of readiness was an important explanation for failed projects. In four cases, clients concluded (with the benefit of hindsight) that the original concept for the project was wrong because other organizational issues needed to be addressed first. The consultants, however, did not diagnose these issues, and proceeded instead with an inappropriate project.

4. Some nonprofits are not ready for assistance. Organizations were not ready for assistance for several reasons. In the fundraising study, three of six unsuccessful consultations were in relatively new organizations with inexperienced boards, while the boards in four unsuccessful projects had no prior involvement in fundraising. Two boards were unwilling to play an active role in fundraising, and board training was not effective at building commitment to undertake the work.

Why do organizations ask for assistance when they are not ready to benefit? It seems that young boards simply do not understand what is required to improve fundraising. Board education may be necessary before an effective fundraising plan can be developed. There is also evidence that some organizations are responding to pressure from an outside funder to diversify their funding base. In successful fundraising projects, organizations were better informed about the effort required and ready to move to a new level of functioning.

5. Some projects demand consultants with strong organization development skills. A major conclusion from the fundraising study is that most consultants had to be deeply involved in organization development (OD) issues. When faced with lack of sophistication and readiness, some consultants were sensitive to such issues and had the skills to help their clients make progress. Consultants without OD skills were not successful with such clients, although they might have been successful with more sophisticated clients requiring assistance with the more technical aspects of fundraising.

Many clients in the fundraising study were:

> . . . unsophisticated organizations, most with no development staff, overly dependent on one or two sources of funds, and not knowledgeable about what is needed to tap other sources.

> Consultants had to help them clarify roles of the staff and board, work on board development issues, build the organization's case, set up systems for seeking and acknowledging donations, and plan for the future. . . . They had to be extremely sensitive to the level of development at which the organization was functioning and tailor their approach to both the present reality and the future potential of the agency.[3]

Consultants also helped to develop better program descriptions, advised managers on financial management, helped the executive director to think strategically, and provided advice on staff issues.

A key practice of organization development consultants is facilitating clients to solve their own problems. When consultants produced fundraising plans with little involvement and no follow-up assistance, the plans failed or were never implemented. Consultants played this "expert" role in four fundraising cases, three of which were clearly unsuccessful. In the other 17 cases, fundraising plans were developed in collaboration with staff and often the board. Greater contact with the consultant as the plan was being developed also increased board and staff commitment to implementation.

The strategic planning study found that consultants who specialize in strategic planning brought a particular planning process and format to the work and were more likely to be responsible for writing the plan. OD consultants tended to have a more flexible approach, enabling the executive director or board chair to help shape the process and even take responsibility for the writing.

6. Leaders need assistance with implementation. Some consultants help organization leaders try new ideas or tactics, learn new skills or adjust to new roles, preparing organization leaders for the implementation challenges they are likely to encounter. Other consultants concentrate on developing a plan, leaving nonprofits on their own to implement new ideas that emerge. Several examples illustrate how consultants can prepare clients for implementation.

- **Coaching the executive director.** In the strategic planning projects, work plans rarely included time for coaching the executive director, yet in successful projects, executive directors reported that coaching did occur and viewed it as quite valuable.

- **Set up systems.** In several successful fundraising projects, consultants developed a system for some aspect of fundraising—managing individual donors, seeking corporate and foundation gifts, or direct mail. Staff was able to build on what they learned and fundraising results continued to improve.
- **Follow-up coaching.** Two strategic planning consultants suggested a follow-up visit (at six to twelve months) to assess progress and make adjustments, which clients found to be quite useful. The fundraising study also suggests that grantmakers should make extra money available for periodic consultant follow-up.

7. Leader turnover can bring change to a halt. In several fundraising cases a change of executive director occurred, causing the plan to languish or the finished plan to be rejected by the new director. In addition, several nonprofits were not included in the study because no one in the organization remembered the grant. If no one remains who was around at the time the grant was made, and none have heard of the project, it is doubtful that the plans were ever implemented.

8. Insufficient financial resources prevent progress. Additional funding, particularly for paid staff, may be essential to rapid progress. Two organizations received follow-up grants to hire staff or carry out their fundraising plans and achieved significant increases in funding. In one case, it is not at all certain that significant improvement would have occurred without this additional support. Many projects led to a decision to hire a dedicated or full-time development staff, and the number of organizations with development staff increased from three before the projects to 16 several years later. Two nonprofits that did not hire development staff made progress while consultants were helping, but further improvements did not occur once the project was finished.

Modified Capacity Grants

Two examples of modified Capacity Grants programs are presented below. The David and Lucile Packard Foundation provided $11.9 million in Capacity Grants to support 175 Packard grantees in 2000. With assets of $9.8 billion at the end of 2000, Packard provided program grants to about 2,000 nonprofits in six program areas throughout the country. The Philadelphia Cultural Management Initiative offers several types of support to a pool of more than 80 eligible organizations, including a total of $450,000 per year for Organization Development grants. The Philadelphia Cultural Management Initiative was launched by The Pew Charitable Trusts, a Philadelphia-based foundation with $4.8 billion in assets and $231 million in grants (in 2001).

The Packard Foundation's Organization Effectiveness Grants

The Packard Foundation has been helping grantees strengthen their management capabilities since 1983, and was the largest provider of capacity building Capacity Grants until 2002. Packard's extensive experience in providing Capacity Grants is instructive for grantmakers considering this approach. The description that follows focuses on Packard's Organizational Effectiveness (OE) grants and is based on Packard's program prior to 2003, as are the lessons and challenges.

In 2000, almost 10 percent of all Packard grantees, 189 organizations, were awarded an OE grant (grants averaged about $44,000). OE grants are intended to develop "effective management, sound governance, and continuous learning and improvement of our grantees." Packard is looking for "well-defined projects that improve an organization's skills and systems, or help to define new management strategies or structures." Grants are primarily used to cover the costs of outside experts who assist with assessments and planning. Eligible projects include (from program guidelines, 2001–2002):

- Organization assessment and strategic planning
- Board and/or staff development

- Fund development planning and feasibility studies
- Succession planning and executive search services during leadership transitions
- Market research and development of external communications strategies
- Design and implementation of evaluations related to enhancing overall effectiveness
- Mergers or other restructuring efforts
- Assessments, planning or feasibility studies related to the use of technology for management functions within an organization

Packard does *not* provide funding for staff salaries, administrative overhead, computers or other equipment, recurrent staff training expenses, or evaluation of technical programs.

Application/Selection

Because Packard grantees are distributed across the country, the application and selection process is often conducted long distance. In about 10 percent of the cases a face-to-face meeting is possible, either because the grantee is able to come to Packard's office or Packard makes a site visit. Site visits are at the discretion of the program officer, and are usually reserved for potentially large grants or important grantees. Most often, however, Packard relies on written applications, the support of the relevant program officer, and phone interviews to assess a project's potential. The first step for current grantees is to submit an initial two- to three-page letter that addresses four questions:

- Why do you want to undertake your project at this time?
- What do you expect to accomplish?
- In the long term, how do you see this project enhancing the effectiveness of your organization?
- Who from among your organization's staff and board will provide leadership for the project?

Applications are assigned to an OE Program Officer who consults with the primary program officer who awarded the original program grant. If outside assistance is called for, the applicant will be asked to identify a consultant, provide his or her resume and client list, and submit the consultant's work plan, including outcomes, activities, timeline, and a detailed budget. Packard staff provides several resources to help grantees select an appropriate consultant.

Once a work plan is submitted, the OE program officer uses it as the basis to help each applicant think out loud about what they hope to accomplish, and looks for evidence that the grantee has a deep understanding of the issues that need to be addressed as well the effort it will require from both the board and staff. At times, the OE program officer may explore with the applicant ideas for more productive projects. Otherwise, Packard prefers to devote its resources to organizations that are ready and likely to benefit.

OE program officers are able develop relationships with some grantees, often those that undertake more than one project or larger projects. However, the workload of an OE program officer, who might approve 60 grants per year, does not lend itself to developing many deep relationships. The work plan and follow-up discussions complete the application and the OE program officer makes a final recommendation. Other than the initial letter of intent, which can be shown to the primary program officer, OE program grantees maintain a confidential relationship with OE program staff. Discussions with the applicants are not disclosed to other Packard program officers.

Developing Capabilities

When a grant is approved, the grantee hires a local consultant. Packard does not communicate with consultants. Packard requires a final narrative report for each project, and an interim report may be required for large projects, or projects of long duration. OE program officers may also check on important or difficult projects. As the project work proceeds, grantees initiate contact when they need advice, want to change consultants, or make significant changes to the project scope.

Lessons Learned

Over the years, OE program officers have gained tacit knowledge about the approval, support, and monitoring of grants.

The OE program plays a key role in developing useful projects. Packard has learned that some grantees propose projects that are not likely to address a core issue, and that local consultants simply respond to their request rather than trying to help them diagnose their needs. Thus, an important function of the OE program officers is to challenge grantees and help them think more deeply about their organization in order to develop a useful project. While grantees know their organizations better than a foundation program officer ever will, Packard adds value, largely because it stands apart from the grantee organization and can help with grantee self-reflection. To develop a more candid relationship, Packard considers it important that these discussions remain confidential.

Project work requires flexibility. Over the years, Packard has developed a philosophy of how to help grantees that is less rigid than many grantmakers. While other grantmakers use work plans to hold grantees "accountable" for achieving what they planned and rarely approve revisions, Packard views work plans as the starting point for discussions. Internally, Packard refers to Capacity Grants as "learning grants," fully hoping that grantees will gain new insights from their work with consultants. Packard believes that it can be difficult for a consultant to truly understand an organization's issues during the all-too-brief exchange devoted to developing the initial proposal, and are not surprised when consultants and clients attempt to revise projects or request follow-on work as they reach a better understanding of central issues.

To encourage grantees to adopt a learning attitude and make adjustments as needed, Packard communicates its philosophy in a number of ways. After each grant is awarded, Packard sends a letter spelling out the requirements for the final report, and the rationale behind it, such as:

> The nature of Organizational Effectiveness grants makes each one a learning opportunity, both for the grantee and for the Packard Foundation. In your report, we are hoping that you will take time to reflect upon your challenges and

> successes, and then share with us the insight you have gained from undertaking your project.
>
> Projects undertaken by Organizational Effectiveness grantees often evolve as they move forward and sometimes can have unintended outcomes, both positive and negative. We encourage you to share such experiences with us.[4]

Final reports are Packard's chief tool for monitoring whether the projects accomplished their purpose. While conventional Capacity Grant reports might only ask whether a project is on schedule and on budget and whether the goals have been met, Packard uses the reports to learn about the change process. The questions convey to grantees that it is okay to be candid in describing problems. In the final report, grantees are asked:

- What challenges did you face in connection with this project? How did you address these challenges?
- What was accomplished in connection with this project? Please address each stated objective. If any project objectives were changed, please also explain the circumstances leading to the modification of the objective(s).
- What were the most important lessons learned?
- What advice would you offer to help another organization that is thinking about undertaking a similar project?

With this encouragement, it should not be surprising that grantees approach Packard with requests to change a project. Packard considers each case individually and decides whether to continue supporting the OE work, or perhaps fund additional work. In reaching these decisions, Packard is guided by a set of beliefs about organizational change, described by Barbara Kibbe, Director of the Organizational Effectiveness and Philanthropy Program:[5]

- Management challenges are normal and ongoing for all organizations. A commitment to addressing them is a sign of strength, not weakness.
- Organizational effectiveness grantmakers can and should insist on thoughtfulness, but not on what or how to think.
- There is no quick fix and there is no permanent fix either.
- If you share a common vision/goal with a grantee and they encounter some bumps along the way, their crisis can be an opportunity to rethink, reposition, and reengineer. Your renewed commitment in times of organizational change, challenge, and/or transition can pay big dividends.
- The work of organization building almost always takes longer and is harder than you think. Holding an organizational effectiveness grantee to a tight timeline can actually inhibit learning and lead to posturing and lack of candor in reporting.

Packard Decision to Reduce Organization Effectiveness Grants. Packard Foundation's endowment decreased by 60 percent from the end of 2000 to August 2002. At that point, Packard reevaluated its priorities and decided to reduce its investment in Organization Effectiveness and Philanthropy activities. However, Packard will continue its long-standing commitment to capacity building grants through a small staff and a grants budget of $3 million in 2003, half of what it was in 2002.

The Pew Charitable Trusts' Philadelphia Cultural Management Initiative

The Philadelphia Cultural Management Initiative (PCMI) was launched in October 2001 to support those cultural organizations motivated to address management issues. In 2002, seventy-four organizations that had previously applied for program grants from Pew's Cultural Leadership Program (PCLP) were eligible for PCMI support. Arts organizations could also become eligible by engaging in a PCMI assessment process. In either case, all eligible organizations have engaged in some form of self-assessment. To receive support, nonprofits have to identify areas for improvement and describe how they came to understand their needs.

Pew, in collaboration with Drexel University, set up PCMI as a separate program administered by Drexel's Arts Administration graduate program. In developing PCMI, Drexel worked with an advisory council of local arts leaders to define the philosophy and programs of PCMI and recruited the director. Pew's ongoing role is to review PCMI's strategy and programs and provide funding. PCMI's role is to continue learning about the development needs of organizations, promote its programs and grants to eligible organizations, manage the application process, award grants, and evaluate the progress of grantees. At the same time, Pew also launched a companion program with the Nonprofit Finance Fund to help organizations understand their complete financial picture and to undertake projects around endowment and facilities replacement.

As PCMI develops relationships with eligible arts organizations, it expects grantees to be comfortable revealing their management concerns so that assistance will be productive. PCMI does not share any information about individual organizations with Pew—applications, assessments, consultant reports, and discussions are all treated as confidential. Pew does receive summary reports on the number of applications, grants awarded, and general issues across the sector. A formal assessment of PCMI impact is being planned, and will be shared with Pew.

With a total budget of $850,000 per year to support up to 74 or more organizations, the challenge for PCMI is to develop services that will have the greatest impact on the most organizations. Currently, PCMI provides services that are inexpensive to deliver, such as executive education and small grants, to a large percentage of all grantees and more intensive support to a small number of organizations. Executive education covers a wide range of important management topics such as strategy, managing change, governance, financial models, and strategic human resource management. A series of technology courses for basic skill building and technology planning workshops are offered. Organizations can also apply for professional skills development grants of up to $8,000 over 12 months. The approval process is easy and fast, with a high acceptance rate.

Confidentiality. The PCMI director meets with every eligible organization to promote its programs and grants and to learn more about the organization's needs. The director can be most helpful when grantees are candid about their concerns and capabilities. While the structure of PCMI as a separate organization helps, it does not guarantee that executive directors will be entirely forthcoming. Candor may improve over time as leaders take advantage of PCMI programs and begin to develop a relationship with PCMI.

More intensive assistance is available for a smaller number of nonprofits each year, through the Organization Assessment Fund and Organization Development Grants.

Organization Assessment Fund

An important goal for PCMI is to "stimulate and sustain 'learning organizations' committed to continuous refinement through self-reflection and capacity building."[6] Many applicants for PCMI support have already been through the PCLP assessment process, and have developed insights about their critical needs. Organizations can also apply directly to PCMI for a rigorous assessment by outside consultants that will identify areas of organizational strength as well as challenges. Once an organization has gone through a PCMI assessment process, they are eligible for other PCMI support.

By the end of 2002, seven organizations were in the midst of organization assessments. Eligible organizations must have an annual budget of at least $150,000, two full-time staff and a long-range plan covering at least three years. Those interested contact the PCMI director to discuss what they will learn from the process, the time required, and whether their organization is ready to undertake an assessment. If the assessment seems appropriate, then the organization submits a letter of interest explaining why it is interested. The PCMI director meets with both the board chair and the executive director to further describe the assessment process and determine whether the organization is ready. It is not unusual for organization leaders to have four or five discussions with the PCMI director before they are approved for an assessment.

Assessments are both time consuming for the client and a major investment for PCMI. The organization staff and leadership are expected to devote between 80 and 100 hours to this process. The assessment requires between three and five days of consulting time, using both an organization development consultant and a financial specialist, and costs between $11,000 and $14,000. The assessment process includes:

- An overview survey completed by members of the staff, board, and others related to the programming and mission of the organization, to discern areas of shared understanding and areas of discontinuity.
- An extensive review by the facilitator and outside consultants of documentation such as board minutes, financial statements, planning materials, personnel policies, and other operational documents.
- A facilitated one-day meeting with key organizational stakeholders that measures organizational effectiveness and tests alignment/disagreement within the organization.
- A follow-up and feedback session with the facilitator to discuss results and develop priorities, next-steps, and/or action plans based on the result of the assessment.[7]

The assessment results and feedback are confidential between the organization and the consultant. The PCMI director does not discuss the assessment with the consultant or have access to the final report. It is up to the grantees to share what they learned, if they choose, although their conclusions about critical issues will be important in future applications for PCMI support.

Organization Development Grants

A limited number of Organization Development Grants are provided to organizations with insights about their needs and a clear strategy to build additional capabilities. Organization Development Grants support projects that can greatly enhance sustainability, particularly executive management, financial systems and management, marketing, and fund development. Grants range from $10,000 to $40,000 per year, for a maximum of two years. In March 2002, $333,000 was awarded in the first round of grants, to five organizations from a total of 14 applications. In late 2002, twenty-eight organizations applied for a total of $430,000 in grants, and nine grants were awarded.

Organization Development Grants can be used for the following projects, which are typical of projects supported by other grantmakers with Capacity Grants:

- Planning efforts to consider a significant programmatic expansion or contraction including consultants, facilitators, retreat facility rental, and associated costs;
- Consulting fees to study targeted areas of capacity in areas such as technology utilization, marketing, fund development, or financial management;
- Customized training and skills development programs;
- Addressing the building of an organizational capacity that has been identified through a rigorous process of review and assessment.

Organization Development Grants can also be used for projects that are not commonly supported, such as:

- Implementation of improvements or a new initiative in the areas of management, administrative systems, marketing, etc.;
- Temporary staff positions related to the intended project;
- New staff positions that will be permanent. Applications must indicate how the organization intends on absorbing the additional salary into their budget at the end of the grant period. For multiyear requests, grants for permanent positions will be made on a declining basis from year one to year two of the grant.

Application/Selection. The application process begins with a one-page Letter of Intent to Apply, at least a month prior to the deadline for grant applications. Applicants submit a project narrative of up to four pages that includes expected project outcomes and budget; a description of how the organization came to understand the capacity building issue addressed by the project; and the consultant's workplan and qualifications, if a consultant is used. Applicants also submit fiscal information for the past three years, budgets for the current and next two fiscal years, a long-range plan, and other supporting documents.

Projects are selected based on the extensive written application materials. Selection is determined in a highly competitive, adjudicated process by a panel of arts administrators and experts in organization development. The panel does not make site visits or conduct interviews, although applicants are encouraged to discuss their projects and applications with the PCMI director, who can offer preliminary feedback on the project. The panel uses several criteria to evaluate projects:

- Clarity of project,
- Quality of assessment/diagnostic process in determining the critical issue,
- Quality of consultants,
- Expected outcomes and means of measurement/evaluation,
- Project impact on the organization.

Successful applicants are able to demonstrate that a rigorous assessment process was used to identify the intended project. The panel is looking for a high level of self-awareness and candor about weaknesses and underlying causes. Applicants are advised to describe the diagnostic process that occurred, who participated within the organization, and the path that led to the specific area of request and why it is of critical importance at that time.

PCMI takes advantage of the opportunity to provide feedback to organizations not selected. The PCMI director meets with each applicant and explains the panel's reaction to their project. The goal is to help the organizations gain insights about how to proceed, without telling them which issues to address or how to do it. The director also explains other support available from PCMI that may be appropriate.

Developing capabilities. Once a grant has been made, nonprofits often ask for assistance in identifying appropriate consultants. While PCMI does not endorse consultants, they do pass along names of consultants who have worked successfully with other grantees, and encourage grantees to call references and conduct interviews. The PCMI director checks in with grantees during the period of the Organization Development Grant, and serves as a resource when needed. He does not talk to consultants. PCMI asks for a final report for each Organization Development Grant and an interim report for two-year projects.

Example of Organizational Development Grant. Painted Bride Art Center is a community-based performing arts organization with expenditures in 2001 of just under $1 million. In March 2002, the Painted Bride Art Center received an $80,000 grant over two years to hire consulting services to develop a new marketing plan and to establish a new position of audience development coordinator. Strategies developed by the consultant will help the Center to increase community investment, membership, and box office efficiency. Implementation of these strategies will help the Painted Bride to become less reliant on contributed income and contribute to the overall capacity of the organization.

Lessons Learned

PCMI philosophy. The specific services and application process distinguish PCMI from most grantmakers providing Capacity Grants. The differences are intentional and reflect a different view about how to help organizations develop capabilities. According to Martin Cohen, "PCMI's philosophy is to encourage organizations to learn about themselves, and as such we provide a menu of opportunities to support the building of skills as well as engage in self-reflection. Funds are available through different parts of the program to address critical issues to those who engage in self-reflection and come to an understanding of their strengths and challenges."

Encouraging participation. In getting to know grantees, Cohen has concluded that "budget size is not an indicator of effectiveness," and that capacity building would help arts organizations of all sizes. A large percentage of eligible organizations receive some type of services from PCMI, by attending workshops or obtaining grants. Thus far, twenty-three out of 74 eligible organizations have received grants from the professional skills development fund. While most of the applicants are of moderate size, with budgets between $400,000 and $4 million, organization budgets have ranged from $150,000 to $18 million.

As an MSO, PCMI has no leverage over grantees, but can continue to develop relationships, build its reputation for effectiveness, and respond to the needs and interests of different types of arts organizations.

Pew's Leadership Grants provide an incentive to improve. Pew began a new approach to grantmaking in 1997; the Philadelphia Cultural Leadership Program (PCLP) offers three-year grants for unrestricted operating support. A "comprehensive review" including site visits by a team of consultants is used to select applicants that "demonstrate artistic accomplishment, financial and management excellence, and audience and community support." Organizations can reapply for additional three-year grants if they maintain a high level of excellence, but the bar may rise over time. Since 1997, PCLP has awarded $30 million to 50 groups in the Philadelphia region. In 2001, $7.8 million was awarded to 15 organizations, with grants ranging from $45,000 to $2.4 million over three years, a contribution representing from 1.5 percent to 8 percent of the grantee's annual expenses.

About half of the organizations undergoing the time-consuming application and on-site assessment process are approved for PCLP grants, as a reward for good management practices. Pew staff concluded that additional assistance would help all applicants achieve a higher level of excellence, and decided to make all applicants to PCLP eligible for support from PCMI, a new capacity building program.

Pew's PCLP grants provide an important source of pressure (or incentive) to improve capabilities, for both large and small organizations. Judging from grants awarded, it seems that large arts organizations find the grants significant enough to subject themselves to the scrutiny of a comprehensive review. While a $1 million grant may be only 2 percent of an organization's budget, it represents unrestricted funding that can otherwise be difficult to come by, and needed to support administration, expansion, or the development of new programs. For organizations of moderate size, there is an even greater incentive to meet the program's standards of excellence, as PCLP grants can represent from 5 percent to 8 percent of annual expenses for budgets between $150,000 and $3 million.

Clearly, PCLP grants are coveted by arts organizations. The question is whether they motivate organizations to address issues and seek assistance. Another source of motivation for current grantees is Pew's intention to raise the bar for standards of excellence. Already, some former grantees have not been renewed. An interesting question is whether those asking for and receiving assistance from PCMI are current grantees seeking to address weaknesses or declinees. The evidence as of 2003 is telling. Of those organizations that were successful in obtaining a PCLP grant, 88 percent have sought assistance from PCMI. Of those applicants to PCLP that were unsuccessful, 35 percent have sought assistance from PCMI. It appears that stronger organizations are interested in building on their strengths or addressing weaknesses.

Conclusions

Both Packard and PCMI have improved upon conventional Capacity Grants by using a capacity program officer to provide assistance to grantees, hoping to improve the level of candor of grantees. Capacity program officers can improve grantee reflection, leading to more useful projects. PCMI goes further, requiring applicants for OD grants to engage in an intensive self-assessment with outside assistance. Despite efforts to improve the impact of Capacity Grants, there are several limitations that have not been addressed.

Quality of consultants is uneven. Research suggests that effective consulting is often critical to project success and long-term impact. Yet, funders of Capacity Grants generally leave grantees to their own devices to select a consultant. Neither Packard nor PCMI recommend consultants. Packard does provide reference materials on working with a consultant, yet Packard's study showed that even with this help, grantees have little understanding of what to look for in a consultant or how to find one.

No structure for long-term coaching. Both research studies found that coaching is valuable when it occurs during the project. Capacity Grants don't provide access to an advisor who knows the organization well, is brutally honest, and can be trusted, unless the capacity program officer is able to fill this role.

Mismatched consultant incentives. The client's interests sometimes fall short of what is needed to build long-term capacity, and consultants play an important role in helping clients recognize and address such issues. As long as clients use Capacity Grants to hire consultants directly, consultants can only go so far in pushing clients. Consultants have financial incentives to complete the project, whether or not they feel that is very useful.

Funding for capacity needs. While consulting may be enough to get an organization moving, many nonprofits run into significant barriers that require additional funding. All too often progress depends on additional resources for administrative support, technology, facilities, working capital, or maintenance reserves and few nonprofits have sufficient discretionary income to fund these needs. The Pew PCMI program is unusual because Capacity Grants can be used to fund internal positions.

Key Features of Capacity Grants

- Grantees define the project and apply for grants
- Only motivated grantees apply
- Grantmaker reviews the project; decides if it is worthwhile
- Grantee selects consultant from the marketplace
- Projects are short term

Alternatives to Capacity Grants

Two additional approaches to capacity building have been developed that provide long-term coaching and more effective consulting. In the first approach, grantmakers build a relationship with a Development Partner who provides ongoing support to a set of grantees. In the second approach, Structured Programs, grantees establish improvement goals and are provided substantial support and coaching to achieve those goals. Designers of both approaches expect greater long-term change than from Capacity Grants. These approaches are described more fully in Chapters 4 and 5.

Capacity Grants remain an important alternative for many grantmakers. It is clear that Capacity Grants produce significant improvements in some grantees. The critical question is how often do lasting improvements take place, a question that can only be answered by tracking a larger group of grantees over time. In the meantime, grantmakers can take steps to improve grantee candor and reflection and provide project flexibility.

Notes

1. Berger and Vasile, 2002.
2. Fletcher, 1994.
3. Fletcher, 1994, p. 33.
4. From a sample grantee letter.
5. David and Lucile Packard Foundation, 2000.
6. Philadelphia Cultural Management Initiative Program Guidelines 2001–2002, p. 3.
7. Philadelphia Cultural Management Initiative, Guideline revisions for 2002, p. 5.

CHAPTER 4

Development Partners

Another approach to capacity building calls for a grantmaker to select a consulting group, referred to as a Development Partner, to work with its grantees. The grantmaker purchases a block of consulting time, directs interested grantees to get assistance from the Partner, then steps back and lets the Partner assume substantial responsibility for helping grantees develop their capacity. The general contract for consulting time covers a group of grantees for several years, and can be renewed if both parties are satisfied with the arrangement. Some Partners have provided support to grantees for ten years or longer. This approach addresses three limitations of Capacity Grants by making long-term coaching available, controlling the quality of consulting, and creating strong incentives for consultants to focus on long-term change.

A Development Partner approach is not for everyone, as grantmakers have to be willing to give up direct control over resources and to trust consultants. Grantmakers are willing to do so because they believe that the quality of consulting is paramount and that a carefully selected Development Partner is better positioned than the grantmaker to deal with readiness to change.

In limiting grantees to working with a Development Partner, grantmakers hope to improve the consistency and impact of consulting. In contrast, when grantees select their own consultants, results are often mixed—while some projects are of the highest quality, others never get off the ground or have limited impact. An important reason that consulting can be more effective is that strong relationships can develop between grantees and Development Partners over the years. Also, long-term support means that the focus of consulting shifts from short-term project success to long-term change, which has a profound impact on the way consulting is performed.

The funder's dollars may also be stretched further with a Development Partner approach because Partners are better positioned than grantmakers to decide which grantees offer the greatest promise for improvement. It is the Partner, rather than the funder, that makes most decisions about which grantee gets support, which projects are worthwhile, and how much time to allocate to each. This arrangement also gives Partners considerable flexibility to adjust projects as conditions change, allowing them to shift resources to their best use.

A Development Partner relationship does not exist unless a funder has a general *contract* for a block of consulting time. It should be noted that many grantmakers provide general funding for local MSOs, but this relationship does not offer the advantages of a Development Partnership. It is more common for MSOs to compete for consulting contracts, one project at a time, in the marketplace.

Three examples of Development Partnerships are described below, two of which have existed for at least 20 years and the third for seven. These partnerships have persisted because grantmakers find them effective. Community Resource Exchange (CRE) is an independent management support organization based in New York City, and it has had an important partnership with the New York Foundation for more than 20 years. Both organizations are dedicated to community-based nonprofits that serve disadvantaged communities. CRE is a Development Partner with several other grantmakers as well.

SHATIL, another management support organization, was specifically created in 1982 by the New Israel Fund to provide extensive management support and training to its grantees. The New Israel Fund, an Israeli-European-North American partnership, was founded in 1979, and has granted over $120 million to more than 700 organizations in Israel—

organizations dedicated to safeguarding civil and human rights, bridging social and economic gaps, and fostering tolerance and religious pluralism.

The third partner described in this chapter is the Management Assistance Group (MAG), a Washington-based MSO that partnered with the Ford Foundation to design and deliver a program called the Capacity Building Initiative (CBI). CBI is designed to bring about organizational change at a modest cost per grantee for around 100 of Ford's Peace and Social Justice grantees.

Grantmakers sponsor these partnerships and create a structure—the pool of consulting days and multiyear funding—so that experienced consultants can have the greatest possible impact with grantees. The funding structure is not difficult to implement and the challenge of making it work rests largely on the shoulders of the Development Partners. The three Development Partners highlighted here have worked for years to figure out how to have the greatest possible impact. Each has a strong view about "what works" and many of their practices set them apart from more traditional consulting. Key practices are described below, such as how services are allocated, issues are diagnosed, consultants' time is used on projects, time is monitored and billed, consultants are recruited, and feedback is obtained for learning.

Community Resource Exchange

For more than 20 years, Community Resource Exchange (CRE) has been a Development Partner of the New York Foundation. The New York Foundation grantees work with disadvantaged communities in New York City, with a particular emphasis on youth and the elderly. Founded in 1979, CRE has provided management assistance to over 2,000 community-based organizations and institutions serving those affected by poverty in New York City. CRE's mission is to improve the lives of New Yorkers most in need by ensuring the stability, growth, and effectiveness of community-based organizations. In 2002, with 24 consultants on staff and a budget of $3 million, CRE provided one-on-one consulting to more than 300 clients.

Nearly 80 percent of CRE's work is paid for by a network of funders. These relationships have largely been modeled after those with the New York Foundation. Through a general fund for "walk-in" clients, about

75 organizations that are not otherwise covered by a funder obtain assistance each year. Over 20 percent of CRE's clients pay for assistance, billed at a rate of $100 to $150 per hour; often the funds have been given to the client by a local funder in the form of a Capacity Grant. CRE has an understanding with each of its major funders that CRE's consulting relationships are confidential.

CRE believes that clients who cannot otherwise afford high-quality assistance should be able to obtain it, at no direct cost, and with a minimum of hassle. New York-based community organizations simply call CRE to request services. There is no formal application process. An intake person collects enough information about the client's situation and needs to determine whether the organization should become a client; if so, which staff should handle the assignment; and enough background information to determine whether the nonprofit qualifies for funding under a specific partnership contract. CRE's goal is to provide comprehensive services to clients. Former clients can obtain quick advice over the phone; CRE provided 400 phone consultations in 2002. CRE has developed a range of services in addition to direct consulting, such as executive search and a peer learning/networking series. They also provide some support grants, called "Reality Checks," to fund immediate needs that arise out of consulting work.

CRE consultants are committed to help those affected by poverty and have great respect for the work of community-based organizations. Most CRE consultants have been active in community organizing, more than half of the consultants are of color, and a third are fluent in a second language. CRE consultants bring strong credentials to their work, and have experience in either community organizing, consulting, or nonprofit management. Two-thirds of the staff have advanced degrees and 17 have more than ten years of consulting experience. While all CRE consultants have technical skills in areas such as fundraising, board development, and strategic planning, senior consultants also bring general organization development skills that are particularly important to the initial diagnosis and design of interventions. Junior consultants often begin with technical skills and acquire generalist skills through CRE training and on the job mentoring by more senior consultants.

By focusing on New York City, CRE has developed extensive knowledge about the local nonprofit environment. Staff consultants are able to draw on the knowledge of their CRE colleagues and offer clients advice on specific funders, funding strategies, community needs, program strategies, opportunities for collaboration, as well as political strategies. CRE goes even further, and offers to use all of its contacts and resources to help clients, which may mean calling a funder on their behalf or providing a political contact.

In 1999, the New York Foundation made program and support grants averaging $40,000 to 120 organizations. In general, grantees are supported for five years, and about a third of the grants are for general support of fledgling community organizing or advocacy groups with budgets of under $100,000. Since the early 1980s, the New York Foundation has contracted with CRE to provide an agreed-upon number of management consulting hours to grantees. This support provided an average of 60 hours of assistance for each grantee in 2002.

Program officers at the New York Foundation play an active role in capacity building as well, making numerous site visits and raising questions intended to help recipients think about management issues. Program officers do not try to diagnose the grantees' situation, but encourage them to seek help from CRE. The role of program officers is to stimulate interest, while CRE consultants work with grantees to identify and address issues. The New York Foundation believes that nonprofit managers must ask for help, and that every one of their grantees can benefit from some assistance. They also believe that development is a long-term process, and that three to five years of program grants and management assistance can help nonprofits start on a development path.

New York Foundation funding is not conditional on whether an organization receives assistance or makes improvements. Grantees approach CRE for assistance with issues such as board development, financial management, fundraising assistance, human resources, strategic planning, and organizational development. The consulting relationship is completely confidential and CRE provides the New York Foundation with only a summary report of CRE's activities without details about the client's situation. Grantees can describe their improvement work in greater detail to the foundation, if they choose.

Allocation of Consulting Time

One of the biggest challenges for CRE is deciding how to allocate consulting time when the demand for services outstrips the supply. In general, it assigns one of three types of relationships to each client after an initial assessment:

- *Consultations* usually involve a short session or two in which CRE offers advice for handling a specific issue or problem.
- *Standard* relationships are most common and involve one or two relatively well-defined workplan areas, usually requiring 4–7 staff days over a period of 3–6 months.
- *Comprehensive* workplans cover multiple areas of assistance and may require 10 or more staff days over 4–12 months.

When a potential client calls for assistance, a CRE consultant contacts them within a day or two to obtain a more complete intake. The consultant then has an assessment meeting with the leadership of the organization to identify what is needed, determine how to proceed, and clarify the role of both CRE and the client in the actual work. Experienced consultants, knowledgeable about organization change, ask insightful questions to assess the client situation; a formal "assessment tool" is not used for diagnosis. CRE consultants typically ask about prior efforts to address the issue; whether key leaders and staff are committed to addressing the issue; obstacles that would prevent the issue from being addressed; and possible underlying causes. Consultants are alert to the leaders' readiness to change, the quality of leadership, as well as the organization's culture and politics. Clues about the client's readiness to change might include:

- **Candor.** There is a lack of trust, openness, honesty, or genuineness on the part of the client. The client will not share financial information with the consultant.
- **Receptivity.** The client is resistant to CRE's input in shaping the work. CRE does not believe it can influence the organization.
- **Lack of motivation.** The group has asked for help only as a precondition to obtain funding. There is no evidence that leaders feel personal ownership of the proposed work with CRE.
- **Lack of leadership.** The work plan requires internal leadership, but leadership is lacking. The organization's point person lacks the authority needed to implement the work plan.

In addition to readiness, CRE's assessment also considers the organization's importance to the community, the time required to address the organization's issues, whether they are covered by available funding, and funders' priorities. For a client project that is apt to demand an extremely large number of hours, CRE confers with the relevant foundation to make sure the client has high priority. If a work plan is not adequately covered by funding, CRE will sometimes use funds from their pro bono "walk-in" account to supplement other funding.

If the consultant concludes that either a standard or comprehensive relationship is warranted, he/she will try to reach agreement on the issues, approach, and roles during the initial assessment meeting. More than one meeting or conversation may be needed, but when an agreement is reached, CRE submits a proposed work plan to the client. Work plans are tailored to the unique needs of each client and specify goals, timeline, and budgeted consulting time. Work plans help both parties to reach a meeting of the minds before work begins, and also serve as an internal management tool for CRE to motivate staff to stay within the estimated time covered by funding.

Consulting Approach

CRE work plans address issues familiar to other technical assistance providers, such as board development, strategic planning, financial management, fundraising, organization development, and personnel issues. Yet, the approach of CRE consultants in managing these projects differs greatly from that of many nonprofit consultants. While "projects" (consulting engagements) are the vehicle for much of their work with clients, CRE is equally concerned with project success—whether project goals are met and whether the client is satisfied—*and* sustainable change within the client organization. CRE feels that the following practices distinguish its approach and have been crucial to its success with clients.

Develop trusting relationships with clients. Nothing is more important to CRE's success than having client trust. CRE wants clients to understand that CRE exists to help them succeed. CRE builds relationships in several ways, first by having staff that share a commitment to the mission of community-based organizations and are sensitive to cultural diversity. CRE also conveys their dedication to clients by providing free, no-hassle services for those who cannot afford to pay directly, and assuring that relationships are confidential. Trust also builds as clients find that CRE's assistance and advice are helpful.

Finally, CRE believes that respect for clients is essential for building trust. CRE strives to treat clients as colleagues, rather than as a set of problems, recognizing that nonprofit leaders bring extensive experience, knowledge of their community, and passion to their work.

Challenge clients to confront issues. In general, CRE's greatest contribution comes from influencing the way clients think. CRE is best able to do so when a strong relationship exists. With most clients, CRE consultants offer an important perspective on the client's own diagnosis of issues as well as insights on how to initiate change. The more sensitive the issue, the more forcefully consultants may have to challenge the client's ideas. There are times when CRE consultants are "brutally honest" about a client's funding situation, financial health, the need for major restructuring, or how leaders have contributed to the organization's problems. With strong relationships, clients are more candid about problems and more willing to listen when the consultant raises difficult issues.

When a strong relationship does not exist, such as with a new client, CRE may simply respond to its needs and demonstrate the value of assistance, while laying the groundwork for the client to work on more significant issues in the future. CRE believes that it is often most able to effect deeper change in an organization on the second or third consulting project, building on the relationship established in its first engagement.

CRE seeks a delicate balance between respect for the client and desire to be responsive to the client's needs on the one hand, and the desire to help the client confront issues that are important for long-term success. Occasionally, CRE faces a difficult dilemma when a returning client seeks assistance but remains unwilling to change. As much as CRE wants to help every grassroots organization in New York City, it also wants to use its time productively. In the end, CRE may delay assistance until there is agreement on a productive work plan or provide only minimal assistance until there is a change in circumstance.

Use in-house staff. All consulting is provided by CRE staff, who share a common approach to consulting and participate in substantial training and development. Sharing client experiences helps to build institutional knowledge and improve the quality of work.

Use broad diagnostic skills. CRE considers it important that a "generalist" rather than a specialist is the primary consultant for each client. For every client, a senior consultant handles the diagnosis and develops a work plan or supervises a more junior consultant throughout the engagement.

Build client commitment. CRE has learned that collaborative consulting—helping clients to honestly diagnose their own issues and develop solutions—leads to greater client commitment and improves the chances that changes will be implemented. CRE will not play the role of the expert and take on solving the client's problem for it. Instead, CRE makes it clear from the outset that leaders, particularly the executive director, are expected to play an active role in overseeing the project and managing change.

Work plans often include group meetings and individual interviews designed to build organization support. For many projects, CRE suggests forming a working group to oversee the change process that includes staff from different functions and levels, and possibly board members. The working group provides useful input and is a vehicle for building support for ongoing change from key organization members.

Coach organization leaders. Because consultants need access to leaders to jointly diagnose issues, resolve problems, and decide on specific next steps, work plans include face-to-face meetings with the client. During these discussions, which are central to a successful project, the consultant has an opportunity to influence the executive director's thinking. Only through such opportunities for "face time" with leaders can a deeper relationship begin to develop.

Without having asked for it, executive directors often receive considerable coaching from CRE consultants, not only on the project at hand, but on other issues that either the executive director or consultant considers important. This is where consultants lay the groundwork for addressing other issues relevant to long-term success. As clients develop greater trust, they may also ask for advice on sensitive issues—how to handle a difficult board member, how to resolve a staff conflict, or even feedback on their own management style.

Assist with implementing change. CRE rarely agrees to work plans that only involve planning without any implementation steps. CRE often works with clients to develop new systems or structures, and continues to assist as new systems are introduced or new roles are being tried. Training or coaching may be needed to help staff develop new skills and adopt new behaviors.

Set limits on consulting. Over half of CRE clients each year have had a prior relationship with CRE, many for ten years or more, and CRE believes that it is most effective with multiple interventions over an extended period of time. CRE faces a dilemma because it encourages clients to develop long-term relationships yet limits the work on an individual project so that clients do not become dependent on outside assistance. To achieve closure on individual projects, CRE formalizes the end of each work plan with a close-out letter and invoice that shows how the project was funded. Clients are encouraged to continue working on issues, but to call for advice if they encounter roadblocks or their situation changes. CRE also encourages organizations to return when they are ready to address other important issues.

Management of Consulting

CRE believes that its consulting approach and the quality of consultants are critical to its success with clients. Their overall impact also depends on their ability to allocate consulting time to its best use. CRE has developed important internal management practices that enable it to develop consultants, evaluation systems that allow consultants to learn from client feedback, and a billing system that helps consultants manage their time.

Billable structure. In the early 1990s, CRE began to link funding to each project based on an estimate of consulting days, which required a significant cultural change for both clients and consultants. Rather than viewing CRE as an *unlimited* free resource, clients had to consider how to get the most out of the limited time available. Consultants had to shift from the ideal of "availability to anyone for anything" to figuring out how to minimize the time required to accomplish key goals. Work plans force both CRE staff and clients to recognize the constraints on CRE's time, and to work toward maximizing the impact of CRE's assistance within the time allotted.

The billing system creates a strong incentive to assign all work with clients to a funding source. Consultants are also pressured to be efficient in their use of time by the strong demand for services, and the desire to keep billable rates low. To meet client demand, each consultant is given a target rate of billable hours against which they are evaluated. While the rate takes into account administrative tasks and staff development, the pace of the work is brisk.

Consultant development. The CRE consulting staff devotes considerable effort each year learning from successes and failures and altering practices for greater impact. To assure some level of consistency across consultants, CRE conducts technical training on a variety of topics, and also holds general sessions twice a year for the entire staff that allow for more wide-ranging reflection about practices and impact. In addition, CRE has a weekly two-hour staff meeting, and twice-monthly case conferences. In total, roughly 5 percent of each staff consultant's time is dedicated to staff development each year.

Evaluation of Impact

CRE collects information about every project's outcome, at least in the short term. A close-out report on every project gives the consultant's perspective. To get the client's perspective, follow-up interviews are conducted with a sample of clients once a year. These calls provide valuable information about CRE's impact as well as common barriers to progress. Such information has led to new practice areas and changed consulting practices. More specific information is collected about the work of each consultant, his/her relationship with the client, knowledge, and overall effectiveness. This information is summarized for each consultant and informs individual development plans.

In 2003, CRE began an evaluation of the long-term impact of their work with clients. It involves collecting information from both the client and consultant at the beginning and close of each project. A follow-up survey of the client two years later repeats the original client survey to reveal changes in the client organization. CRE serves about 300 clients each year, and will be able to collect complete cases on 500 or more clients within a few years. With a large sample of cases, it will be possible to learn a great deal about factors that lead to long-term change in capabilities, and organization capabilities that correlate with high performance. This evaluation promises not only to improve CRE's consulting practice, but to provide valuable insights to other consultants and sponsors of capacity building.

Lessons Learned

Much of what CRE has learned over the past 20 years is reflected in its consulting approach and management practices. Following are a few additional insights on topics of general interest to capacity building.

Learning the CRE way. CRE has found that consultants with prior consulting experience, particularly with larger, private sector firms, often find it difficult to adjust to the "CRE way." While they bring technical knowledge, they are often less familiar with assessing client readiness or developing commitment. They may also be more comfortable with projects structured for outside experts, and less adept at building client relationships based on mutual respect.

Screening for readiness. Other providers question whether clients will be uncommitted to project work if they do not pay some portion of the consulting fee. CRE has found that clients are committed if there is effective screening.

More complex, longer work plans. For clients that are ready to make changes, CRE has learned that providing assistance in an isolated management area can be of limited help, and that involvement in multiple areas (such as fundraising and board development) is more likely to result in lasting improvement. Given finite resources, CRE will always face a trade-off between helping more clients or having longer projects that improve long-term impact. CRE feels strongly that comprehensive relationships of ten days or more have a greater impact than shorter consultations.

SHATIL

SHATIL is the "Empowerment and Training Center for Social Change Organizations" created by the New Israel Fund (NIF) in 1982 to provide assistance to beneficiaries, potential and former grantees, and other organizations. NIF supports public interest groups in Israel working on issues of democracy, civil rights, pluralism, and social justice. In 2002, it provided $4.4 million in support to 148 grantees.

Because the Israeli public interest sector is comparatively new, many groups seeking support are young and small. In dealing with these groups, NIF frequently provides general operating support based on a funding "track" in which funding begins as a large percentage of the annual budget and decreases over time to under ten percent. At this point, a final grant usually is made. Depending on variables such as grantee capacity and availability of other sources of funding, an organization may complete its "track" in as little as three years or in more than ten. Grantees understand that the goal is eventual independence from ongoing support. During the grant lifecycle, NIF also provides specific sub-grants to promote administrative and fundraising capacity and free organizational consulting by SHATIL.

During the final grant, SHATIL assists organizations in finding new sources of funding so that they can continue their activities. One source of ongoing support is New Israel Fund donor-advised gifts, in which New Israel Fund serves as the fiscal agent. Organizations continue to receive support from SHATIL (as first-priority clients) during the first two years after the final grant. It should be noted that SHATIL also provides consultation to some organizations that are not yet grantees, to *help them apply* to NIF for a grant.

A final grant can also be made if the organization's work is no longer consistent with New Israel Fund's goals. Some organizations continue to receive support, at less than ten percent of the total budget, because they have special significance to NIF's strategic goals. At times, NIF graduates turn to the New Israel Fund for emergency funding due to an organizational crisis.

While SHATIL has a close relationship with the New Israel Fund, which provides major funding for its capacity building assistance, SHATIL functions as an independent organization and maintains full confidentiality for its clients. SHATIL provides training and consulting in four major areas:

- **Organizational development and management:** improving board, committee, volunteer, and staff performance; strategic planning and program planning; assessing decision-making processes and improving organizational structure and effectiveness; building an active membership base; financial management and legal aspects of an NGO.
- **Advocacy:** organizing issue campaigns; formulating objectives, developing strategies, and identifying targets; and negotiating effectively for change.

- **Media and public relations:** generating media interest and attention; developing public relations strategies; preparing promotional materials; and improving public speaking skills.
- **Resource development and marketing:** identifying potential sources of support and writing proposals; establishing and stewarding relationships with donors; designing, implementing, and managing fundraising events; and cultivating strategic alliances with the business sector.

With an annual budget of $3.5 million, offices in three locations, and a staff of over 60, SHATIL has provided direct consulting to 400 organizations. Over 1,000 people representing 300 organizations attended SHATIL training workshops and courses. Training formats are diverse and cater to both junior and senior staff of organizations. Fledgling organizations or staff members may attend one-day introductory workshops on how to write grant proposals, use volunteers, or comply with laws governing nonprofits. For senior staff, there are more intensive formats, including semester-long courses in conjunction with local universities on nonprofit management and community organizing.

SHATIL consultants bring strong credentials to their work. In addition to experience in community organizing and nonprofit management, many speak multiple languages and are able to provide assistance in Hebrew, Arabic, French, Spanish, and English, as well as Russian and Amharic (Ethiopian), the first language of many recent immigrants to Israel. SHATIL is recognized for its knowledge about civil rights and social justice as well as the challenges of the advocacy environment in Israel. Consultants provide significant "added value" to the bread-and-butter issues of organizational and financial management.

Relationship with Funder

The New Israel Fund's program officers evaluate applicants on many dimensions—the organization, activities, and community impact—as part of the grantmaking process. Following the diagnosis and evaluation process, NIF's program officers submit their recommendations to the board regarding grantmaking. It is SHATIL's role to diagnose the organization's consulting needs and provide assistance accordingly. Program officers do not advise grantees on how to address organizational problems.

New Israel Fund program officers *do* discuss developmental milestones with grantees and point out issues that might affect future organizational sustainability. Development and maintenance of clear programmatic priorities, board and staff development, membership recruitment, and financial management are typical issues that might be discussed in conversations with a program officer. Grantees understand that failure to make progress on these capabilities may affect future grants, and program officers regularly suggest that grantees turn to SHATIL for assistance. Future grants are never, however, conditional on receipt of SHATIL assistance. The majority of NIF grantees receive some type of SHATIL assistance, which varies in substance and intensity over the organization's life cycle.

The close relationship between New Israel Fund and SHATIL—the organizations are governed by the same board of directors, are housed on different floors of the same building, and share some administrative functions—creates certain tensions. During the first decade, the option of separation between SHATIL and NIF was raised from time to time by each side. Both decided that it would be preferable to maintain the current relationship, despite the inevitable tensions.

While an external evaluation of SHATIL services carried out in the mid-1990s indicated that some grantees are anxious about the relationship between assistance provider and funder, most clients appear to believe that SHATIL's promise of confidentiality will not be broken.

Both the New Israel Fund and SHATIL go to great lengths to ensure that confidentiality is maintained. Program officers may inquire whether an organization is receiving SHATIL services and receive a brief description of the type of assistance (e.g., financial management, strategic planning). No additional details may be shared. Frequently, however, the *grantee* may choose to share results of consulting with the program officer, particularly when assistance has identified needs that require additional funding, such as computers, a fundraising coordinator, or additional personnel.

Allocation of Consulting Time

SHATIL offers a range of services and resources that can be accessed by organizations based on the urgency of their needs, the priority of the group to New Israel Fund, and the availability of resources. Grantees of NIF are the top priority and are eligible for the full range of services that

SHATIL provides. In special cases SHATIL offers consultation to grantees of other foundations, such as the New York Foundation, based on similar attitudes toward grantee development.

Organizations that are recruited through outreach projects are second priority. They also access the full range of services but sometimes at a lower level of intensity. Other organizations are not likely to receive individualized consulting but do access SHATIL workshops and conferences. It is rare for SHATIL to expend significant energy on an organization or issue area that is not a priority for NIF.

In recent years, SHATIL has begun providing services to non-priority groups on a fee-for-service basis in order to create a revenue stream. In some cases, this has involved contracting directly with other foundations that subsidize the purchase of consulting hours and access to workshops for their grantees.

Consulting Approach

SHATIL employs a staff of organization consultants with general skills; specialists with specific expertise in areas such as fundraising, media, or lobbying; and issue or population experts such as environmentalists, Ethiopians, or Russians. Generalists are trained in organizational development and/or community organizing, and work with clients on the full range of developmental and strategy issues. Specialists provide skills training and hands-on consulting in specific areas such as fundraising, volunteer management, or media relations. Issue/population experts manage outreach projects to specific populations such as Bedouin women or Russian immigrants. Training and consulting are provided through the project and are tailored to the language and cultural needs of the population in question. Most of the SHATIL staff function as both trainers and consultants.

Most organizations approach SHATIL by phone or letter to request services, although SHATIL also engages in outreach for a new project or population. While New Israel Fund program officers may recommend that an organization seek SHATIL services, the program officer does not serve as an intermediary in brokering the relationship with SHATIL. The fact that the organization seeks out SHATIL services is an important indicator of its willingness to address challenges. Organizations fill in a brief application that serves as the basis for an initial intake. During the intake, a consultant is assigned to assess the organization's fit within New Israel Fund priorities, its immediate needs and interests in terms of assistance, and its capacity to benefit from SHATIL services. When possible, SHATIL requests that the intake discussion include multiple stakeholders, including board, staff, and activists. The consultant writes up the intake along with recommendations for assistance (length of assistance, types of assistance, and intensity of assistance) that are approved by senior staff. Assistance may be provided by several consultants.

A senior generalist consultant is assigned as contact person for each organization and serves as "case manager," helping the organization to access the appropriate mix of SHATIL training and consulting. The "case manager" works closely with other consulting staff, often sitting in on initial consultations to ensure that there is alignment between the proposals of various consultants.

Philosophy and Approach

The goal of SHATIL consulting is to strengthen capacities within the organization and increase effectiveness over time. Along with New Israel Fund grants, SHATIL views its consulting as a long-term investment in the organization and therefore strives to establish a fluid relationship that enables the organization to address multiple issues over time. Each organization defines the starting point and specific topics for initial assistance. SHATIL is aware that the "presenting need" is often not the only or most pressing need. For example, organizations often seek help with fundraising when they also need extensive help in planning. Once SHATIL consultants have established rapport with the organization, they may suggest additional or alternative areas of assistance.

SHATIL consulting is "hands on." Together with organizational stakeholders, issues are identified and solutions pursued. Consultants work with organizations on implementation and increasing their capacity for self-reflection and organizational learning. The consulting relationship is informal. Aside from the initial intake, consultants rarely provide formal reports or engage in classical "organizational diagnosis."

SHATIL's consulting model is influenced by the fields of community organizing, organizational development, and change theory. SHATIL places strong emphasis on empowerment of indigenous leaders, disenfranchised populations, and organizations working on the margins of society. SHATIL works with these individuals and groups to identify and cultivate their strengths. SHATIL helps organizations to engage in power analysis—both as it relates to the internal structure of their organization and as it relates to the broader environmental context in which they operate. SHATIL works with organizations to implement democratic practices and ensure that they are truly representative of the populations and communities they purport to represent.

Consultants

SHATIL staff have a wide range of professional backgrounds, including social work, community organizing, organizational psychology, philosophy, and international relations. Many SHATIL staff are former activists from organizations to whom SHATIL has provided services (although there is an express policy of not "poaching" staff members from current clients). SHATIL has found it challenging to recruit staff with the right combination of nonprofit experience, consultancy and training skills, and commitment to low-income and disenfranchised groups. In order to build a pool of qualified consultant/trainers for social change organizations, SHATIL serves as a field placement site for social work and organizational psychology students, including interns from the U.S. and other countries. Some of these students have been hired as staff upon graduation.

In recent years SHATIL has augmented its staff with freelance and part-time positions. This model has enabled SHATIL to respond to cultural and geographic considerations as well as to maintain a top-flight consultant pool. Because SHATIL serves a diverse and geographically dispersed population, it often requires a consultant with hard-to-find specifications (for example, a woman who speaks Amharic and lives in northern Israel). To meet these demands, it often makes sense to hire a part-time or freelance consultant. Also, SHATIL has found it difficult to retain its most talented senior consultants because the SHATIL salary scale is well below that of private consulting firms. With the flexible staffing model, consultants whose services would otherwise be out of the range of SHATIL's pay scale provide discounted services on a part-time or retainer basis. This enables SHATIL to draw on a varied and talented pool of consultants and for these consultants to have opportunities to work with social change nonprofits. In addition to the 60 SHATIL staff, of which 38 are part-time, there are about 30 freelancers who work on retainer.

Basket of Services

Services range from low intensity to high intensity based on the amount of staff time required to provide them. High-priority groups often receive the full range of services and many hours of consulting (the most intensive service offered). Services include those described below.

Information resources. SHATIL writes and publishes "how-to guides" on various aspects of organizational development and advocacy. Guides are published in four languages and are sold to the public for a token fee. SHATIL also maintains a computerized fundraising library with a database of local and international funding sources and a database of businesses interested in cooperating with NGOs.

Workshops, conferences, and seminars. SHATIL organizes more than 100 training events per year, including workshops, conferences, and courses. Topics range from volunteer recruitment to proposal writing to media relations. Workshops are skills-focused and designed to provide basic information, hands-on experience (through simulations, role plays, and exercises), and instructional take-home materials. Some workshops are open to the general public for a fee, while others have closed registration for priority clients only.

Courses and forums. In the mid-1990s SHATIL began offering more multisession courses, and in response to participant feedback, placing greater emphasis on peer learning. SHATIL also identifies specific positions within organizations where staff are in need of "on-the-job training." Young organizations tend to promote former activists to staff positions, often with little background or prior training. SHATIL offers courses with a combination of basic professional training and ongoing staff development to staff in specific positions, such as fundraisers, volunteer managers, spokespersons, program coordinators, executive directors, and board members. As follow-up to the courses, SHATIL offers ongoing forums to provide regular opportunities for networking, peer support, and supplemental training. Some forums offer two versions, one for beginners and another for advanced participants.

Consulting. Approximately 400 organizations per year receive individualized organizational consulting. A consultant is assigned to the organization and together the organization and consultant identify a range of issues to address over a six-month period. Every six months the consultancy agreement is evaluated and revised.

Coalition building. SHATIL works with groups of organizations to develop effective collaboration and joint action around advocacy issues. SHATIL provides a wide range of support to coalitions including coordination, training, strategy development, and staffing. SHATIL assists an average of 30 coalitions per year.

Lessons Learned

With support, activists can learn on the job. A majority of the organizations that receive New Israel Fund support are started by passionate activists with little background in nonprofit management. In many cases these activists are responding to conditions or issues that affect them personally. Often the organization is run on a meager budget with the central activists financing most operations out of pocket. Under these circumstances, organizations need a consultant/trainer who is empathetic, responsive, and creative. They need a program where you can "learn as you go" and organizational support that is practical, accessible, and low cost. Because much of their work is advocacy oriented, they need a source of support that is culturally and ideologically attuned to their needs.

Organizational capacity is built through a combination of training and consultation. SHATIL's experience has demonstrated that training and consultation are highly complementary. Training is an excellent means of imparting information, exposing participants to new ideas and practices, and teaching basic skills. However, it is not sufficient to change organizational behaviors or help organizations to navigate transitions. On the other hand, focusing exclusively on consultation does not help organizations to build internal capacities and skills. Consultation does not typically help to support individuals within the organization or groom them for future leadership. The combination of training and consultation over time helps organizations to integrate new skills, improve effectiveness, and navigate change.

Evaluation of Impact

While many grantmakers have no data on whether their capacity building investments produce long-term improvements, New Israel Fund can point to dozens of organizations that have become self-supporting and are able to describe a clear mission, set goals and priorities, manage finances, raise funds, and deliver services. NIF provides evidence that at least this approach to capacity building works for many of its grantees.

An outside evaluation of SHATIL's capacity building services was conducted in the mid-1990s, utilizing both a questionnaire format and focus groups of staff from organizations that had received assistance. Client organizations reported that during the period covered by the study, their budgets and paid staff almost tripled and the number of funding sources almost doubled. Clients attributed at least some of this success to SHATIL's assistance.

When asked the question "What, in your opinion, was the consultant's most important contribution to your organization," clients tended to cite developmental and problem-solving tasks. Organizations felt that the consulting process had helped them with normative developmental tasks such as establishing roles within the organization, defining programmatic goals, and preparing work plans. Clients also felt that consultants successfully served as a "mirror" for their organizations, assisting them to clarify issues, providing feedback, giving understanding and insights, and providing options. Organizations particularly emphasized the emotional nurturing and support that they received from SHATIL consultants and the importance of practical coaching and problem-solving.

Management Assistance Group

Management Assistance Group (MAG) is a nonprofit management support organization based in Washington D.C. that works exclusively with justice organizations across the country that are "grappling with organizational problems, challenged by change or growth, or striving to become strong." After 25 years, MAG has developed a distinctive philosophy about organization change and how to work with clients. The following five steps provide an overview of how MAG engages clients, offers feedback, and provides support:

- **Exploration.** We meet with key members of the organization to learn about its structure and issues, to gain their trust and confidence, and to make sure they are open to change. We need permission to look broadly because it is not always possible for those inside an organization to see clearly what is missing.

- **Study.** We carefully review written documents, such as budgets, by-laws, financial reports, work plans, and job descriptions, and conduct in-depth interviews with a broad cross-section of the board and staff, in order to explore their concerns and help them to think about their problems in new ways.
- **Analysis.** We then analyze what we have learned, diagnose and reframe the issues. We are committed to getting to the root of each problem and we do not duck tough issues. For example, when we find that an executive director's failure to delegate disempowers the staff and blocks growth, we help the director to see the costs of that behavior and to develop new, more effective ways of operating. In partnership with the staff or board, MAG then designs solutions tailored to the organization that address not just symptoms but underlying causes. If an organization's difficulties stem from an outmoded structure, we help it to design a new one, with job descriptions clearly spelling out each new role.
- **Communication.** We usually present our findings in written as well as verbal form to ensure that they are understood, and communicated in a way that empowers the staff and board to make changes. We help each group to determine which changes it will make and embrace as its own.
- **Implementation and follow up.** Our work does not end with the submission of a report. We continue to work with an organization to help implement the needed changes. It is hard to change and easy to slip back into old, familiar ways of operating. We help the group to stay the course by providing ongoing guidance and, sometimes, mid-course reviews. Follow-up work is absolutely integral to MAG's process.[1]

Capacity Building Initiative

In 1995, the Ford Foundation asked the Management Assistance Group to design and deliver the Capacity Building Initiative (CBI), a program to help Ford's Peace and Social Justice grantees achieve systemic organization change. All grantees have a common mission to deepen democracy, strengthen citizen participation, combat discrimination, and foster true international cooperation. Most are large and generally sophisticated. About 80 percent are national organization and some are international. Grantee budgets range from $500,000 to $10 million, with $2 million being typical, and most have at least six full-time staff.

Despite their sophistication, Ford staff believed that some justice organizations were reluctant to invest in organization development work. Ford wanted a program that would educate grantees about how better management practices could further their mission and then support leaders who were ready to undertake improvements. MAG was well known to Ford, having worked with many of their grantees over the years. Undertaking CBI as a Development Partner with Ford was a major departure for MAG.

The goal for CBI is ambitious: to achieve systemic change for about 100 nonprofits on a limited budget that amounts to an annual expenditure of $6,000 to $7,500 per organization. It is not possible to provide one-on-one assistance for that amount, and MAG was not convinced at the outset that significant change was possible using group interventions. Through their experience with CBI, MAG has concluded that group interventions can be powerful—in some situations even *more powerful* for changing attitudes and perceptions than one-on-one assistance. MAG has recently expanded its consulting approach to include group interventions as an important component of their work.

Before embarking on the design, MAG first interviewed more than 80 grantees. Simply asking grantees what they needed was not helpful, as most asked for individual assistance and help with fundraising. Through the interviews, MAG was able to get a better sense of what the grantees' real needs were, and what would motivate grantees to take advantage of the services. Two principles were developed to guide the design of services: responsiveness and practicality. MAG decided to tailor all services to the unique challenges facing peace and social justice organizations. In addition, services are designed to enable participants to immediately put into practice what they have learned, with a goal of concrete, positive change for each organization. Grantee participation is guided by four principles:

- **Confidentiality:** MAG holds in strict confidence everything said or done by participants in the course of CBI services, and everything MAG learns about them.
- **Voluntary participation:** Grantees are free to choose to sign up for CBI services or not, based on their organizational priorities. Participation is not a condition of continued funding, nor is the Ford Foundation given any report on which groups participate in the services.
- **Active participation:** If grantees do sign up for a service, they are expected to follow through and participate fully in every component. The more time and effort they invest in each service, the more value they will get out of it.
- **Institutional commitment:** CBI custom-designed services aim to produce systemic organizational change. It is therefore essential for participants to have strong institutional support and for the leaders of their organizations to be committed to putting the insights and knowledge gained to work.[2]

The funding for CBI totaled $750,000 per year for the first two years and $600,000 per year from 1999 to 2002. Ford program officers selected grantees to be eligible for CBI services, and the total number has varied from 90 in 2000, down to 70 in 2001, and back up to 112 in 2002. The initial contract for a two-year program began in 1997 and was renewed twice, finishing in 2002. While there is some funding left for a reduced program in 2003, Ford does not plan to continue the program beyond 2003. At that point, some grantees will have had access to CBI services for a total of seven years.

Description and Allocation of CBI Services

MAG provides two types of services: 1) inexpensive educational services accessible to most, if not all, grantees, and 2) intensive services, available to a limited number of nonprofits that are ready to undertake development work. A brief application is required for each service and all services are free to grantees. The challenge for CBI is allocating resources to impact the largest number of grantees.

Intensive services are more expensive to deliver. An organization diagnostic requires three days of consulting and is available to 25 grantees per year. Capacity Grants are available to about 15 organizations each year. Approximately $300,000 out of the total annual budget of $600,000 is allocated for organization diagnostics and Capacity Grants. Finally, two "guided change processes," an innovative group intervention, are available to 15–20 participants per workshop each year.

Workshops, organizational diagnostics, and stipends are relatively inexpensive to offer and popular with grantees. One- or two-day management workshops are offered on different subjects: successfully supervising staff; effective budgeting and financial management; forwarding your goals through the media; making more effective use of technology; and raising money from individual donors. These workshops are presented by outside consultants rather than MAG staff. Five to six workshops are offered each year, typically in Washington, and between 15 and 30 participants are accepted for each workshop. CBI also provides stipends enabling grantes to attend a variety of training courses not provided by MAG—leadership/management training courses, local workshops on computer technology, media strategies, proposal writing, and other topics.

Organizational diagnostic. While grantees are not required to sign up for an organizational diagnostic, they are encouraged to do so. MAG views the diagnostic as a valuable educational step that offers grantees a realistic assessment of their organization's strengths and challenges and often provides the impetus for leaders to make improvements, with or without additional CBI services.

MAG uses a low-cost, long-distance approach to reach grantees all over the country. A senior MAG consultant is assigned to each participating organization. After an initial conversation with the executive director of the grantee organization, a diagnostic questionnaire is sent to both staff and board members. The consultant reviews the responses as well as background material on the organization. The executive director and consultant jointly decide on four to six key people for further in-depth interviews, including the executive director. The consultant then conducts phone interviews, analyzes the responses, provides feedback to the executive director that distinguishes between symptoms and core issues, and makes recommendations for action. This feedback often leads to a number of lengthy discussions to help leaders gain a new perspective and develop a project to address core issues.

Capacity Grants. A small number of grantees each year engage consultants to help with organizational development work using grants of up to $25,000. Originally, Ford program officers selected organizations to receive Capacity Grants, but two problems became evident. Groups that received the grants were not necessarily addressing core issues, and groups that emerged from the organization diagnostic with a better understanding of issues often could not follow through without additional funding. After a couple of years MAG decided to require an organizational diagnostic before grantees could apply for a Capacity Grant. While obtaining a diagnosis does not guarantee that a grantee receives a Capacity Grant, about 70 percent get further assistance with their projects. MAG concludes that the combination of required diagnostic and follow-up grants has been extremely effective.

MAG believes that grantees should choose their own consultants. At the same time, to increase the odds that consulting will be effective, MAG developed a list of consultants across the country who are compatible with MAG's approach to consulting, have experience working with social justice clients, and in their view, are effective at organization change. Consultants are not included simply because they are experienced or have a good reputation. When a grantee is awarded financial assistance, they are given a list of three consultants to interview, often including a MAG consultant. Around two-thirds of grantees decide to use MAG consultants, in part because a positive relationship has been established during the diagnostic process.

Guided change process. A major innovation of the CBI program is the development of a guided change process that uses two group workshops as a vehicle for significant organization change. MAG identified two topics—diversifying the funding base and developing an effective board—that involve significant organization barriers and concluded that training courses would be ineffective, as the knowledge and skills acquired by participants can be difficult to apply. Instead, they designed a five-part change process—pre-screening, first workshop, interim work and coaching, second workshop, and follow-up coaching—to support participants as they begin to introduce changes in their organizations. Participants often have questions or encounter problems and value having an outside "coach" as a sounding board.

After the initial application, a light screening of applicants takes place to make sure that all participants are ready to tackle the issues in the workshop. The facilitator gains insights into the core issues facing each organization by conducting phone interviews and reviewing a pre-questionnaire from each participant. This information also allows the facilitator to make sure that the session addresses all significant issues. For the workshop on developing an effective board, executive directors attend a two-day workshop that allows time for each participant to diagnose his/her organization's issues, develop a plan to introduce changes, and discuss strategies for overcoming potential barriers. Based on what they have learned, participants have to decide if they really want to develop a different type of board. Those who proceed go on to produce a board development plan and have three months to begin changes before attending the second workshop. During this period they receive coaching from MAG consultants. For the second workshop, participants attend with a board partner and work together to review their progress, identify continuing barriers, and plan next steps. After the workshop, MAG provides additional coaching for each participant.

Managing change and growth workshop. When the CBI offerings were first introduced, MAG found that groups simply did not know enough to know what they needed. Large numbers signed up for the fundraising workshop, but were less interested in other offerings. MAG developed an introductory one-day workshop on managing change and growth to help grantees gain insights into their organizational needs, explain how they can use CBI services to address those needs, and begin to establish a relationship with MAG consultants. MAG strongly urges grantees to take the workshop. Seventy-five percent of grantees have done so and give the workshop high ratings.

For both the guided change process workshops and the managing change and growth workshop, facilitation is key to their effectiveness. Facilitators use a Socratic method to lead discussions, posing questions and letting the group provide the answers. For example, the managing change workshop describes several transitions that are common to justice organizations, pointing out signs of trouble, tensions that emerge in organizations, and adjustments to improve organization effectiveness. The workshop helps grantees see that their problems are not unique, but a normal part of organization development.

Group discussions are particularly powerful, as participants are able to recognize their situations in the examples offered by the facilitator and in the stories told by other participants. According to Susan Gross, executive director of MAG, "In a group setting, grantees are able to recognize their problems by seeing them in other people. It takes them much longer to get to that point on their own." The final hour of the managing change and growth workshop is devoted to describing the CBI services that will help grantees address their issues.

Evaluation of Impact

The primary concern with the design of CBI is whether less-intensive, long-distance interventions will deal with important issues for each grantee and stimulate concrete changes and learning. To address this concern, Ford commissioned a five-year evaluation, conducted in 2000, that focuses on grantees' opinions of CBI's impact.[3] The study surveyed clients about the value of CBI and specific changes that have occurred because of CBI. Many of the respondents had used more than one service from MAG over the five-year period, so the responses reveal the cumulative impact of CBI services rather than the impact of an individual service.

Overall the study shows that CBI has had a significant impact on Peace and Social Justice grantees that have used the services, and that grantees view the service as valuable. Perhaps most telling, when asked whether Ford should increase their grants by $750,000 (about $7,500 per organization) or continue CBI, eighty percent favored keeping CBI.

A few other key findings, include:

- When asked if they would have engaged in significant OD work if CBI had not been available, 34% said yes, 34% said no, and 19% were not sure.
- 86% said that they would continue with capacity building work, 6% were unsure, and 6% thought not.
- 86% felt that CBI helped their organization better identify and understand its OD and capacity building needs.

- 86% felt that CBI helped their organization develop action plans to address important organizational issues.
- 91% agreed that CBI services address the most pressing challenges of Peace and Social Justice grantees; 91% agreed that CBI has been a valuable use of their time.

Organization change. In addition to changes in attitude and perspectives, grantees were asked about specific organization changes that occurred in their organization. Most grantees reported at least one specific area of change, while many reported that change had occurred in more than one area. Forty-six percent reported that the *board was strengthened* and 40 percent reported that CBI helped to *expand or diversify funding*. In general, CBI contributed to organization change and improvement for 82 percent of respondents, while 17 percent reported that knowledge and skills were enhanced but there was no evidence of organization change. Overall, more than half of respondents reported that CBI helped identify and address key barriers to capacity building (57 percent), that mission focus or priorities were clarified (51 percent), that roles and responsibilities were clarified (53 percent).

Lessons Learned

1. The power of group process. The most important lesson for MAG is the power of group process as a vehicle for organization change. The design of the guided change process, using multiple workshops, is a significant innovation and a key component of CBI. Like many other programs, CBI offers low-cost training for many and high-cost on-site consulting for a few. The key difference for CBI is the ability to achieve significant change for a larger number of grantees through two lower cost innovations—the guided change process and the long distance organization diagnostic.

2. Let organizations choose to participate. In the beginning, Ford program officers selected grantees without any guidance, and the participation rate was 50 percent. In the third year MAG developed selection criteria. Eligible grantees received a special letter from Ford inviting them to participate, but asking them to decline if they were not interested.

Twenty-five percent declined, and of those that accepted, 90 percent participated in at least one service.

3. CBI reaches grantees who are not quite ready for help. In MAG's traditional consulting work, all clients have reached a point where they recognize the importance of addressing organizational issues and ask for help. Many groups never reach that point, and never approach MAG for assistance. The CBI program, however, is able to reach some of these groups, as one-third of all participants said that they would not have engaged in OD work without CBI. MAG has been able to introduce nonprofit leaders to the notion that they have to work on their organizations, not just their programs.

Conclusions

Development Partners demonstrate that low-cost, long-term assistance is possible and offers an intriguing option for capacity building, particularly for local or regional funders that can partner with a regional MSO. The funding arrangement offers important advantages over Capacity Grants by improving the allocation of consulting time to clients most likely to benefit, and improving the consultant's incentive to offer candid feedback and focus on long-term change.

1. Similarities in consulting approaches. Each of the three Development Partners described here have remarkably similar philosophies about consulting. Their practices, developed over years of working with grantees, may well serve as a model for how to effect long-term change in organizations. Each relies on interviews by experienced consultants to diagnose the client's issues, paying particular attention to client readiness. Each works to develop confidential relationships based on respect and trust. Each uses a collaborative approach, rarely shaping a project to simply produce recommendations or a report. At the same time, each brings considerable expertise to their clients—from management topics to fundraising and the political environment—but uses their expertise to help clients learn and develop their own ability to diagnose and solve problems.

2. Grantees benefiting from Development Partners. An interesting question is whether the Development Partner approach can be effective with all types of organizations. SHATIL and CRE are dedicated to working with grassroots organizations that deal with social injustice or poverty. MAG has been equally successful working with larger, more sophisticated social justice groups. One characteristic of both SHATIL and CRE clients is that boards and staff often have limited management experience. There is a significant need for assistance to develop skills and introduce systems for financial management, planning, fundraising, human resource management, and information technology. Ongoing support helps grantees to acquire skills and knowledge when they need it.

Two characteristics of all grantees may also explain why Development Partners are particularly effective. These groups may be more reluctant than most to seek assistance with management issues—signing up for a Structured Program or applying for a Capacity Grant.

- Management practices are sometimes viewed by clients with suspicion as "private sector" ideas and contrary to the organization's mission.
- Building trust, based on shared values and respect for the grantee's work, may be particularly important in order to provide assistance to these groups.

In each of the three Development Partners described, the consultants understand social justice issues, and are sensitive to the management issues that confront such organizations.

3. Low cost. While the Development Partners highlighted here have a significant impact, all are doing so with limited funding. Organizations that have an "intensive" relationship with SHATIL are offered about ten hours of consulting per month, which is about 15 days per year. CRE devotes about six days to a "typical" client and 12 for an "intense" relationship. MAG is serving about 90 grantees on a budget of $600,000, for a little more than $6,000 per grantee. While grantmakers may assume that ongoing assistance, available whenever clients need it, is a more expensive proposition than individual Capacity Grants, it appears that the costs here are quite low. One reason is that the supply of consulting days is lower than demand, forcing consultants to limit the time with any one client in order to serve more organizations.

Another source of cost savings comes from the elimination of significant marketing expenses. Development Partners, such as CRE and SHATIL, invest little time in marketing. For most independent consultants, 30 percent or more of their billable time is needed to meet potential clients, respond to requests that may or may not turn into a contract, and diagnose organization issues in order to submit a proposal. CRE and SHATIL are able to keep their rates low, in part by avoiding these costs.

4. Reduced client choice. Some funders prefer to let grantees select a consultant in the marketplace, rather than limiting them to a specific Partner, arguing that there is a better selection of consultants and that clients are more committed if they exercise choice. Barbara Kibbe from the Packard Foundation suggests, "You will get more leverage out of coaching a grantee on how to select a consultant than from choosing the 'best' consultant for the grantee. In fact, the more decisions the grantseeker makes, the more committed they will be to the process and the project."[4]

Development Partners agree that forcing an organization to use a particular consultant can be counterproductive, and provide some degree of choice. SHATIL and CRE both conclude that offering unlimited choice is less of an issue for their grantees than whether they provide high-quality consultants with the skills and expertise needed to help grantees. SHATIL has 20 organizational consultants on staff, while CRE has 25, and are able to offer clients a choice. An evaluation of SHATIL found that one of the primary criticisms was from long-term New Israel Fund grantees who felt that they were "outgrowing" SHATIL staff and wanted more options in terms of consultants with skills appropriate to larger organizations. They responded by bringing other consultants on staff and allowing some grantees to use outside consultants subsidized by SHATIL. They also have developed new courses to meet specific needs identified by clients.

MAG agrees that grantee choice is important, and addressed it in two ways. First, by offering invitations to potential participants they allow each grantee to choose to participate in the CBI program. While some do not, those that do have exercised some degree of choice and are more committed to participate. Second, they use the Managing Change and Growth introductory workshop to introduce themselves to participants. When participants sign up for services—a workshop or organization diagnostic—they are making a more informed choice based on having met the MAG staff. If they have an unfavorable impression, they won't sign up.

5. Candid feedback to grantees. As a Development Partner, consultants have a built-in incentive to offer candid feedback if it is helpful to address long-term issues. Certainly some independent consultants consider challenging clients an important part of their approach, though many are more cautious if there is a risk of getting fired. Clients can fire an independent consultant, whereas a Development Partner is not fired from the Partner contract, and simply moves on to help the next organization waiting for assistance.

While grantmakers, clients, and consultants provide a strong endorsement of the Development Partners approach, additional research is needed to confirm the long-term impact and compare Development Partners with other approaches. Overall, the New Israel Fund provides the strongest evidence that a Development Partner can help grantees develop lasting capabilities. NIF forces grantees to develop their capabilities because it is clear from the beginnng that program funding will decline and then stop. Despite the enormous challenges facing these newly formed or emerging organizations, most of them survive after NIF support has stopped.

Ford's evaluation research shows very positive initial evidence of changes in attitude and perspective, and some evidence of organizational change. A high level of client satisfaction is evident as 80 percent of respondents prefer having access to CBI services than a direct grant for the equivalent funds. Further longitudinal research is needed to track more closely how capabilities change, and the impact on organization performance.

CRE has not formally tracked the survival or performance of its clients over the past 20 years. But CRE knows a great deal about the progress and setbacks of many long-term clients and believes that they have had a substantial impact on the vast majority of clients. The New York Foundation and other funding partners agree, based on visible evidence of grantee improvement and voluntary reports from some grantees.

Key Features of Development Partners

- Assistance is available when grantees are ready
- Grantees are referred to Development Partner by grantmakers
- Consultants influence grantee's perception of issues
- Consultants can develop long-term relationships with grantees
- Consultants provide ongoing coaching
- Consultants have incentives to focus on long-term improvement

Notes

1. Management Assistance Group web site. “How We Work: An Overview of Our Approach.”
2. Management Assistance Group web site: “Basic Principles Guiding MAG’s CBI.”
3. Marble, Melinda, 2000.
4. Kibbe, Barbara, David and Lucille Packard Foundation, 2002, p. 2.

CHAPTER 5

Structured Programs

Structured Programs are an ambitious form of capacity building that focus on long-term performance improvement. Participants are required to engage in specific steps, such as organizational assessment, comprehensive planning, and setting performance goals. They then devote several years to making improvements so as to meet their performance targets. In exchange for agreeing to these steps, participants receive substantial consulting support and often financial incentives as well. Consultants often assist throughout the multiyear change process as new practices and systems are put into place.

Sponsors of Structured Programs believe that improvement occurs when nonprofit leaders try new ideas and practices. Programs are designed to either entice or require participants to take specific actions that nonprofits rarely undertake of their own volition—such as implementing a system for outcome measurement, engaging in comprehensive planning, or setting aside funds for working capital. Only by implementing such practices do nonprofit leaders begin to appreciate how they contribute to organization stability or program quality.

Structured Programs are based on a combination of required educational steps and substantial support—so that well-thought out plans have the resources required for implementation. Even if nonprofit leaders know precisely what they need to do, they often lack financial resources for administrative positions, working capital, or technology to implement their plans. At the same time, some funders have learned from experience that offering general operating support without insisting on educational steps—assessments and thoughtful planning—is not effective at bringing about change.

Finally, programs that require specific performance measures have a mechanism to evaluate not only the progress of participants, but also the overall impact of the program. It is the *only form* of capacity building for which assessing organization improvement is automatic. With most forms of capacity building success is based on whether specific capabilities are implemented, rather than whether performance improves. It is assumed, but rarely tested, that specific management practices will improve performance for a given organization.

Sponsors play a central role in the change process, helping participants to shape goals, pushing them to address critical issues, and monitoring their progress. While a funder can sponsor a Structured Program, there are advantages if an intermediary, such as an MSO, plays this role and the funder is one step removed from the capacity building work. Then participants don't worry whether revealing difficult management issues will affect future program grants. When sponsored by an intermediary, the funding for the programs often comes from a coalition of grantmakers.

This chapter presents four examples of Structured Programs, each illustrating a different way of utilizing this approach. Three are designed and delivered by an intermediary—either an MSO or a consulting firm. These are National Arts Strategies, the Nonprofit Finance Fund's Building for the Future^{SM} program, and Matrix. National Arts Strategies, a national MSO that has used a Structured Program approach for close to 20 years, provides substantial support and ongoing coaching of grantees for five years or more, as well as significant payouts when grantees reach agreed upon goals. Building for the Future^{SM} (BFF), designed by the Nonprofit Finance Fund, a national MSO, focuses more narrowly on building financial reserves, and combines ongoing consulting with challenge grants to help participants build their reserves over a ten-year period. The Matrix program is a low-cost alternative that does not offer financial incentives but uses group workshops to supplement limited on-site consulting. Developed by a consulting firm, Community Impact Consulting, this 15-month program requires each organization to develop a system for outcome measurement to track performance improvement over the longer term.

The fourth example, the Edna McConnell Clark Foundation (EMCF), has developed a Structured Program that represents a radical shift in its grantmaking practices. Previously supporting 150 or more grantees, EMCF now concentrates its resources and efforts on helping a small number of organizations willing and able to engage in significant capacity building. EMCF provides substantial consulting assistance and multiyear support linked to milestones set by the grantee.

National Arts Strategies

National Arts Strategies (NAS) is an independent MSO that serves arts organizations throughout the country. Founded in 1983, NAS has a clear purpose: "Believing that organizational health supports artistic excellence, we work with communities to strengthen arts organizations by developing the managerial and financial skills required to adapt and thrive in today's changing environment." That mission statement encompasses two key aspects of NAS: 1) it utilizes a community approach, encompassing many arts organizations; 2) it focuses on management areas that affect financial stability and places capacity building within the broader artistic objectives of the organization.

To date, NAS has conducted stabilization projects in eight geographic communities: Boston, Kansas City, New York, Arizona, Seattle, Baltimore, Columbus, and New Haven. In each community, NAS collaborates with foundation, corporate, individual, and government donors, who invest in a multiyear funding and technical assistance program designed to strengthen the community's organizations. These dollars must be over and above normal operating grants and gifts to the arts. As of early 2003, seventy-two arts organizations have been served in stabilization projects with a total investment of $46 million. Since 1997, NAS has expanded its focus from large arts organizations to include those with budgets of $250,000 to $1,500,000.

NAS is one of the few assistance providers that bring funders together to supply working capital to their grantees. Even small funders can join in the effort and help to provide significant incentives for grantees to improve. More recently, NAS has experimented with a single funder model, working closely with the Cleveland Foundation to help arts organizations in that community.

Thus, NAS does not take on individual clients; rather, it works with groups of clients in a region as part of a communitywide stabilization project. While it works together with funders in each region, NAS is an independent advisory service that develops close and confidential working relationships with its clients. In addition to ongoing management support, coaching, and technical assistance, the stabilization project provides an infusion of cash to create or augment working capital reserves (generally speaking, up to 25 percent of an organization's total budget). The working capital reserve grant is made after changes to management practices have occurred so that the organization is prepared to manage the additional resources. NAS is typically involved in a community for five to eight years before the arts organizations "graduate" and working capital reserve grant restrictions are lifted.

The National Arts Strategies approach is based on years of experience with arts organizations that have excellent programming but precarious finances. The latter are often due to a lack of sound financial management systems or sufficient working capital. NAS recognizes that resolving the financial issues requires a great deal of learning and improvement in other areas—from planning and improved governance to more effective use of technology. In a typical stabilization project NAS provides individual organization assessments, technical assistance, and ongoing management support for up to eight years. The program seeks to stabilize the finances of arts organizations by working with them on an appropriate capitalization structure and a range of management issues that may affect long-term stability, such as long-range planning and governance.

Application and Selection

When local grantmakers call NAS for assistance in their community, they are often frustrated by the precarious financial situation of important cultural organizations. Arts leaders may also call for assistance, concerned specifically about their organization. Key community funders invite NAS to meet with both leaders of arts organizations and funders to describe the NAS philosophy, experience in the field, and nature of the work. If the arts organizations express an interest in such a program, community funders form a committee, and NAS conducts an initial assessment of local conditions and needs. The local committee then identifies arts organizations to join the project, based on both need and interest in participating. NAS looks carefully at available financial information, and may make a site visit to each organization. NAS works with as few as five and as many as thirteen organizations in a region.

Developing Capabilities

At the beginning of an engagement, NAS consultants assume the primary consultative relationship with each nonprofit, a relationship that continues throughout the project. These consultants begin by conducting a comprehensive management assessment that serves to educate them about the unique circumstances and aspirations of the organization as well as to educate the client about underlying issues. The assessment also allows each consultant and client to reach a common understanding of issues to be addressed. Each client then develops a long-range plan that addresses issues raised in the assessment. Grantees have often felt greater responsibility for and ownership by developing their own plan, and often hire a local planning consultant. For this reason, NAS does not feel that their direct involvement in planning is necessary, but does offer advice on the structure of the process and reviews and critiques drafts of the plan.

NAS consultants have found that face-to-face time with the client is critical and staff make site visits at least once every two months throughout the project. Yet, NAS is able to help clients with relatively few consulting days each year by overseeing the organization's progress on a few central issues—financial systems, planning, and performance—but requiring clients to do the work. In a typical five-year project, direct contact declines from ten days in the first year to six by the final year. Consultants are also available by phone and email.

NAS consultants are particularly effective because they focus on educating and coaching clients. Their primary role is to ask challenging questions on issues such as survival, mission deviation (such as when a group pursues funding at all costs), or board performance.

NAS consultants can be more candid than most, as clients who don't like what they're hearing cannot terminate the relationship without losing important financial payouts. NAS consultants offer clients a confidential relationship; details about the nonprofits' management challenges are not shared with local funders. Instead, the committee of local grantmakers receives reports of financial progress on several indicators, and an overview of organization progress. Grantmakers are cautioned that additional information might compromise NAS's work with a client.

Once the plan is complete and other benchmarks met, such as thorough and timely monthly financial reports, NAS recommends the local committee approve a multiyear working capital reserve grant for the organization. Progress is monitored by NAS over the course of the grant, usually five years. Plans are evaluated and updated annually to take into consideration changes in external conditions. At the end of the grant cycle, the organization completes a new long-range plan in order to continue their work on financial stability.

On rare occasions (seven to date), an organization does not make sufficient progress to be awarded a final working capital grant.

FIGURE 1. National Arts Strategies—Capacity Building Steps

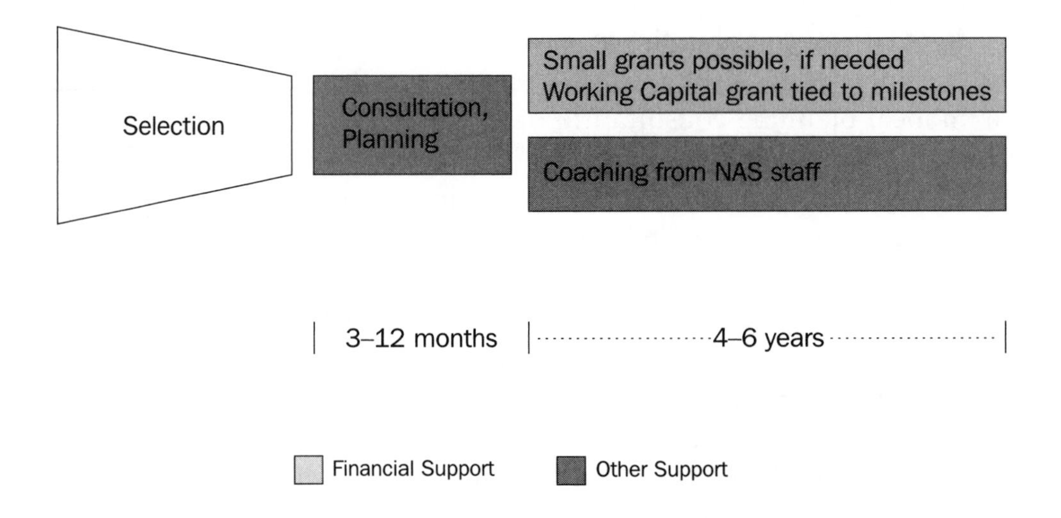

Evidence of impact. Because it tracks working capital and net assets for each participant in every community program, NAS has strong evidence that their intervention improves the financial health of participants. The following charts show net assets for six communities, over a period of about ten years. The data shows clear improvement in net assets from when each project was launched. In most cases, financial indicators have held steady or even improved over time.

The dramatic progress cannot be attributed only to NAS consulting, however. Each participant received an additional grant for working capital during the assistance period, which clearly affects financial indicators. It may also be that local funders provide additional funding or general operating support for organizations that have participated in the program. Finally, general economic conditions can play a significant role in any community.

National Arts Strategies Project Sites Net Assets

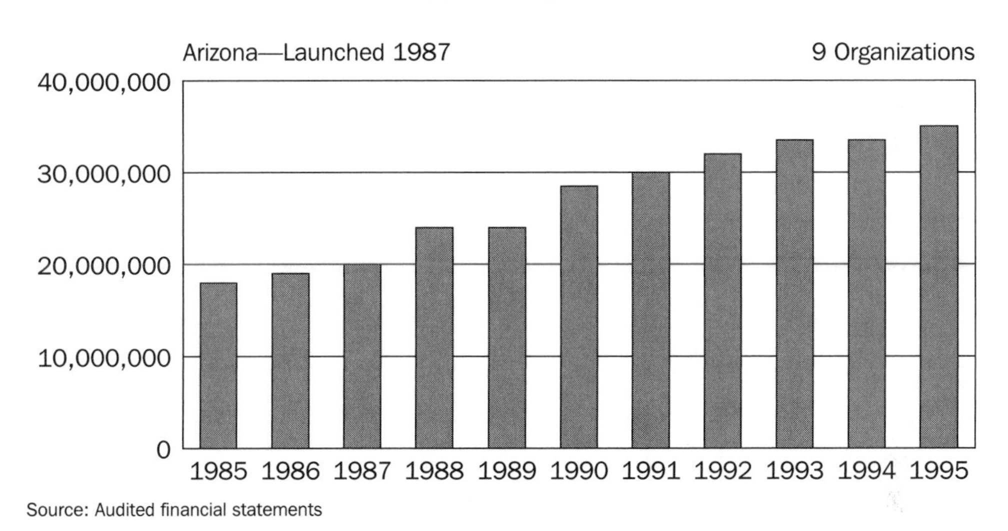

Source: Audited financial statements

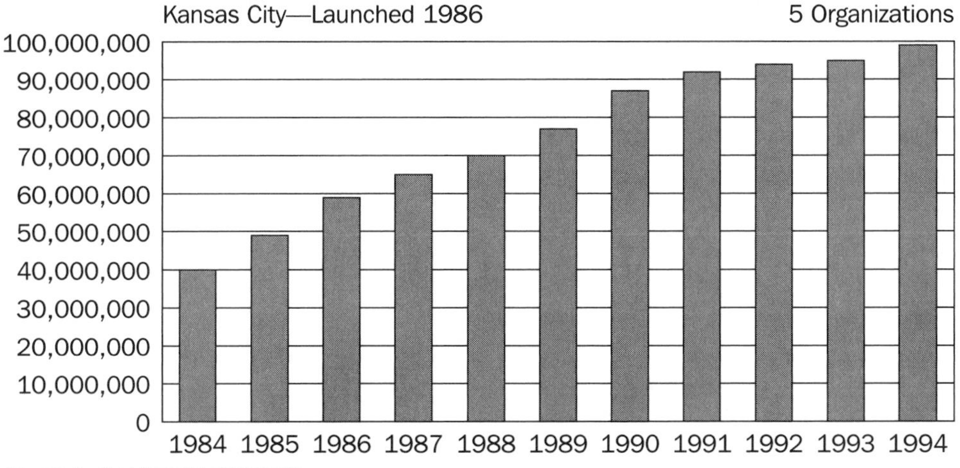

Source: Audited financial statements

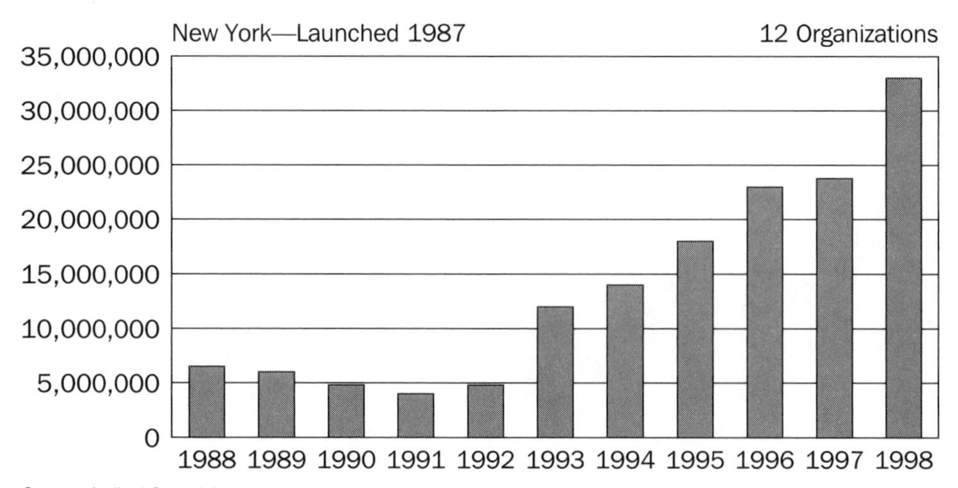

Source: Audited financial statements

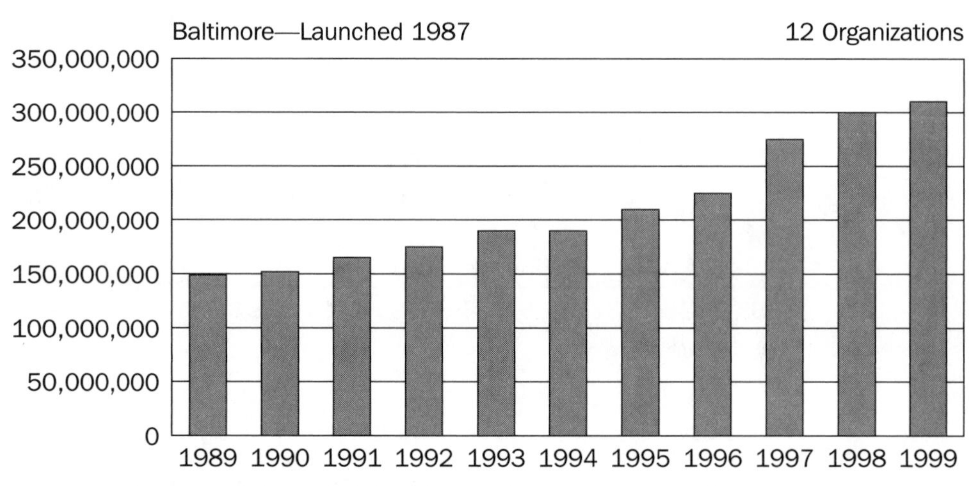

Source: Audited financial statements; FY 1999 is a six-month fiscal year for one organization

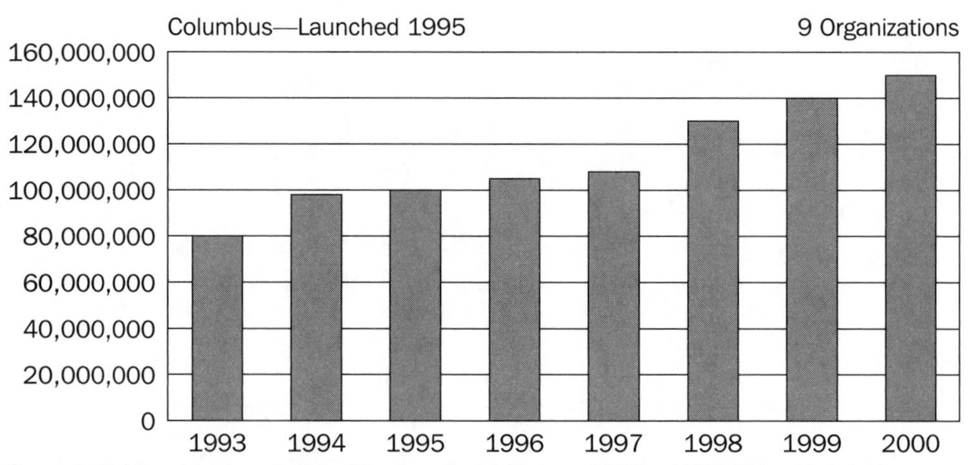

Source: Audited financial statements; Data of the six month period between 7/1/97 and 12/31/97 is not included for one organization due to change in fiscal year. FY 2000 is a 13-month fiscal year for one organization.

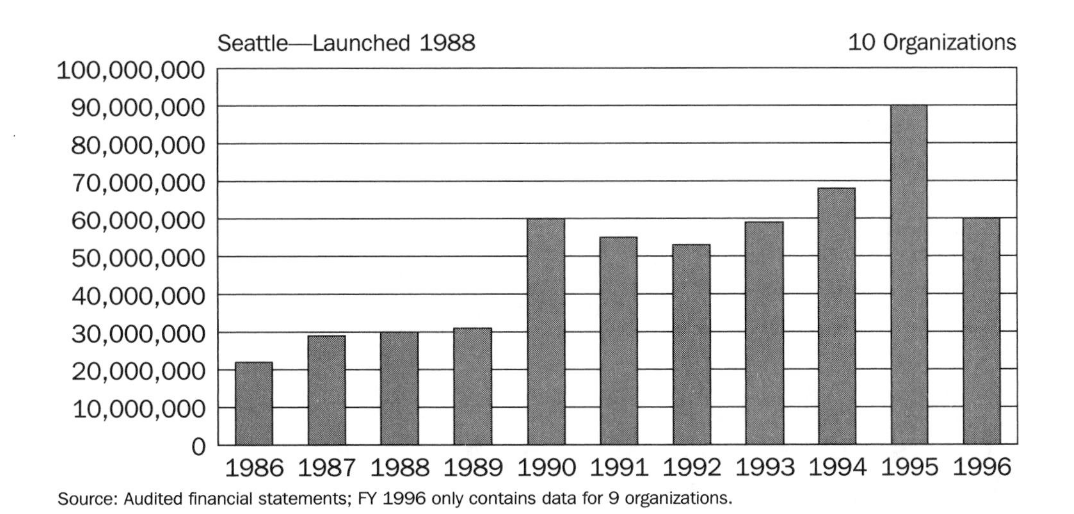

Source: Audited financial statements; FY 1996 only contains data for 9 organizations.

Lessons Learned

In working with more than 72 arts organizations, NAS has learned a great deal about organizational change and the specific challenges facing arts organizations. Seven of the most important lessons are presented below. In addition, NAS itself has learned from its findings and has refined its consulting approach over time.

1. Address the whole organization. In the early 1990s, NAS often worked only with the financial officer, executive director, and board chair, and focused on improving the financial management system and developing long-range financial plans. This narrow focus on financial stability proved ineffective, however, in cases where the issues were largely cultural. NAS recognized that a different approach was needed to have a broader impact on the organization and to change the way leaders and staff think about investing in program rather than working capital or building reserves; the way they think about current needs versus future needs. The NAS process now involves the entire board, top management team, and much of the staff in implementing changes.

2. Let client issues dictate work plans. Over time, NAS has learned that progress is greater when they are more flexible about the order in which critical issues are addressed and the methods used. For example, nonprofits do not have to conform to a particular financial reporting model, as long as they find something that works for them and that meets an NAS standard. The client's leadership decides how rapidly issues are addressed and in what order. To encourage more rapid engagement, NAS has learned to balance its interest in capitalization with management's preoccupations.

3. Coaching works. In NAS's experience, coaching from its staff has the greatest impact on clients, changing the way they see issues and building their commitment to take action. It is always important to help clients diagnose and address underlying issues and coaches are often required to present clients with harsh realities.

4. Clients with low commitment can make progress. The NAS program provides some evidence that the combination of a strong financial incentive and a well-constructed process can bring along organizations that might otherwise be considered "not ready." The local funders committee presents NAS with a slate of clients, at varying stages of readiness. From the outset, some clients are skeptical about external interventions or the need for change, and remain guarded throughout the project. Nevertheless, even these clients learn something from the program and are able to comply with the grant terms, confessing at the end that the new management practices are valuable tools.

5. Don't impose "best practices." NAS has learned that nonprofits don't operate the same way, that each has unique qualities, and that there does not appear to be one best way to manage. They view the imposition of best practices out of context to be dangerous because it does not account for the individual circumstances of each organization.

6. Funders change too. Long-term stability often depends as much on changing the grantees' relationship with local funders as it does on their own ability to manage their resources. Through the NAS process, funders better understand why management problems develop and how to help. Many change their grant review practices to include an analysis of long-range capitalization and a review of the organization's long-range plans. Others provide ongoing support for capacity building, recognizing that new issues arise as organizations continue to develop.

7. National consulting staff offers advantages. NAS has been able to retain high-quality consultants as either full-time or associate staff by providing a regular flow of work. Having worked together in other projects and communities, the staff has collectively learned about capacity building and developed a shared perspective on how to help arts organizations. Colleagues also provide a valuable sounding board when individual consultants face difficult issues. An important disadvantage is that consultants must travel extensively, have less face time with clients because they are not local, and cannot continue the relationship once the project is completed.

Nonprofit Finance Fund—Building for the Future℠ Product

The Nonprofit Finance Fund (NFF) was founded in 1980 to provide management assistance to nonprofits and loans for facilities projects and working capital to support their businesses. NFF is an independent MSO, serving nonprofits in Washington, DC, the San Francisco Bay area, Greater Philadelphia, New York City, New Jersey, Massachusetts, Detroit, and Chicago, and makes available some services to nonprofits throughout the country. NFF is funded by national and regional grantmakers, financial institutions, and government agencies. Clients served typically have budgets between $250,000 and $10 million.

Building for the Future (BFF) is a financial product developed by NFF to help nonprofits plan, build, develop, and manage cash assets such as building reserves and endowments. BFF combines financial assistance and advice to help organizations strengthen their balance sheets. The combination of management assistance and financial support provides nonprofits with an incentive for sound management and provides funders with a structured funding practice. BFF has been used to help Boys & Girls Clubs in the Northeast as well as human services organizations in the Detroit area to develop building reserve funds. BFF has also helped jazz-presenting organizations nationwide to plan and develop endowments. To date, BFF has added $5.8 million in combined deposits and matching funds to the endowments and building reserves of 35 organizations.

One version of BFF is designed to encourage sound building management practices, such as preventive maintenance and regular replacement of major systems. NFF research on Boys & Girls Clubs shows that even well-funded, well-managed organizations that have received high-quality technical assistance on building management often do not implement sound building management practices.

> For most managers of youth-serving organizations, including those at Boys & Girls Clubs, this pattern of not implementing building management practices persisted despite knowledge that such measures save money and are effective. The problem was, in part, a result of the realities of the funding environment. Clubs and other youth-servers reported that virtually all their funders favored dramatic 'rescue' grants for emergencies or 'one-time opportunities' while rejecting general operating support or 'overhead' that would fund ongoing management improvements. The unintended effect of such policies was to provide an expensive incentive for poor management.[1]

Launched in 1999, Building for the Future has been piloted with 19 Boys & Girls Clubs in New York, New Jersey, and Boston, and has $4.5 million of funding provided by the Charles Hayden Foundation, Citigroup, and the U.S. Treasury's Community Development Financial Institutions Fund.

Developing Capabilities

Once a Boys & Girls Club is selected for the program, NFF staff and a facility consultant conduct a site visit and assess the club's facilities and financial position. Each club develops a 20-year schedule for building replacement, and a plan to build an adequate reserve within ten years. The reserve is built with a combination of monthly contributions from grantees and matching contributions from NFF over the ten-year period. The size of matching grants and the club's contribution depend on the age, number of square feet, and overall physical condition of the club, and the financial strength of the organization. To encourage clubs to engage in sound building management, NFF also provides matching funds for preventive maintenance, as needed, and loans if building replacements are required before sufficient reserves are in place.

About 12 to 15 hours of initial consulting time is required to complete the assessment and plans for each club. NFF staff also offer ongoing regional workshops for grantees on facility-related topics and are available to grantees to deal with issues as they arise. Currently there are approximately six NFF staff members, representing administrative, financial, and program functions, who share responsibilities related to BFF. One NFF program staffer is assigned to manage the primary relationship with each participating club and checks in with the executive director about once every two months. Altogether the investment of NFF staff time is about a half a day per month or less, for each club.

Building for the Future is designed to impose a minimal burden for grantees while affecting the behavior and attitudes of grantee boards and staff. Over ten years, they expect clubs to get used to the management processes of developing building replacement plans, regular building replacement, preventive maintenance, and making regular deposits. After a long period of using such systems and practices, NFF expects that grantees will find it difficult to live without them, and will continue to plan and fund building needs even after the financial incentives of BFF have disappeared.

Results to Date

As of January 2003, nineteen clubs had on-site visits, and 16 had formally enrolled in the program and begun making deposits. The three clubs that had not yet enrolled have faced multiple changes in executive directors since January 2000. Matching grants (in current dollars) to each organization range from $52,200 to $506,530 over ten years, with an average allocation of $194,000. The average monthly matching grant for each club is approximately $1,600. As of January 2003, a total of $520,000 in grants has been provided, stimulating $900,000 in matching deposits from the clubs, and producing $787,000 in building system replacements.

Nine of the 16 clubs were on time or ahead of schedule with deposits to their building reserve accounts, although only two or three clubs were making deposits to their reserve accounts on a monthly basis as planned. Instead, many were making annual or semiannual payments, often when they receive capital funds such as Community Development Block Grants.

Nine made replacements to building systems. The replacement schedule has proven to serve as more of a general guideline as equipment thus far has generally lasted longer than expected. Matching funds for preventive maintenance have not been used to the extent planned. Clubs are required to submit receipts for maintenance contracts or actual work performed, and few have done so. It seems that many clubs use their own staff to conduct preventive maintenance, and do not have receipts. In other cases, staff simply lack the time to submit the paperwork.

Thirteen clubs received follow-up site visits from the facility consultant or NFF program staff. Two workshops were conducted on building management practices in October 2001, and 60 precent of the clubs attended.

Lessons Learned

1. Leadership turnover can delay improvement. Of the 19 participating clubs identified by January 2000, nine had changed executive directors by January 2003. Five clubs have had more than one change in leadership during this period, and one club endured four transitions in leadership. Turnover has had a clear impact on NFF's ability to establish Building for the Future and influence management behavior.

2. Medium-size clubs benefit most. A preliminary conclusion is that clubs with budgets between $750,000 and $2,000,000 benefit the most from this program.[2] Few medium-size or smaller clubs have either a building replacement schedule, a systematic process for putting funds aside, or a proactive approach to preventive maintenance and replacement. For these organizations, management assistance to assess the financial systems and develop plans is an important contribution. Medium-size organizations have found the replacement schedule a useful tool not only for facility planning but for overall financial and fundraising plans.

Small clubs don't benefit as much, because they have trouble keeping up with the administrative requirements of the program. They often lack the management and administrative support to copy preventive maintenance contracts, establish financial systems, and make monthly payments. They also have not taken the extra step of using these plans for larger planning purposes. Larger clubs don't benefit as much from the management assistance because they already have building reserves and facility plans in place, although reserves may be somewhat underfunded. Larger clubs are attracted to the program primarily by the matching funds.

3. Need to relax some restrictions. Overall, with the exception of the smaller clubs, grantees have not found the requirements to be overly burdensome or onerous. One improvement would be for NFF to relax the requirement for competitive bids for building work. NFF is also considering more flexible and customized schedules for payment, to better reflect the cash flow situation of clubs.

4. Grantees want additional requirements. Recognizing that unused reimbursements for preventive maintenance represent a substantial sum, some clubs suggested that NFF should *require* them to submit paperwork for reimbursement.

5. Culture is changing. NFF has learned from grantee focus groups that the attitudes of board and staff are changing to a more proactive approach to building maintenance. The fact that a funder is behind this change in management practices is particularly persuasive for nonprofit boards. The Hayden Foundation has considerable influence as one of the few funders for capital needs. Equally important has been the cultural change of the Hayden Foundation, as they came to learn that their earlier practices, sometimes in the form of a "hero rescue grant," were actually counterproductive.

FIGURE 2. Building for the Future Program—Capacity Building Steps

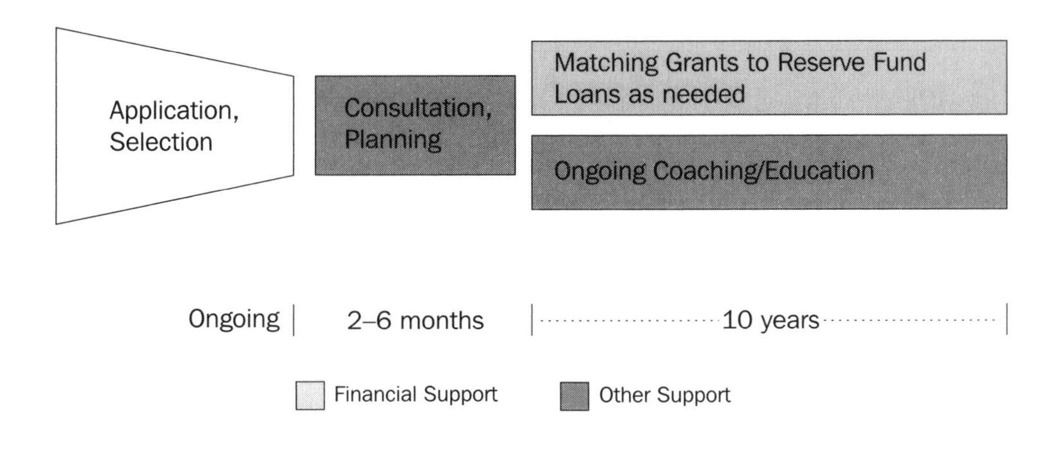

The Matrix Program

Matrix is a 15-month comprehensive management assistance program for a group of up to 20 agencies working toward a common outcome in a geographically defined community. The program offers workshops, monthly coaching, and some on-site assistance at no cost to participants. It does, however, require a significant investment of time and energy, particularly for the executive director of each agency. In joining Matrix, participants agree to four requirements: a comprehensive external assessment conducted by a team of experts; the implementation of a quality improvement project arising from the assessment; the implementation of an outcome measurement system that tracks at least one program outcome; and participation in 12 full-day workshops. One board member as well as the executive director from each agency are required to attend the workshops. In addition, executive directors are asked to take one idea from each workshop to implement in their organizations. Agencies earn a certificate of completion if they meet all four requirements.

Matrix was developed by Community Impact Consulting (CIC), based in California, with strong support from the Stuart Foundation. Much like National Arts Strategies, any community can request a Matrix program, which CIC delivers for a fixed fee. A primary sponsor in each community, such as a community foundation or United Way, takes the lead in preparing for the Matrix program. Matrix is unique because the sponsor not only identifies a community issue to be addressed, but works with CIC to identify an appropriate indicator for the issue that can be measured in the community. The sponsor is responsible for collecting baseline data on the issue, and repeating the data collection a year or two after the completion of the Matrix program.

Nine communities engaged in a Matrix program between 1998 and 2002. In each case, one or more funders (including Stuart) sponsored the program to address an important community issue. Between six and 12 agencies participated in each community, with the result that 76 agencies have completed the program. The primary sponsor, with CIC assistance, hires a Matrix Coordinator, a local consultant who runs the 15-month program on a half-time basis. The Coordinator organizes 12 local workshops, selects local trainers, arranges for teams of volunteers to conduct assessments, arranges for technical assistance, and meets monthly with each grantee.

Matrix is a low-cost version of a Structured Program. Much of the on-site consulting for the quality improvement project is arranged pro bono by the Coordinator. Matrix is also less expensive because it uses a workshop format rather than on-site consulting to educate participants about management topics that may be relevant. The greatest cost is for the Coordinator. CIC will deliver a Matrix program for $175,000, which can cover up to 20 participants.

There is no financial enticement to enroll in a Matrix program, in the form of challenge grants or program support. For organizations interested in internal improvement, Matrix offers substantial value—free workshops, monthly coaching from the Matrix Coordinator, and free on-site assistance with the improvement project and outcome measurement system. Only organizations that are committed to capacity building and place a high value on the support provided enroll.

Application and Selection

The primary sponsor invites all agencies that share a common community issue, such as "reducing youth and family violence." Matrix differs from most forms of capacity building in that enrollment is open to every nonprofit active in a program area. Typically, forty organizations are invited. Of these eight to twelve decide to participate. Of those that begin, about ten percent drop out. CIC believes strongly that capacity building should be voluntary and that everyone should be able to participate. According to Rudeen Monte, the designer of Matrix, "These people are grown-ups. We don't pressure them. They know if they have the time to devote to this process. We also don't talk about failure if someone does not complete the program. They are choosing not to participate. It is a decision to put their energy someplace else."

Developing Capabilities

The nonprofit assessment begins with a survey that is completed by board members, staff, volunteers, funders, and clients. The Coordinator assembles an assessment team (typically local volunteers) that includes experts in human resources and information technology, a lawyer, and accountant. The team reviews internal documents and the surveys, but does not conduct on-site interviews. A detailed report is prepared in each of seven management areas, with recommendations for improvement. A typical report might suggest 30 areas for improvement. The Coordinator meets with the executive director to review the findings. By the time the assessment is reviewed, it may be three months into the monthly workshops, and each executive director has developed some relationship with the Coordinator.

Quality improvement project. Once the assessment is complete, each executive director defines a critical management area to tackle. The Coordinator's role is not to offer advice on which issue to tackle, but to help the participant think through the options. Coordinators are trained to use a cause-and-effect model that helps participants identify underlying issues and link a quality improvement project to improved program outcomes. So far, executive directors have chosen important and sometimes difficult areas to improve. CIC believes that it is important to create an environment where the executive director feels comfortable enough to take on difficult issues. Specifically:

- Matrix uses neutral experts. Each member of the assessment team signs a confidentiality agreement and none provide any consulting for participants.
- The Matrix Coordinator also signs a confidentiality agreement, and does not provide any direct technical assistance to the grantees. The assessment report is private and only seen by the Matrix Coordinator and client.
- Participants also sign confidentiality agreements to improve the level of candor in the workshops. As executive directors learn that other participants are also undertaking difficult issues, they are reassured that progress is possible.

The Matrix Coordinator arranges for technical assistance to help each organization with its improvement project.

Outcome measurement. Each agency is required to identify an important program outcome related to the central community issue, and put in place a system to measure the agency's performance on that outcome. During the course of the Matrix program, as management improvements are put into place, Matrix expects to see the outcome measure for each agency improve as well. Most importantly, as each agency improves its outcomes, there should be a corresponding improvement in the community indicator.

Outcome measurement serves two purposes. First, by collecting data on a specific community outcome, as well as agency outcomes, CIC hopes to demonstrate that the Matrix program has an impact. Very few capacity building efforts attempt to demonstrate impact by linking organization changes with improved organization performance or community impact. Perhaps more important, by forcing the measurement of one outcome, nonprofit leaders will learn the value of data and its potential for program improvement. Even a limited outcome measurement system is a very important first step for most nonprofits.

Every agency receives assistance from evaluation consultants to develop a logic model and implement a tracking system. While some agencies already have systems in place to measure program "outcomes," the evaluation consultants have found that nonprofits were measuring process (or activity levels) rather than outcomes. By the end of the program, every executive director has learned the value of tracking outcomes, developed tools, and begun to collect data.

Workshops. Twelve full-day workshops emphasize a few central themes, in particular that all management actions and program planning should be connected to client outcomes. In addition, the Matrix coordinator and workshop trainers use information from the individual assessments to identify topics of common interest. Because of their general importance, seven core topics have been presented in every Matrix program: strategic planning, board development, financial management, outcomes, human resource management, fundraising, and information technology. In each session, participants identify an improvement idea related to the workshop topic that they will implement in their own organization. Participants are expected to complete each "homework" assignment before the next monthly workshop. Executive directors and board members are learning new information that may change how they think about current practices and lead to further change at a later date.

In the first hour of each workshop, participants report briefly to their colleagues on the progress they have made in the past month and other developments. Throughout the workshops there is a great deal of sharing between participants, as they bring up situations from their own experiences and exchange ideas on how to address particular problems.

Coaching. The Coordinator meets monthly with each organization to monitor progress on their improvement project, outcome measures, and homework. Coordinators also offer advice and help the executive director develop strategies to overcome obstacles and push the improvement efforts forward. Participants often describe the individual coaching they receive over 15 months as the most valuable part of the program. CIC trains both the Coordinator and workshop facilitators and provides coaching "on call" throughout the program. CIC prepared a Coordinators Manual that proved to be helpful as well.

Matrix Results

The Matrix information about organization change at the end of each community program is largely based on exit interviews with participants. A follow-up study of agencies would yield valuable information about the sustainability of new practices reported at the end of the program, whether management improvements continue, and changes to program outcomes, financial health, and program growth.

Every agency that has participated in a Matrix program completed their quality improvement project and implemented outcome measurement systems. Exit interviews reveal a high level of satisfaction with Matrix. In every community, participants rate coaching from the Coordinator as very important, saying that it not only provides individual support, but also helps them to tie together topics and relate them to specific agency issues.

An example of specific findings comes from a Matrix program sponsored by the Whatcom Community Foundation in Bellingham, Washington, from July 1998 to December 1999. The 12 community organizations that participated were the largest and most important providers of services related to "youth and family violence." Exit interviews revealed specific improvements already achieved:

- All reported an increase in functional management documentation, such as new financial statements and personnel and board manuals.
- Five of seven agencies that were already collecting outcome data reported improvement over prior-year results.
- An additional five agencies implemented new systems for tracking client outcomes.

- Eight reported improved financial management; some improved their financial management systems, while others either reduced their debt or increased revenue.
- Ten reported improved board/executive director relations.

Matrix is the only program that attempts to track community outcomes. Undoubtedly, a wide range of factors can affect community outcomes, so a causal relationship cannot be shown. At the same time, there were agency improvements during this period, and these agencies do represent a large portion of the services provided in the community. Perhaps the greatest value in defining a community outcome is increased clarity about what each agency is trying to achieve. An outcome focus is brought to bear throughout the workshops and coaching, whether the topic is strategy and program priorities, human resource management, fundraising, or information technology. A constant refrain is, "How will this management idea lead to a reduction in youth and family violence?"

FIGURE 3. Matrix Program—Capacity Building Steps

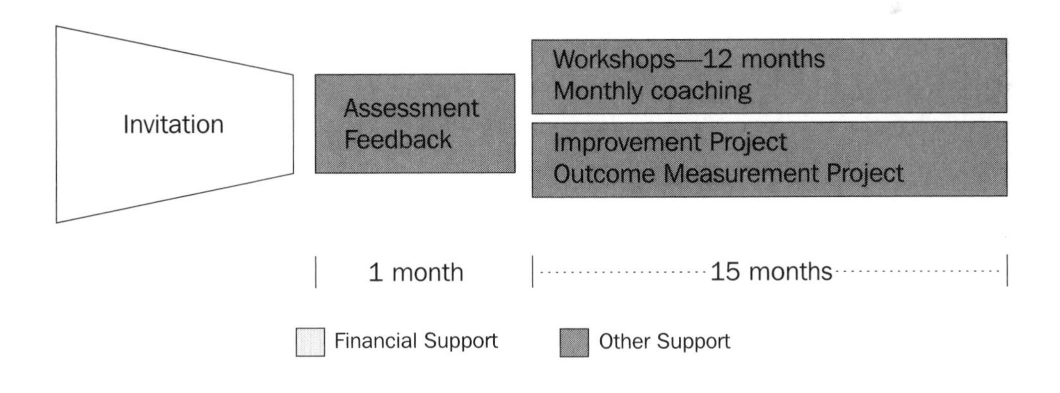

Lessons Learned

Require early assessments. Though the goal was to complete assessments for all participants and begin improvement projects at the beginning of the 15-month program, not all agencies completed surveys and provided documents in a timely manner. In order to get all participants moving ahead on both the improvement project and the outcome project at the beginning of the program, CIC decided in 2002 to require assessments before the workshops begin. Assessment information will also allow the early workshops to better reflect the needs of the agencies.

Emphasize outcomes thinking. CIC has been surprised at how weak or nonexistent the systems are for tracking outcomes in every agency, especially considering that almost every funder sponsoring Matrix requires outcome measures for their grantees. More importantly, nonprofit managers do not use data to make program improvements, and may not consider it important. CIC has decided to put more emphasis on linking management actions to program outcomes throughout every workshop, rather than limiting the discussion to the session on outcomes.

Improve engagements in workshops. CIC was not satisfied with the level of participation in each workshop. To reduce the number of participants who miss workshops, arrive late or leave early, CIC is rethinking the format of the workshops.

Edna McConnell Clark Foundation

Over the past few years, the Edna McConnell Clark Foundation (EMCF) has developed a new approach to grantmaking, called Institution and Field Building (IFB). This approach seeks to address their frustration with their past, often ineffective, efforts to reform public sector systems—criminal justice, schools, and child protective services. Having concluded that the resources available to the foundation were relatively small compared to the task, they decided to focus their resources on a single, broad area: youth development. Specifically, EMCF supports nonprofits that serve young people from low-income circumstances during their "non-school" time. Next, they concentrated their efforts on organizations beyond the start-up phase, located in the urban Northeast Corridor.

EMCF also recognized that capacity building would be important to the success of the new approach. In the past, some grantees provided excellent programs and services, but the organizations were unstable and unable to maintain quality programming over the longer term. Others lacked the resources to improve program quality or expand services to meet the needs of the community. IFB was designed as a more comprehensive and long-term approach to capacity building and invests significant resources in a limited number of youth-serving organizations.

To be selected, organizations must have excellent programming and be at a stage of organizational development suitable for undertaking significant growth. Once selected, grantees are required to go through a multistage process that includes assessment, business planning, and goal setting. EMCF works hard at creating a close working relationship based on mutual goals. It also provides support to complete the business plan and makes a significant investment toward the plan's implementation. The relationship with grantees can extend up to six years and grants are large, having ranged from $1.75 million to $5.5 million. There is no expectation that sizable grants will continue past this period, and each grantee must develop an exit strategy in order to sustain its new activity levels.

EMCF decided to create the position of Portfolio Manager, to work closely with each grantee throughout the planning process and implementation of the plan. Generally, these Portfolio Managers might work with only four or five grantees at a time. EMCF piloted this approach with four organizations beginning in 2000, and announced a total investment of $10 million in May 2001. Four additional organizations were selected in early 2002. Though EMCF is now helping fewer organizations than before, it hopes to have a more lasting impact on those it is working with. EMCF expects eventually to work with a total of 20 to 30 grantees.

> Our goal is that, after five years, each grantee will be stronger, more solvent, more sustainable, more effective, and able to serve—with high-quality programs and services—three to five times as many young people as it did before entering into the institution building relationship with the Foundation.[3]

Application and Selection

EMCF uses a rigorous process to identify grantees that have a very high probability of success. Organizations cannot apply for funding. Instead, EMCF searches for candidates through networking and referrals, in a process they refer to as "sourcing." The executive director is contacted, and if there is interest, the organization is asked to send documents describing the program, financials, and history for a preliminary review. EMCF may decide not to proceed based on this information.

Once an organization has passed a preliminary review, EMCF engages in a due diligence review. Led by a Portfolio Manager, the EMCF team includes experts in youth development, evaluation, information technology, finance, and administration, and makes site visits to observe the program and conduct interviews with key parties—the executive director, key staff, board members, service recipients, key stakeholders, and funders. Additional documentation and data are collected. The due diligence analysis leads to a recommendation to invest, not invest, or return to pipeline.

A key challenge to any selective process is the identification of criteria that will predict whether an organization is capable of moving to the next stage of development. EMCF has developed a set of issues and questions that they consider critical to a successful relationship:

- **Compelling product or service:** does the organization show plausible or demonstrated effectiveness in making a difference in the lives of young people served?
- **Leadership and management:** does the organization have a track record of achieving its objectives and serving its mission, with a vision for future growth, depth in senior management, and a recognition of the need to fill gaps?
- **Operational viability:** do the organization's structure, processes, systems, and relationships have the potential to support growth?
- **Financial health:** are the organization's finances in order and does it show a capacity to manage its financial affairs?
- **Outcomes measurement:** does the organization show concrete efforts at measuring its performance and a commitment to developing systems to evaluate and improve its outcomes?
- **EMCF compatibility:** are the organization's culture and management suited to a highly engaged relationship with the Foundation?[4]

A total of 150 to 200 hours of staff time is invested up front in the due diligence process and 70 to 80 measures and indicators, both hard and soft, are used. Soft issues, such as leadership and commitment to outcomes, are more difficult to assess, and call for careful questioning and a lot of interaction over an extended period. EMCF has considered how to deal with each of these issues:

Management capabilities. EMCF expects to find weaknesses as part of the due diligence process in areas such as: financial health, operations, systems, depth of management, skill level of staff, board development, and fundraising. While some weaknesses—such as a precarious financial situation—may eliminate a candidate from consideration, the IFB approach is intended to select organizations that require additional support in order to grow. The important question for EMCF during this assessment is whether organization leaders know that they need to develop their internal capabilities, evidenced in part by their candor in discussing challenges and weaknesses.

Quality of existing programs and services. While EMCF selects candidates based on their reputation for high-quality programming, few youth development organizations conduct evaluations to show impact. With limited data to judge program effectiveness, EMCF uses program experts to help assess programs. Some of the questions considered include: Is there a compelling product? Is the program based on research? If not, are there comparable models in use? In the absence of strong data, such questions are intended to gauge whether there is plausible effectiveness.

Leadership. EMCF has to determine whether the organization's leadership is committed not only to growth, but to making internal improvement to support that growth. While EMCF can take risks on other weaknesses revealed by the due diligence process, committed leadership is not one.

Evaluation system. Since few organizations have an evaluation system in place, EMCF looks for leaders who are highly committed to implement outcome measures. EMCF has learned that talking about wanting data is not enough to predict a grantee's ability to use data. Instead, organizations that currently collect and use data for management purposes are likely to use outcome data to improve program quality.

Organizations have to be interested in doing good assessments, using intermediate and long-term measures derived from research, where possible. EMCF expects to work closely with grantees to develop appropriate measures, and some will be comparable for all grantees.

Planning and Goal Setting

After clearing the due diligence review, each organization is required to work on a long-term "business" plan. If a high-quality plan is already in place, EMCF uses that as the basis for discussions about goals, milestones, and levels of support. If not, EMCF makes an initial investment to underwrite developing a business plan and refers grantees to a specific consulting firm that understands EMCF's grantmaking approach. The three entities—EMCF staff, the outside planning consultants, and the grantee—typically take five to six months to develop a business plan that covers specific growth targets, program outcome goals, organization improvement steps, performance milestones, and clarification of the resources required to achieve them.

> The intent of our approach to business planning is for each grantee to work with the Foundation's staff and The Bridgespan Group to develop a comprehensive, five-year business plan that is grounded in a robust theory of change which the grantee will "own" and use to achieve its mission-driven goals and objectives. These plans build on the grantee's strengths, but also address all organizational weaknesses or challenges that were identified during the due diligence assessment.[5]

The plans describe how specific investments and improvements to organization capabilities will improve programs and client impact. This "theory of change" also guides the outcome evaluation work. Each grantee defines measures and allocates resources for a high-quality evaluation system that will track service recipients and eventually provide data for the formal evaluation of outcomes. The requirement of a high-quality evaluation system is critical to EMCF's approach, and sets it apart from all other capacity building programs.

EMCF role is to review the consultants' diagnostic information and recommendations, ask questions, clarify options, suggest avenues for inquiry, or point out issues that were overlooked. During this process, EMCF gains a greater understanding of an organization's critical needs and where investments would be most useful. EMCF believes that it is critical that the grantee feels completely responsible for each decision reflected in the plan. Once the organization has identified its goals and required resources, EMCF reviews the proposed performance measures and performance milestones and negotiates the sequence and structure of grants to fund the plan. The plans and funding commitments are also reviewed with the organization's board of directors.

It is important to note that EMCF only makes a commitment if it has developed a high degree of confidence in the organization, a confidence based on interactions during the due diligence process, and even more importantly, during the planning process. In total, EMCF works closely with potential grantees for nine to 12 months before reaching a firm commitment on future funding. EMCF publicly announces a long-term commitment to the grantee, and discloses the total commitment of funding over a multiyear period.

The funding provided by EMCF funds the growth plan. EMCF does not view the multiyear commitment as "program grants," as the intention is not to fund the organization's current operations, but to fund the means to achieve improved quality and growth, such as the implementation of measurement systems, improved infrastructure, and staffing. EMCF does not attach funding to any particular budget line, position or function. The grantee has flexibility to allocate funds as best it sees fit to implement its plan and achieve its goals.

Developing Capabilities

Since EMCF is in the early stages of work with an initial group of eight grantees, it cannot describe concrete results. Yet from the earliest planning of this new approach, EMCF anticipated that the development phase would present a number of challenges and devised a philosophy of how they would like to work with grantees. Most importantly, EMCF does not want to simply wait four years and see whether or not grantees were able to make their milestones. Instead they want to work with the organizations to help them achieve their goals and to make adjustments in plans as needed. During this phase, EMCF Portfolio Managers are the primary contact for grantees, responsible for monitoring progress and helping grantees anticipate problems and resolve issues as they arise.

The due diligence and planning process sets the stage for a meaningful partnership, as Portfolio Managers develop an accurate and detailed view of the organization's capabilities. The level of candor is expected to be significantly better than is typical, even for highly engaged grantmakers.

Unlike other Structured Programs, EMCF does not pay for or provide additional consulting after planning is complete. Each grantee can hire consultants to help with organizational or technical needs, paid for out of its overall multiyear budget, which includes substantial EMCF funding.

FIGURE 4. Edna McConnell Clark Foundation—Capacity Building Steps

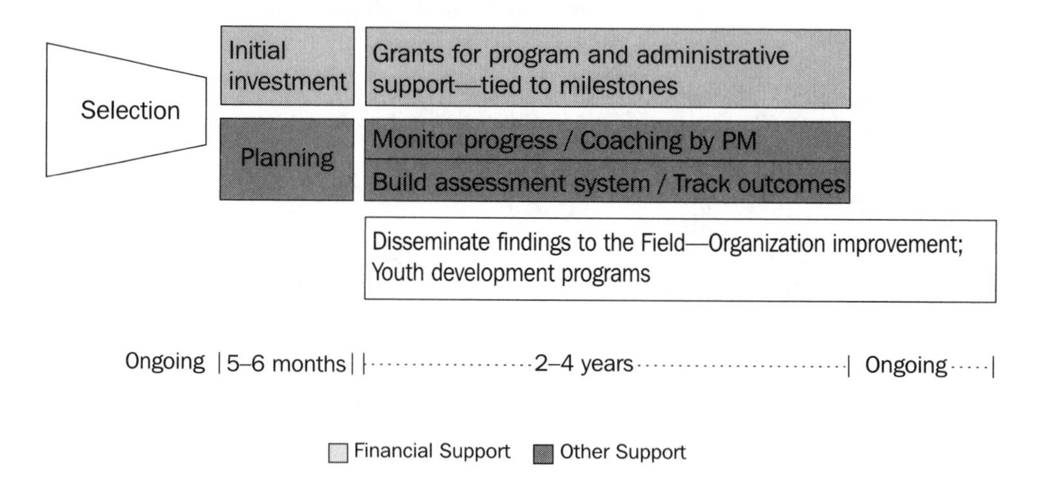

Grantee Profile

Michael Bailin, president of the Edna McConnell Clark Foundation, offers three examples of the progress grantees are making:

> While business planning was something new to the grantees and a remarkable challenge to their organizations, in looking back on it they uniformly recognize the benefits this process yielded to them. . . .
>
> Business planning at Harlem Children's Zone (HCZ) required the organization to make several key and occasionally tough decisions to better align the organization's range of programs with its mission as well as make significant changes in its organizational structure. For instance, when it found that a senior center for the elderly was diverting a large proportion of resources away from the organization's primary goal of improving the lives of Harlem's children, HCZ transferred this service to another nonprofit agency. In addition, HCZ fully restructured its senior management team and made several key hires, while simultaneously reconstituting

and revamping its entire board of directors. And very recently, to demonstrate its long-term commitment to the neighborhood's youth and children, HCZ broke ground for its new, state-of-the-art facility in Central Harlem.[6]

An important perspective on the value of the IFB program comes from Geoff Canada, President/CEO of Harlem Children's Zone:

> Truthfully, the process was harder and more time consuming that I'd expected. When we worked with consultants before, it usually involved spending a day with them, talking about a particular issue. I thought the work with Bridgespan would take an hour or two a week at most. Instead it was four to five hours a week of thinking, and talking, and working through the issues that came up. If someone had asked me before we began whether I had that kind of time available for planning, there's no way I would have said I did. And if they'd told me that was what it would take, there's no way I would have gotten involved. But I didn't know, and no one told me, and I'm glad that was the case, because the payoff has been tremendous.
>
> For one thing, we came out of the process with a blueprint for change and growth that's like a Bible for us, we follow it religiously. The details of the business plan—like the new organization structure and management positions—allowed us to take goals and turn them into concrete actions we could undertake without being overwhelmed. The plan also enabled our board to align itself strongly with our strategy and strengthened its capacity to raise the major new dollars we'll need to support our goals.
>
> Just as important, working on the plan with Bridgespan really improved our ability to think strategically. For example, we'd always had solid information about our program costs; but the financial analysis that was part of the business planning process helped us see these programs more clearly and concretely in terms of their comparative costs. It created a pause moment, when we could step back and look at how each of the programs related to our mission. The data alone didn't drive our decisions about which programs to eliminate and which ones to deepen. Those decisions will always be a

> matter of judgment. But it did help us look ahead and think strategically, because it presented concrete information about where the agency was in the context of where we wanted it to go. . . .
>
> Most executive directors, people in my position, are caught between the desire to plan for the future and the things we have to do right now to survive, and almost always, we shortchange tomorrow for today. What we need to do is shift our thinking, but I couldn't have said that before going through this process. Time spent up front on planning is priceless, but I had to live that to learn it. Business planning is the way you get answers to the questions you have to answer in order to grow. It's a way of opening doors you didn't even know were closed.[7]

IFB helped Harlem Children's Zone turn its ambition for growth into well thought-out, concrete plans, and provided funding for internal investments to get the plans moving. Some of the highlights of HCZ's nine-year expansion plan include:

- Expansion of current management and administrative staff; investment in information systems; development of an evaluation system for each program to measure and improve program impact.
- Complete new headquarters building, open by 2004.
- Open Head Start program in 2001; expand in 2004 using headquarters space. Launch a new Charter School, Beacon School (after school) program, and a Medical and Dental Clinic, all to be located in new headquarters space.
- Critical Mass: Increase the number of parents and children participating in programs within the defined Children's Zone neighborhood—a 24-block area of Central Harlem. Increase the participation rate of children in each age group to the following levels:

Age Group	Percent Participating in HCZ Project Programs
0–2	80%
3–4	70%
5–11	60%
12–13	40%
14–18	30%

- Geographic Expansion: increase the Zone from 24 to 60 square blocks in 2004 and to 91 in 2007. This expansion will add an additional 3,800 and 8,000 children under the age of 18 to the target population, enabling HCZ to serve a total of 16,754 children by 2009.

FIGURE 5. Harlem Children's Zone Business Plan

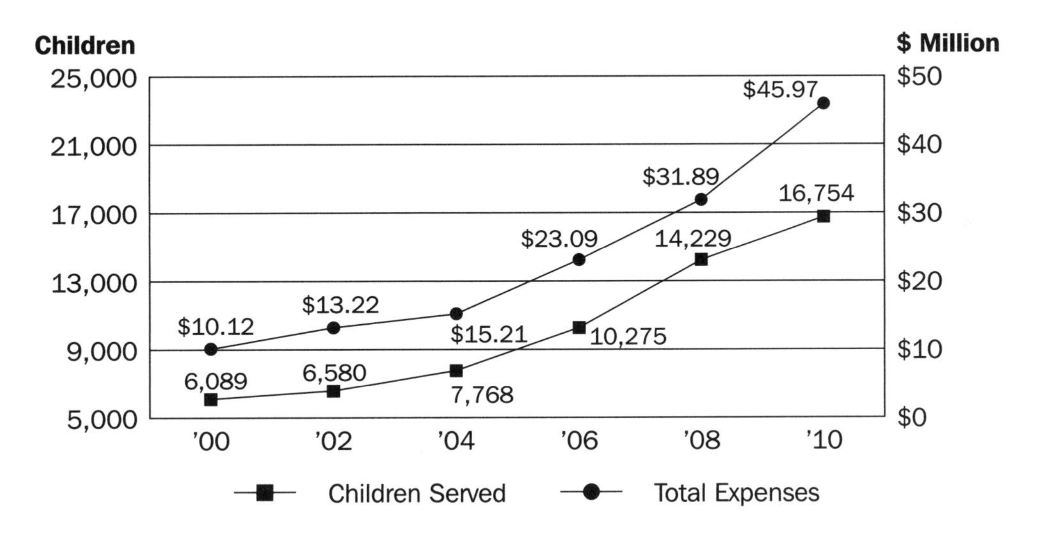

Lessons Learned

Though EMCF cautions that, "all assertions we make and conclusions we have drawn from our work to date are tentative, and should be treated as interesting hypotheses at best,"[8] the progress to date is encouraging. Michael Bailin reports that all grantees are "moving ahead successfully, hitting all the ambitious targets and milestones set forth in their business plans."[9]

EMCF believes the most important lesson thus far has been a confirmation that its prior, more traditional approach to grantmaking cannot work. Though EMCF had been more involved with its grantees than the vast majority of funders, they did not know the operations of these organizations as well as they thought they did. This became painfully apparent when they engaged in the work required for due diligence. In one case, they discovered that a former grantee had, in the past, been in severe financial crisis, at times unable to meet its own payroll. Throughout this period, EMCF had been a major funder and maintained close contact with the grantee, yet was completely unaware of its financial problems.

From this and other cases, EMCF drew two important lessons. First, a traditional "project grant" relationship with grantees rarely, if ever, involves complete candor. Funders are deluding themselves if they think that they are well informed about important issues. They are well informed only about the issues that the grantees choose to reveal. Second, grantees often get into financial difficulty not as a result of negligence or poor financial management, but rather because of the funding environment itself. EMCF realized that they had contributed to the difficulties. Organizations found themselves pulled off mission in an effort to satisfy a range of demands, and incurred higher costs as they took on disparate activities.

The insights gained from due diligence confirmed for many on the staff and the EMCF board of trustees that the previous approach to grantmaking was inherently flawed. They concluded that it is important for nonprofits to have the resources to define their mission and develop thoughtful plans so that they can be proactive in seeking funding and stay on mission. EMCF's role, they decided, should be to fund their ability to develop these plans, and provide significant support toward it. They also concluded that a new type of relationship is required, where selective sharing of information is no longer possible. According to Mike Bailin, "When we described this case to the board, that sealed the change to a different approach. There was no doubt that we had to find a different way. Some on our staff have said that they could never do grantmaking like that again."

EMCF is on a steep learning curve as they work with additional organizations through the due diligence process, business planning, and the development of capabilities. Since 2000, a number of other lessons have emerged:

- Few youth-serving organizations have established the quality of their programs and services through some effort at systematic data gathering and analysis.
- The Portfolio Manager's skills and experience are critical to his/her effectiveness. It is not enough to select someone who has

worked in nonprofits. Candidates need a solid understanding of the nonprofit field and relevant business skills. In addition, they need to understand the challenges of organization change, either through experience building an organization or having worked on such issues as a consultant.

- Managing relationships with grantees during the planning phase is much more intensive, requiring more time and energy, than anticipated.
- The foundation staff need to learn more about business planning, personnel, financial controls, office technology, and the inner workings of organizations.
- In their initial plans, grantees chose to focus on strengthening their internal capacity and improving program quality before attempting to scale up services. EMCF's investments for the first few years did *not* go directly into program expansion.

Critical Features of Structured Programs

Structured Programs can put an organization on a path of learning and improvement that continues long after the program is completed. For nonprofits that complete a Structured Program, there should be strong documentation of improved capabilities, as well as evidence of improved performance—financial stability, program quality, or growth. Equally important are changes less visible to outsiders. Throughout the process, many leaders and staff embark on a steep learning curve as new systems and practices are adopted, often accompanied by a shift in attitudes and beliefs.

The ability to assess whether programs worked is built into each Structured Program. For EMCF and NFF's Building for the Future it is too soon to evaluate success. Matrix has short-term results collected at the end of each 15-month program. Only NAS has long-term data on program participants, going back as far as 1984.

For EMCF, the test of IFB will be, "whether, at the end of the day, it has resulted in better outcomes for substantially more young people living in poor neighborhoods."[10] Because every grantee is required to track the impact of its youth-serving programs, EMCF can use program outcomes as one measure of its own impact, along with grantee growth rates and financial stability.

Building for the Future provides NFF with a straightforward mechanism to track outcomes, as each grantee accumulates funds in a separate account earmarked for building maintenance. The program is successful if grantees are able to stick to a schedule that builds an adequate reserve over ten years. In addition, NFF tracks each organization's overall financial health.

To the untrained eye, Structured Programs may appear straightforward, and even simple to implement. They are not. In the highlighted programs, sponsors struggled to ensure that applicants were committed to the work and stuck it out; that projects addressed the "right" issues for each nonprofit and resulted in improved performance; that outside assistance was of high quality; and that grantees were held accountable for progress.

Incentives to Participate

Without a high level of commitment to change, Structured Programs are doomed to failure. Potential participants belong to one of two camps. In one camp, organizations are *already motivated* to develop internal capabilities and believe that development is critical to their stability and program success. Such nonprofits apply for capacity building assistance and support even if program grants are not included. In the second camp, nonprofits are attracted to capacity building *only if* significant funding is attached. Improving management is viewed as a necessary hurdle imposed by the sponsor to receive additional funding.

Sponsors have learned that dangling the possibility of a million dollars of long-term support in front of applicants makes it difficult to evaluate the level of internal commitment during the selection process. EMCF addresses this problem by getting to know potential grantees over a nine- to 12-month period of intensive work. They believe that a single site visit does not come close to revealing the true level of commitment. The advantage of significant funding is that nonprofits, particularly established organizations that would never apply for capacity building assistance, may find it worthwhile to jump through a few educational hoops and commit to specific improvements. For funders interested in the stability and program quality of larger, established nonprofits, significant challenge grants may be the only way to support organization change.

Matrix has been effective at attracting participants without offering any financial incentive. Because participants are attracted by access to education, on-site consulting, and ongoing coaching, internal commitment is less of a concern. Matrix simply lets any agency participate that is interested.

Similarly, Building for the Future appeals only to those interested in improving their management of buildings or developing endowments.

The following chart summarizes the incentives offered by each of the Structured Programs—the use of program grants, funds for stability or overhead, and consulting support.

FIGURE 6. Incentives to Participate in Structured Programs

<table>
<tr><th></th><th colspan="4">Structured Programs</th></tr>
<tr><th>Incentives to Participate</th><th>NAS</th><th>Building for the Future
(Boys & Girls Clubs)</th><th>EMCF</th><th>Matrix</th></tr>
<tr><td>Program funds</td><td>None
Increased odds of future program grants from local funders</td><td>None</td><td rowspan="3">Substantial Funds are provided to cover any budget category required by the business plan.</td><td>None</td></tr>
<tr><td>Overhead funds for staff positions, technology, financial reserves</td><td>Working capital grant—from local grantmakers</td><td>Matching grant—for building reserve
Loan - replacement</td><td>None</td></tr>
<tr><td>Small grants</td><td>As needed—to support capacity building work</td><td>None</td><td>None</td></tr>
<tr><td>Consulting support</td><td>NAS staff support</td><td>Nonprofit Finance Fund staff support
Consulting provided</td><td>Consultants and foundation staff for development of business plan
Ongoing support from Portfolio Managers and foundation staff</td><td>Coaching from coordinator
Workshops
Assessment
Limited on-site technical assistance</td></tr>
</table>

Provide Access to High-Quality Consulting

Consultants play an important role in helping grantees achieve the ambitious goals expected in a Structured Program. High-quality consulting is needed for effective assessment, planning, and coaching. NAS and CIC have staffs familiar with the challenges of long-term change and knowledgeable about the sectors in which they work. NAS uses only their own staff for initial assessments and long-term coaching. Matrix hires and trains local consultants in each community to act as Coordinator and deliver their program. Workshop facilitators are experienced consultants with extensive subject matter knowledge, but still receive training in the Matrix approach to workshop design. NFF's staff has extensive experience serving the financial needs of the clients with whom they work, and supplements this knowledge with consultants who are experts in topics such as facilities, real estate, or endowments.

EMCF selects consultants to assist grantees in developing their business plans. EMCF is the only sponsor that does not provide consultants for ongoing coaching and organization development work. Instead, grantees are free to hire consultants as needed. In addition, the Portfolio Manager's role is to help each grantee succeed. If grantees are willing to discuss unexpected problems and setbacks without fear of losing the funder's confidence and resources, then Portfolio Managers may be effective coaches.

Devise Methods of Accountability

Accountability is always easier in theory than in practice. With milestones and incentive payments, Structured Programs have a mechanism to hold organizations accountable for progress. Practice shows, however, that it can be difficult to adequately capture capacity in the form of measurable objectives, and it is not always clear what funders should do if a milestone is missed.

While some capacity building goals can be easily quantified, many cannot. Fundraising targets, number of clients served, or number of new board members are relatively easy to track; it is more difficult to assess whether new board members are of high quality and likely to make a contribution. NAS, for example, monitors whether a client has produced monthly financial reports containing specific information, a clear milestone on the way to financial stability. A more important question is whether managers use financial information when making decisions, or whether managers believe that financial stability is important enough to divert funding from program. Goals are helpful to the change process, even if they are not perfect. Simply discussing specific goals helps to achieve a meeting of the minds at the outset of an ambitious undertaking, and makes funders more comfortable committing to substantial multiyear payments. Goals also pressure grantees to devote more time and energy to the capacity work.

While helpful to the change process, milestones may force sponsors to face a difficult situation—if milestones are missed, should a funder withhold payment or future support? The answer depends on the grantmaker's ultimate objective. Funders may choose a strategy of betting on winners—making small investments in many organizations, watching how they perform, and investing larger amounts only in those able to perform. With this strategy, accountability is simple, and withholding payments from "losers" may be appropriate.

Accountability is far from simple if the goal is to build capacity rather than to separate winners and losers. If a grantee fails to achieve a milestone, it is important for the sponsor to understand why. Sponsors may well decide to stop supporting an organization if there is a consistent lack of effort over an extended period, despite discussions and warnings. On the other hand, if a grantee is motivated, but improvement is more difficult than expected or unanticipated events have diverted the organization's attention, then a renegotiation is warranted.

To make such judgments, a high level of involvement is required, either by an assistance provider such as NAS, Matrix, or NFF, or by a careful funder. Both NAS and Matrix have told participants not making progress that they should leave the program.

Careful study of Structured Programs can greatly improve our understanding of the costs and challenges of capacity building, as well as the benefits. Milestones are an important mechanism for grantees, consultants, and sponsors to learn about the process of performance improvement, as they reveal how the reality of organization change differs from initial perceptions and plans. Much can be learned from how and why grantees deviate from plans, the order in which issues are actually tackled, and the type of changes that are particularly difficult for nonprofits. In addition, careful tracking of grantees over time provides valuable insights about how nonprofit leaders are able to transform their organizations while also tending to the immediate needs of programs. Documentation of the time required of nonprofit leaders and staff, as well as the investments of time and resources from sponsors, would greatly inform our understanding of the costs of capacity building.

Structured Programs are promising, but can also be expensive. It will be important for the field to experiment with low-cost models. Programs that offer grants of $1 million or more per grantee, such as EMCF, are only feasible for funders who are willing to focus their investments. Building for the Future's costs are more modest, and the approach may be applied to other issues of financial stability. Matrix represents a holistic but low-cost approach that may be of interest to smaller, regional funders.

FIGURE 7. Key Features of Structured Programs

	Structured Programs			
Key Features	NAS	Building for the Future (Boys & Girls Clubs)	EMCF	Matrix
Primary Management Goal	Improved planning, governance and financial management	Creating reserves for future facility needs	Improved program outcomes	Program Outcomes Client-defined management goal
Range of issues addressed	Broad	Targeted	Broad	Broad
Assessment	Comprehensive	Comprehensive	Comprehensive	Comprehensive
Coaching provided by	NAS staff	NFF staff; selected consultants	EMCF Portfolio Managers	Workshop consultants; Coordinator
Challenge grants	Yes	Yes	Yes	No
Onsite support	Yes	Yes	Yes	Limited
Funder involvement	No direct	No direct	Direct	No direct
Length of capacity building relationship	About 5 years	About 10 years	About 5 years	15 months
Cost	Moderate	Moderate	High	Low

Key Features of Structured Programs

- Required process of education and learning
- Long-term support and coaching
- Grantee sets goals
- Continued support depends on progress toward goals

Notes

1 Nonprofit Finance Fund, Youth Servers Facility Study, p. 1.
2. Nonprofit Finance Fund, Building for the Future, Review of Program Effectiveness, January 2000–June 2002.
3. Edna McConnell Clark Foundation, Mainstreaming Evaluation, p. 6.
4. Edna McConnell Clark Foundation, Due Diligence.
5. Edna McConnell Clark Foundation, Mainstreaming Evaluation, p. 7.
6. Edna McConnell Clark Foundation 2001 Annual Report.
7. Harlem Children's Zone: A Case Study in Learning to Grow with Purpose, p. 12–13.
8. Edna McConnell Clark Foundation 2001 Annual Report, p. 3.
9. Edna McConnell Clark Foundation 2001 Annual Report, p. 5.
10. Edna McConnell Clark Foundation, Mainstreaming Evaluation, p. 2.

CHAPTER 6

The Developmental Consulting Approach

There is widespread concern among experienced consultants, grantmakers, and nonprofit leaders that the overall quality of nonprofit consulting is poor, and needs to be improved. There is little agreement, however, on how to improve consulting effectiveness. While many grantmakers, clients, or even consultants recognize the need for better training on management topics, few recognize the importance of the consulting approach, which lays a critical foundation for all consulting work. This chapter analyzes common problems in consulting and offers a more effective approach, which I call "developmental consulting."

Why Consulting Fails to Produce Change

Normally, consultants view a successful project as one that meets its goals and satisfies the client. From this perspective, many nonprofit projects are successful. The goal of capacity building, however, is long-term change and improved performance. Viewed from this lens, projects that do not result in lasting change and improved performance are not successes, even if the client, consultant, and funder are pleased with the results. On the other hand, a project that fails to achieve short-term objectives but stimulates change may well lead to new capabilities and eventually be considered a success. Viewed from the more ambitious perspective of capacity building, it seems that much consulting fails to achieve these goals. To improve the impact of consulting, it is useful to first understand why change is difficult and the limits of outside assistance.

1. Weak Client Commitment

When consulting projects fail to produce change, it is often because the client was not committed to the work, as evidenced by a failure to follow-through and implement changes. Consultants often view lack of follow-through as the client's problem. According to Robert Schaffer, a leading consultant, "Consultants will thoroughly research a client's problems but pay virtually no attention to assessing the client's willingness and ability to implement the suggestions that the consultant might make to solve those problems."[1] Consultants often act as outside *experts* who analyze the situation and recommend solutions. Often, clients don't follow through because the expert's recommendations are flawed. An outsider often has little time to conduct interviews and collect data, and can be given inaccurate data. Staff can be less than candid and unwilling to reveal sensitive information. With an incomplete picture of the organization's situation, the consultant's recommendations may be off the mark or unrealistic.

Even if the recommendations are sound, staff often resists an outsider's solutions. According to Ken Lippitt, a prominent researcher and consultant, this approach is based on ". . . the assumption that knowledge about something means that there will be some resultant intelligent action or change. This notion has been demonstrated in both research and experience not to be true . . . change involves confrontation."[2]

Other prominent consultants also conclude that client commitment is the primary reason for failed projects and point to the consultant's role as a solution. Peter Block emphasizes "collaborative" consulting, in which the client and consultant jointly diagnose issues and develop a work plan, as more effective than "expert" consulting. Similarly, Edgar Schein promotes "process consulting" as more effective than the "doctor-patient model." According to Schein, the central premise of process consulting is the client owns the problem and continues to own it throughout the consulting process. A process consultant helps clients to figure out the solution for themselves and facilitates their own problem solving, which often means *not* sharing with the client what seems to the consultant as an obvious solution. He advises:

> Even if the consultant feels he or she knows exactly what is wrong and what to do about it, such diagnostic and prescriptive ideas should probably be withheld early in the process for three basic reasons:
>
> 1) the consultant is most probably wrong to some unknown degree because of the likelihood that there are hidden cultural, political, and personal factors operating;
>
> 2) even if the consultant is right, the client is likely to be defensive, to not listen or deny what is being said, to argue, or to misunderstand and thereby undermine the possibilities of solving the problem; and
>
> 3) even if the client accepts the consultant's diagnosis, he probably fails to learn how to do such diagnoses in the future himself.[3]

The expert model is popular, and persists for a number of reasons. Even experienced consultants, well aware of the advantages of process consulting, can find themselves sucked into an expert role; there is often great personal satisfaction in being an expert and providing answers. Clients also can be swayed by the notion of outside experts to the rescue.

> Throughout our lives, we are trained to depend on the experts to give us the answers. . . . Conventional consulting methodologies reinforce this perception by putting consultants in the lofty role of diagnosticians and solution providers. This mystical faith in what the consultant's magic potions

> can accomplish often motivates otherwise hardheaded business executives to spend huge sums and considerable time and energy on consulting projects that have no demonstrable connection to bottom-line achievements.[4]

Understanding the risks, there are times when consultants can provide advice or expertise in a way that does not undermine the project's success. During the course of a project, the consultant may feel it both appropriate and useful to make a suggestion, offer warnings about a proposed solution, provide information, or teach a concept. The key consideration for the consultant is whether in briefly shifting roles, the client continues to *own* the overall problem and solution. The question is whether nonprofit consultants understand how their actions impact client commitment and whether they proactively shape the project to improve the client's commitment to action.

In developmental consulting, the consultant pays careful attention to client commitment throughout the project. Internal motives—such as a desire to expand programs and services, improve the quality of services, address internal conflicts, or improve the organization's stability—often lead to greater commitment. External motives—funder insistence that they get help or a sudden reduction of funding—need to be internalized first to inspire real effort. The consultant can suggest steps to help the client and the rest of the organization improve commitment prior to undertaking the project work.

2. Important Issues Aren't Confronted

Another common reason for disappointing results is that projects address only symptoms of a problem, or tackle unimportant issues that are only marginally connected to performance. This is not a criticism of the client, but a natural part of the consulting process:

> In my experience, however, the person seeking help often does not know what she is looking for and indeed should not really be expected to know. All she knows is that something is not working right or some ideal is not being met, and that some kind of help is therefore needed. Any consultation process, then, must include the important tasks of helping the

> client figure out what the problem or issue is and—only after that—deciding what further kind of help is needed.[5]

Successful projects often begin with a client who is unsure of the causes of poor performance and simply asks for help. The consultant is able to help the client identify important issues and shape a useful project. Projects can get off track when the client (or funder) insists on the presenting issue and is not interested in a joint diagnosis, or insists on a particular solution. The consultant may be hired simply to provide technical expertise or to facilitate work sessions. In theory, such projects can be successful if the client is correct in its diagnosis and insightful about strategy for improving performance. In practice, clients are often neither.

There are two additional reasons that nonprofit consultants may have limited influence over a project. First, the consultant is often unable to develop a meaningful relationship with the client. It simply takes time to overcome the client's sense of vulnerability by having asked for help:

> Because of this vulnerability, potential clients often do not reveal their 'real' problems, deny that they really have a problem, claim that everything is already under control, and in other ways 'test' the willingness of the helper to be really sympathetic and trustworthy in the relationship. As any helper has learned over and over again, only after much listening and being supportive will the real problem surface. From this perspective, the client's response is a normal and expected one, one the helper must be prepared to accept.[6]

As much as the consultant would like to offer insights and suggestions, he or she may have to wait. Schein continues, "The issue is not whether the observation is valid. The issue is whether the group is able and ready to understand and learn from the observation. Such ability and readiness must be built up before feedback can be useful." Until there is a relationship, the client is neither candid about the organization's issues, nor willing to accept feedback from the consultant. It requires significant time to develop a strong relationship, yet nonprofit projects are often of short duration—perhaps ten days or less.

A second explanation for a consultant's limited influence is that the approval process for capacity building grants creates inflexible work plans that miss the mark. Typically, grantees complete an application that describes a specific issue or capability to be developed and how the requested funding will be used. Funding is provided if the program officer agrees that the issue is important and the project is realistic. The consultant provides a detailed work plan and budget based on perhaps a single meeting with the client, or only a phone conversation. Even though the consultant has not diagnosed the issues, many funders view work plans as firm commitments and allow very little flexibility to change course once the consultant begins to work and learns more about the organization. For some grantmakers, the entire process reflects two fundamental beliefs:

- Nonprofit managers can correctly diagnosis their *own* issues.
- Consultants cannot be trusted. Given an opportunity to change a project, consultants will take advantage of the grantmaker's lack of information.

A critical question for capacity builders is what to do if a project does not address important issues, and therefore is likely to have little impact. While the best result for capacity building success may be to redirect consulting assistance to another grantee, there is little financial incentive for a consultant to speak up. Once a proposal has been accepted and is under way, the consultant has little incentive to stop or delay a project, even if it is obvious that the client is not ready. Weisbord explains, "Consultants must learn to say 'not now' more often—the rock-bottom 'consulting skill.'"[7] Capacity Grants create a significant risk for the grantmaker that useless and ineffective projects are completed, which may be considered successful by the grantee, but offer little, if any, chance of real improvement.

3. Insufficient Emphasis on Change and Learning

In the end, improvement occurs when new capabilities are introduced in the organization. Many projects do not develop these capabilities, but organizations expect them to appear after the project is completed. Planning projects, in which all of the implementation occurs after the consultants have left, are perhaps the best example. Robert Schaffer describes the problem:

> The design of most consulting projects reflects the flawed assumptions of conventional consulting. Most are completely dedicated to providing managers with insights and ideas about change but pay virtually no attention to helping the client effect change. In fact, client limitations in this area are generally not viewed as an appropriate focus for the consultant's attention. Rather, they are viewed as hazards to the practice of consulting, like sand traps on a golf course. Over and over again, I hear consultants complain about organizational barriers that prevent their clients from achieving good results from their recommendations—almost as if it were unfair to have to deal with these obstacles.[8]

Many improvement projects depend on changing staff behaviors or organization culture to take advantage of new strategies, systems, procedures, or organization structures. Yet behavioral change is difficult, and nonprofit leaders need help to deal with resistance and develop interventions that accelerate learning.

Developmental versus Traditional Consulting

While consultants are *not responsible* for whether a client organization achieves meaningful change, a developmental approach increases the likelihood of such change. If a developmental approach is clearly designed to build long-term capabilities, why isn't it more common, particularly within capacity building programs? Ed Schein raises a similar concern for the entire field of consulting:

> I cannot really figure out why the learning we have acquired in the other helping professions—about client involvement, about people having to learn at their own pace, about helping clients to have insights and solve their own problems—has not generalized more to the field of management and organizational consulting. If I take a cynical view, I think it is easier to sell products, programs, diagnoses, and sets of recommendations than it is to sell a helping attitude."[9]

There are a number of reasons why consultants have not adopted a developmental approach; why clients have not demanded it; and why grantmakers have not encouraged it.

Consultants gravitate toward traditional consulting. It should not be surprising that most consultants assume that their role is to provide outside expertise. Many enter the field wanting to share insights gained through years of experience in management, or perhaps through management training. Having worked in one or more nonprofits, perhaps as executive director, consultants have a strong urge to share "how they did it" with others. To the extent that consultants bring expertise to a project, it is often technical. Graduates of business schools and public policy schools are trained in technical skills, but rarely in disciplines such as Organization Development that underlie developmental consulting. Large consulting firms also train consultants primarily in technical skills. Few consultants come equipped with skills in facilitation, feedback, coaching, or an understanding of change management.

Even if consultants have appropriate training and skills, a developmental approach may be less lucrative. Traditional (expert) consulting is an attractive business model. Teams of people descend on the client organization to collect information and perform analysis, perhaps living with the client organization for extended periods, working closely with the staff to develop solutions. Such an approach is expensive for the client and profitable for consulting firms. There may also be a greater upfront investment of time and effort with a developmental approach. Additional time may be required with each potential client to "sell" a different approach and discuss the merits of collaboration. Also, by paying particular attention to client readiness, consultants may walk away from more projects than before. Turning down a project is a difficult decision for any consultant, and pits the desire of consultants to do valuable work against the economic realities of consulting.

Once engaged in a project, financial incentives can also lead the consultant to undertake work that is not likely to lead to long-term change. There are times when the consultant should stop or delay a project, but once it is under way, there are strong financial incentives to continue if the consultant cannot easily replace the work on short notice. For example, one consultant interviewed described a large strategic planning project where the board president confided that the executive director was going to be replaced. The consultant was convinced that the strategic planning process should be put on hold until a new director was in place, but did not share this view with the client, primarily for personal financial reasons.

FIGURE 1. Contrasting Approaches to Consulting

Traditional Approach	**Developmental Approach**
Goal is a successful project	Goals is long-term improvement in capabilities and performance
Accept the client's issue	Engage in joint diagnosis; reach agreement on important issues
Limited ability to challenge client's views	Challenge the client's view, when needed; Necessary to raise difficult issues
Impress the client by doing the work	Build a relationship Recurring or long-term projects allow for a relationship of trust
Collect data; do the analysis	Help the client analyze the situation
Make recommendations	Help develop a productive workplan that includes action steps
No role in implementation	Remain involved during implementation Advise on managing change
Limited coaching	Seek opportunities for coaching
Limited learning	Design projects that maximize opportunities for learning
Risk—low commitment to plan; little implementation	**Benefit**—high commitment; develop capabilities

Little awareness of developmental consulting. Few grantmakers or even consultants are aware that different approaches exist, or that a consultant's approach might be related to the client's progress. While there is widespread concern among grantmakers and consultants about the quality of consulting available to nonprofits, most assume that poor results are related to a consultant's lack of experience or limited knowledge of management practices. Similarly, clients are often unaware that different approaches exist and do not seek a developmental approach.

How Developmental Consulting Works

It is important for grantmakers and nonprofit managers to appreciate the profound differences between consulting approaches. To illustrate how the consultant can influence the client and shape a project, three common consulting situations are described. First, the consultant encourages the client to be candid. Second, the consultant steers the client away from an expert project, and defines the role of the consultants and client during an early meeting. Third, the consultant tries to shape a project that offers greater potential for learning.

1. Encourages Client Candor

A successful developmental consulting relationship requires client candor. To encourage this, the consultant must be respectful of the client, the organization, and the situation. At the outset, a client often feels vulnerable and exposed, having initiated a call for help. There is some willingness to discuss the presenting issue—one safe enough to call for help—but the client is often very guarded and will only discuss less threatening and embarrassing problems. If the consultant can help a client to feel supported, it is more likely that underlying issues will be exposed. More threatening issues might include: internal conflicts, power struggles, ineffective board members, unproductive patterns of behavior throughout the organization, or the client's own management style or feelings of inadequacy. To support the client, the consultant can make a number of points, such as:

Consultant: These issues are very common in organizations like this. They tend to arise because (. . . some analysis of the causes. . .). There is no reason that this organization cannot get back on track.

Consultant: I have helped a number of organizations deal with this type of transition. It took a few months, but they quickly adjusted. . . .

Consultant: I have a few ideas on how to get your managers and staff on board. You said that you have never faced a change quite as difficult as this. Many managers find themselves in the same situation, with little experience managing a difficult cultural change. They are not sure how to build support, handle resistance, and anticipate barriers. You can do it, but you will need to try some new techniques. I can talk to you as often as you like during this process, and help you think through how to handle problems as they arise.

The willingness of the client to be candid will be influenced by other factors as the relationship unfolds. First, if the consultant is not particularly knowledgeable or insightful, the client will have little motivation to open up or continue meeting with the consultant. Clients listen carefully during the initial meetings. If the consultant provides insights or asks questions that are helpful to the client, they will find it useful to continue meeting with the consultant. If the consultant is not viewed as helpful, it will be difficult to get time on the client's calendar.

The client's candor will also be affected by the confidentiality of the discussions. If the client believes that the consultant shares potentially embarrassing information with the funder, the client will likely refuse to discuss such issues. The consultant needs to be honest with the client about what type of reporting is required by the funder. It may well be that only superficial "technical" issues are described in a report to funders, and that the rest of the issues remain confidential. In many cases, funders ask for progress reports or a final report directly from the grantee so that the consultant is not put in the a position of informant.

Greater candor is possible when a high level of trust develops with the consultant, and the consultant is viewed as knowledgeable and helpful.

The client finds it comfortable to share concerns and frustrations and ask for feedback and does not become defensive when the consultant offers a different perspective. In such a relationship, the consultant has greater leeway to challenge the client's thinking.

It should be noted that a high level of trust is uncommon in nonprofit consulting. The first issue is funder involvement. A second problem is lack of time. Given project work plans typical of nonprofit consulting, there is often very limited face-time with the client, so the opportunities for building trust and coaching are severely restricted. Such trust is most likely to develop when there are repeated projects over a longer time period, or other opportunities for ongoing coaching.

While coaching is critical to developmental consulting, it is rarely asked for by a client. Instead, coaching occurs naturally as the consultant and client discuss the project, plan next steps, participate in meetings, debrief after meetings, and strategize about obstacles and issues. Coaching can occur before and after important meetings, and continue over the phone in between on-site visits. What is most crucial—when an executive director is unsure of how to handle a situation—is that he or she has access to a trusted advisor. As a high level of trust and candor develops, the consultant can offer more direct feedback, challenge the client's views, and venture into more sensitive topics. The client may eventually recognize this interaction as "coaching," even though it is not requested, and is an integral part of an ongoing project designed to improve some aspect of the organization's capabilities.

2. Defines Roles and Expectations

During the initial meeting with a client, the consultant learns more about the client's situation and both the consultant and client decide whether the consultant can be of help. The client often has some idea of what he or she would like from the consultant, and the consultant may have a different idea about the role that he or she should play. For example, the client may ask the consultant to study an issue, prepare a report with recommendations, conduct a retreat or a training session. The consultant, of course, will try to suggest next steps that are more collaborative and include the opportunity for further joint diagnosis, with particular attention given to assessing and building commitment. As the discussion unfolds, the consultant may feel it appropriate or necessary to explain the advantages of his or her suggestion, or the disadvantages of the client's approach.

While such conversations can unfold in many directions, it is possible to anticipate a few common stumbling blocks and suggest ways that the consultant might handle them. In one scenario the client has suggested a next step, or overall project, that is unlikely to be collaborative.

> **Client:** Why don't you read these reports and write up a diagnosis of what is going on?
>
> **Consultant:** Thank you for the reports; they will be very helpful. It is also important to hear what your managers think about this issue. After all, they are the ones that will have to solve it. The sooner we involve them in diagnosing the problem, the better. Can I meet with the management team sometime this week, for about two hours?

An agreement may be reached quickly if the consultant suggests a specific next step that the client views as useful and appropriate. In other cases, the consultant may have to explain more about the assumptions behind the approach:

> **Consultant:** I know how important this issue is to you and the future of the organization, and it is important that it is addressed soon so that the quality of your programs doesn't suffer. Unfortunately, a report alone won't fix this problem. You know, most consulting reports sit on a shelf and are never implemented. (. . . discussion . . .)
>
> That is why I want your managers involved as soon as possible. The type of changes that you are describing require your managers and staff to do their jobs differently, and won't happen unless they are really committed to resolution of the issue and the plan of action. First, we need to find out how they feel about (. . . the issue . . .). That is why it would be helpful to meet with the team, and for you to be there.

It is not necessary that the client understands or agrees to everything that the consultant suggests, but it is important that the initial steps feel appropriate and useful to the consultant. If not, the consultant may be embarking on a project with little chance of success. The client will learn as the project progresses, and by the end will have a much better understanding and appreciation for a developmental approach.

Another issue that may arise in the initial discussions is whether the client feels that he has the time to play the more active role suggested by the consultant. It often surfaces when the client says that he cannot attend a meeting.

> **Consultant:** I know how busy you are and would not suggest any meetings that don't require your presence. In this first meeting it is important to hear from your managers whether they feel that this project is important. You will need to explain why you think it is important and try to bring out their objections. If you are not personally involved, they may feel that the issue is not important to you. (. . . discussion . . .) Is there a better time for you? Does it make sense to delay the project until you are available?

Another common area of disagreement is the need for further diagnosis. The client may feel that he knows precisely what the issue is, and even have a solution in mind. During the initial discussion the consultant may uncover other important issues, but it is difficult to offer direct feedback or challenge the client's view before a relationship has begun to develop. If the client agrees to further discussions about what is going on in the organization, either alone or with other managers and staff, there will be ample opportunity for the consultant to raise further questions, comments, or ideas. If the client does not agree to steps in which a "joint diagnosis" can occur, there will be little opportunity to change the client's perspective.

Several issues need to be discussed early on in the contracting stage—a collaborative role, the client's own role and time commitment, and involvement of other key players. In particular, the consultant tries to avoid simply studying the organization or suggesting solutions to problems in a vacuum. If these issues do not come up in the course of discussing next steps, the consultant may want to explicitly raise them with the client. However, even if they are discussed, it is likely that differences will emerge throughout the project that require the consultant to repeat many of the assumptions that underlie the developmental approach.

While a collaborative role is essential to a consultant's overall approach to a project, it does not preclude the consultant from playing a variety of roles that vary with each meeting or client contact. Consultants can occasionally provide expert opinions or information, facilitate a discussion, teach a concept, or simply listen.[10] It is important that the consultant understands the advantages and disadvantages of each role, so that he or she can make informed choices about when to switch roles.

3. Incorporates Learning

Lasting change always involves individuals adopting new skills, behaviors, and practices. In the design of projects, consultants can help managers and staff to practice new skills and behaviors. By incorporating new practices into the consulting work, consultants have an opportunity to provide valuable feedback and help staff to become more comfortable, greatly increasing the chances that the practices will persist after the project is completed.

Include coaching. The consultant can add considerable value by coaching the client or other key managers during the project. Clients do not ask for coaching, but it occurs largely because consultants ask for meetings, particularly with the executive director and other senior managers. Consultants constantly look for opportunities to raise important issues not yet on the client's radar screen, to offer feedback, and to change the client's perception on an important issue. These only occur if there are opportunities for face-to-face meetings.

Coaching is particularly valuable during implementation because the consultant can help the client devise ways to handle barriers to change as they emerge. The consultant can offer a valuable perspective on difficult challenges, such as resolving political conflicts, cultural change, and staff development.

High-impact projects. Projects can be designed that produce real outcomes, such as increased fundraising from private donors, rather than simply producing a fundraising plan that calls for increased donations. The difference is enormous because staff is forced to use new approaches and master new skills as they work toward a measurable goal. At the end of a project, not only have specific goals been achieved, the staff has developed new insights, practices, and skills and is poised to create even more ambitious plans and continue to improve results.

Robert Schaffer, in his book *High Impact Consulting*, advocates several techniques to increase the odds of high-impact projects:

1. Define projects in terms of specific performance goals that will be attained.
2. Determine projects' scope based on an assessment of what the client is likely to be willing and able to do.
3. Divide projects into increments, with rapid cycle times, for quicker results.
4. Encourage both parties to work and learn together, in full partnership mode, through every stage of the project.
5. Make leveraged use of consulting inputs.[11]

Schaffer's final point advocates using consultants as little as possible while the staff takes responsibility for improving performance. While it may seem counterintuitive, in many cases this approach is well suited to overworked nonprofit organizations. Because consultants play a limited role, staff spends less time meeting with consultants and more time trying out new ideas. Consultants are helpful in this process, coaching staff when they run into problems.

High-impact projects may be particularly appropriate for nonprofits. All too often the executive director and staff have had limited management training and little experience working in well-run organizations. When clients simply don't know what they don't know, learning begins when they experience new practices—such as goal setting or problem solving—rather than talk about it. Only after using new techniques or skills do they get excited about the possibilities of improvement.

Developmental Consulting Knowledge and Skill Requirements

Developmental consulting requires advanced skills and knowledge. A developmental approach can be learned by both novice and experienced consultants. A solid understanding of organization change is important, as are consulting skills related to building effective relationships with clients.

Developmental consultants are generalists and need to understand a broad range of management topics, so that they can diagnose any major issue and develop a strategy to address it. A generalist need not have additional specialized knowledge; other consultants can be used for more specific technical areas. With knowledge of the topics and skills listed below, consultants can be highly effective:

Management Topics

A generalist needs to be familiar with a long list of management topics, typically covered in any management curriculum. More importantly, these topics are relevant to the job of executive director, and a consultant working at that level should have a similar breadth of knowledge.

- Nonprofit strategies
- Financial management
- Human resource management
- Organization structure
- Risk management
- Performance management
- Decision processes
- Fundraising strategies
- Leadership development
- Problem-solving techniques
- Cost analysis
- Conflict resolution
- Strategic planning processes
- Management information systems
- Coordination and control mechanisms
- Board development
- Marketing
- Productivity improvement
- Meeting management

Change Management Topics

Change management topics are less well known, even to those with management education, as they are often covered in electives rather than core courses. While these topics are central to the effective management of change, relatively few managers and consultants have been exposed to these ideas.

- Diagnosing organization culture
- Resistance to change
- Techniques to overcome resistance
- Techniques to change culture
- Group dynamics
- Adult learning theory
- Techniques to build commitment to change
- Design of group sessions to build commitment

Consulting Skills

Developmental consulting requires greater skill—particularly at feedback and coaching—which are central to long-term change.

- Developing a client relationship
- Leadership coaching
- Facilitation of decision process
- Providing feedback

Capacity Building and Developmental Consulting

While developmental consulting is not common, there are independent consultants and consulting groups using these techniques. Often these consultants have lacked the terminology, framework, and theory to describe it and distinguish it from other approaches to consulting. This overview helps to fill this gap so that nonprofit managers, grantmakers, and consultants can discuss the connection between consulting approach and the long-term change that is often at the heart of successful capacity building.

The consultants at CRE, SHATIL, MAG, and NAS employed remarkably similar philosophies and practices that are consistent with developmental consulting. The critical point, however, is that developmental consulting is made easier when actively *supported* by the capacity building approach. CRE, SHATIL, and MAG operate as Development Partners in the programs described here, while NAS provides assistance as part of a Structured Program.

Effective capacity building and consulting involves two important steps. First, sponsors and funders set ground rules in their *design of a capacity building approach* that can either make developmental consulting easy or make it difficult. With Capacity Grants, grantmakers have little control over the choice of consultant or choice of approach, but impose limitations that make developmental consulting more difficult. While not preventing consultants from using a developmental approach, neither is it encouraged. Developmental Partners and Structured Programs make developmental consulting easier, although it is certainly possible to partner with a consulting group or individuals using traditional consulting tactics. In the second step, consultants make choices in each and every project about how to work with clients. Thus, it is possible for individual consultants or groups like MAG to use a developmental approach even when they are hired directly by a client, or hired using a Capacity Grant.

Capacity building sponsors make a number of choices that support developmental consulting. The three capacity building approaches described in Section II are compared on four different issues.

- Support for defining useful projects (shown in light grey)
- Support for sustained learning (shown in darker grey)
- Incentives to avoid ineffective projects
- The ability to provide high-quality consulting

To more fully compare how each capacity building approach supports effective consulting, it is helpful to distinguish between two types of Structured Programs, those run by an intermediary, such as NAS, BFF, or Matrix, and those run by a funder such as Edna McConnell Clark.

FIGURE 2. Examples of Support for Developmental Consulting

	Capacity Building Approaches				
Features that Support Developmental Consulting	**Conventional Capacity Grants**	**Modified Capacity Grants** Packard, PCMI	**Development Partners** CRE, Shatil, MAG	**Structured Programs (Intermediary)** NAS, BFF, Matrix	**Structured Programs (Funder)** EMC
Assure confidentiality	Possible	Possible	Possible	Possible	No
Time for diagnosis	Limited	Limited	As needed	Required step	Required step
Assurance that useful project identified	Difficult	Possible	Easy	Easy	Easy
Project flexibility	Difficult	Possible	Easy	Easy	Easy
Length of relationship	Short	Short	Long	Long	Long
Coaching availability	During project	During project	Ongoing	Ongoing	By program officer
Project includes implementation steps	Possible	Possible	Likely	Always	Always
Consultant incentive to focus long term	No	No	Yes	Yes	No consultants
High-quality consultants provided	No	No	Possible	Possible	For planning
Primary challenge/ limitation	Grantee candor	No long-term relationship	No performance goals		Grantee candor

Consulting Approach Does Not Guarantee Success

Currently, capacity building programs rely heavily on outside consulting to bring about significant organization change. However, a project's success does not rely solely on the quality of consulting. Even with a developmental approach, projects can fail because of external factors, internal issues, or other uncertainties about organization change. Even the highest quality consulting will not guarantee an organization's survival or long-term success. Instead, this type of capacity building support can greatly improve the odds of survival.

An organization can decline or fail due to *external factors* clearly beyond the control of either grantmakers or consultants. A lack of public support for an organization's mission, a shift of funding away from the program area, an overall decline in the economy, or changes in the political climate can make it more difficult to secure funding. Organizations can get weaker, rather than stronger, and even fail altogether due to external circumstances.

Internal issues can also prevent the organization from developing. When consultants describe failed projects or former clients that never achieved stability or lived up to their potential, the most common reasons cited are internal rather than external. Difficult internal issues might include an ineffective management style at the top, power struggles, and disagreements over strategy or direction. Such issues can make even the most effective outside assistance a waste of time and money. If consultants spot these issues up front and decline to provide assistance until conditions change, then capacity building resources will not be wasted. Unfortunately, such conflicts are all too common and capacity building has little to offer the affected nonprofits.

Finally, using a developmental approach does not guarantee that consulting will be effective. During the course of a project, consultants are faced with innumerable choices that have no clear answers, such as how to build client commitment, what type of planning process to recommend, and which management issues to address first. There is much to be learned about the management practices of high-performing nonprofits and techniques for promoting organization change, and research on these topics will improve the effectiveness of both nonprofit managers and consultants. In the meantime, consultants operate with imperfect information and often limited time to work with clients. As a result, not every project leads to the type of fundamental changes for which clients, consultants, and grantmakers strive when engaged in capacity building.

Notes

1. Schaffer, 1997b, p. 32.
2. Lippitt et al, 1985, p. 35.
3. Schein, 1987, p. 30.
4. Schaffer, 1997, p. 133.
5. Schein, 1999, p. 5.
6. Schein, 1999, p. 160.
7. Weisbord, 1988, p. 71.
8. Schaffer, 1997, p. 31–32.
9. Schein, 1999, p. 247.
10. Lukas, 1998.
11. Schaffer, 1997, p. 30.

CHAPTER 7

Designing a High-Impact Capacity Building Program

Grantmakers support capacity building work in two ways—by designing and funding capacity building programs that provide additional support to grantees, and by using grantmaking practices that support, rather than undermine, sound management. This chapter describes four specific practices that promote the capacity work of grantees, and provides guidance on how to design a high-impact capacity building program.

All grantmakers can adopt practices that promote capacity building work, regardless of whether they have a separate capacity building program. Specifically, grantmakers can promote capacity building through: 1) funding the capacity needs of grantees, 2) providing grants that encourage sound management practices, 3) educating grantees about capacity work, and 4) pressuring grantees to improve their management practices and performance.

Provide Funds for Capacity Needs

A critical question for grantmakers is whether they are willing to fund the capacity needs of grantees. Many nonprofits lack capacity because of the funding practices of foundations and government. Foundations and government contracts pay for programs, and if overhead is included at all, it is often limited to ten percent, which is simply not enough to pay for the administrative and overhead needs of most nonprofits. Nonprofits can only meet these needs if they can generate earned income, attract significant private donations, or are fortunate enough to have a funder that provides significant general support. As a result, there is chronic underfunding of maintenance, building reserves, working capital, technology, administrative staff, and training.

The cost to become financially stable will undoubtedly vary greatly by sector, or even organization. Factors include whether nonprofits own and maintain buildings, whether they are funded largely by government contracts, and their stage of development.

Some grantmakers agree that there is chronic underfunding, yet are reluctant to simply provide 15 percent for general support on every program grant. In their view, relatively few nonprofits have sophisticated insights and thoughtful plans, and extra funding may well end up in program expansion, rather than working capital or administrative support. The Structured Program approach provides some assurance that grantees will address important issues and spend the funds wisely. That is why EMCF, NAS, and BFF require grantees to first go through an extensive assessment and planning process before providing additional funding. Grantmakers interested in financial stability can place restrictions on funds so that building reserves or working capital cannot be diverted, or that payments only occur after appropriate management systems have been put into place. Even more important, Structured Programs can be structured over several years and provide sufficient time for a shift in attitudes toward funding long-term stability.

At the very least, all grantmakers can provide small initial grants for specific needs, identified at the beginning of capacity building work, that will greatly enhance the grantee's ability to move forward with their plans. For example, emerging organizations may need database software so that they can begin an individual donor campaign, or an administrative assistant so that the executive director can take on new initiatives laid out in the strategic plan. CRE provides small "reality checks" for this purpose and NAS sometimes presents such needs to the local funder committee.

Provide Grants that Encourage Sound Management

Grants can also support grantee efforts to develop their own capabilities. If grants are awarded for three years rather than a single year, there are significant benefits to both the grantee and the grantmaker. If a substantial percentage of grants are recurring, grantees can engage in better planning both for program and fundraising. With less time (and stress) devoted to fundraising, executive directors can devote more time to program implementation and quality. Greater funding stability can also improve staff morale and reduce turnover. For grantmakers, there is a reduced workload for program officers, and with longer-term relationships, the possibility of developing a more informed relationship with grantees.

In addition, grants for general support or program grants with overhead built in (15 percent) can help grantees pay for administrative and other overhead expenses. There is some debate among grantmakers, however, about whether simply adding overhead will improve the capacity of most grantees. Some grantmakers feel strongly that discretionary funding should only be given to grantees that have engaged in self-analysis and planning.

Finally, all grantmakers should recognize that some funding practices actually create *disincentives* to adopt sound management practices:

- Denying program grants if the nonprofit has a surplus or significant reserves.
- Discouraging investments in infrastructure because they increase the percent of budget allocated to overhead.
- Refusing to pay for any investments in overhead or infrastructure, while encouraging program expansions that increase the need for overhead.
- Refusing to fund working capital or building maintenance, but providing emergency funds when an organization is in crisis, or when the roof caves in.

Educate Grantees about Capacity Work

Some nonprofits are motivated to build capabilities and improve performance, and don't need to be enticed. Whether due to strong internal leadership, pressing threats, or exciting opportunities, internal motivation is always the most effective way to support capacity building work. The challenge for philanthropy is how to entice *even more nonprofits* to apply for Capacity Grants or a Structured Program, or seek help from a Development Partner. Grantmakers should consider steps to build interest, which can make an enormous difference in the quality of applicants, the level of knowledge and readiness, and the overall rate of participation.

Financial incentives can attract grantees who otherwise would not be interested. Educational programs and voluntary assessments can stimulate grantee learning and generate internal motivation. To reach those who have not been motivated, grantmakers can require grantees to engage in an assessment, purely for the purpose of stimulating grantee learning.

Educational programs. Grantmakers sponsor educational programs to help grantees develop a better understanding of issues facing their organizations. The hope is that a well-designed workshop or assessment will change grantees' perception about the external environment and the capabilities of well-run organizations as well as their own organization's capabilities, and will stimulate an interest in improvement. While many educational programs are voluntary, some grantmakers require grantees to participate.

For nonprofit leaders and staff who have little training in management topics such as financial planning, strategic planning, effective decision processes, or human resource practices, workshops are an effective way to teach vocabulary, concepts, and practices common to well-run organizations. Degree programs or technical workshops, and increasingly distance learning, are effective at closing this gap in knowledge. If, however, the goal is to improve organizations, knowledge about management practices is often not enough.

Currently, there is little data on how often nonprofit leaders who attend informational sessions learn something directly relevant to their situation and follow through on these insights. The general view is that sessions are an inexpensive way to educate many nonprofit leaders about sectorwide issues, but with a low rate of follow-up activity.

Voluntary organization assessments. An individual organization assessment focuses on issues relevant to a specific organization and is more likely to lead to change. Assessments can take many forms—an organization can conduct a self-assessment, using an assessment tool; a program officer can discuss the organization's goals and capabilities with leaders and help to identify opportunities for improvement; an outside consultant can work with the organization to conduct a joint diagnosis; or an outsider can conduct an "expert" evaluation and deliver findings. Each approach offers advantages and disadvantages.

All assessments provide an opportunity for the reflection and group discussions that are often lacking in daily work. A simple self-assessment using a standard tool can be revealing and helpful, particularly for organizations in the early stages of development, or when organization members have little training in management. Simply asking whether an organization has clear goals may be enough to reveal that members do not agree on the goals. Similarly, asking whether the board has committees with well-defined roles can lead to a productive discussion about how effectively the board functions. Used wisely, a self-assessment tool will help an organization facing vexing problems to look for *possible* explanations. Self-assessments can also steer organizations in unproductive directions. Assessments tend to reveal a long list of "weaknesses" without guidance as to priorities or essential issues. Organizations can devote considerable time and effort to installing formal systems and procedures that do not help the organization improve performance.

An assessment process with a skilled consultant is often more effective than a self-administered tool. A consultant can probe more deeply into political and cultural issues that may explain why an organization is stuck. A skilled consultant can diagnose the level of readiness or commitment to action of leaders and staff and feed this information back to the organization. Finally, consultants can challenge organization leaders to face difficult realities, such as how effective is your programming? How do you know? Perhaps most important, do you want to know?

While assessments lead many organizations to take actions, some nonprofit leaders are understandably uncomfortable with perspectives offered by colleagues, staff, and consultants and are not prepared to act right away. It is not unusual for work to begin after a considerable delay, triggered by a change in leadership, a crisis, or an exciting new opportunity.

Forced assessments. Some sponsors conclude that too few grantees have an accurate picture of their own capabilities and opportunities for improvement and have decided to require assessments in a variety of situations. Some require an assessment before a grantee can apply for a Capacity Grant, hoping that grantees will have a better sense of useful issues to address when formulating their request for consulting assistance. Others have taken a more radical step of changing their capacity building grant process to allow for two-part grants. In the first phase of a project, the grantee engages in a joint diagnosis with a consultant, which allows time to develop a relationship, probe for underlying issues, and build commitment for a project that is likely to address important issues. Once a project has been agreed to, a second proposal is submitted to the sponsor with a more specific work plan.

Large organizations are less likely to apply for Capacity Grants, which typically range from $5,000 to $40,000. To interest larger, established organizations in addressing their weaknesses, greater financial incentives are sometimes offered. One major foundation makes significant grants of general, unrestricted support to established grantees with outstanding programming. Along with the generous check is a requirement for a thorough financial review by an outside consultant, to be presented to the board and management, but not to the funder. Such an assessment is designed to educate the organization and can lead to important changes.

FIGURE 1. Use of Assessments to Improve Readiness

	Voluntary self-assessment	**Voluntary assessment with assistance**	**Required assessment**	**Two-part project**
Advantages	Begins with some internal motivation No cost	Greater chance of focusing on important issues	Reach more grantees Only way to reach established grantee?	Same consultant continues with project Greater chance of focusing on important issues
Disadvantages	Can avoid issues	Cost $3–5,000	Not connected to a project; hope that motivation will lead to a project	First part is less structured; funder needs to trust consultant

Pressure Grantees to Improve

Grantmakers not satisfied with the impact of voluntary capacity building can use program officers to pressure grantees to address important management issues. Used cautiously, such pressure can have a significant impact, resulting in a large percentage of grantees that are engaged in capacity building work. For this strategy to be effective, grantmakers must have an informed view about the grantee's management capabilities, as well as an opinion on where improvement is required. Grantmakers hope to stimulate the grantee's thinking by asking questions and offering suggestions, rather than dictating solutions. In the end, grantmakers want grantees to make their own decisions about capacity work and remain accountable for their performance.

The power imbalance, however, can distort messages and make it exceedingly difficult for funders to play a constructive role. Despite the best of intentions, a grantmaker's involvement can actually be counterproductive to the goal of building capacity. It is all too easy for grantees to hear a funder's idle question or passing suggestion as a directive. Some assume that the funder is more knowledgeable and defer too readily to the program officer's opinion. If a funder's ideas do not work out, it can be difficult to hold the grantee accountable.

At the other extreme, many grantmakers prefer a traditional hands-off approach to capacity building, providing funding without getting involved in the organization's issues. While some believe that greater involvement is always inappropriate, others simply feel unqualified to play this role. Grantmakers may not feel entitled to play a more active role if they provide a small percent of a grantee's budget or only single-year funding without a long-term commitment. Others do not have enough personal contact with grantees or information about internal issues to play a constructive role, particularly if grantees are known only through written applications without site visits or personal meetings.

Involved program officers. An involved program officer raises important issues, stimulates the grantee's thinking, and applies pressure to improve in specific areas. To be effective, program officers have to become much more knowledgeable about the grantee organization. While all program officers conduct some level of assessment before making program grants, it is often fairly superficial, based only on information contained in a written application. The type of information that is most important for capacity building—the organization's readiness to improve; quality of leadership; understanding of organization issues; organization culture and politics—are not easily captured in a written application. Involved program officers spend more time with grantees, making site visits and keeping in touch with the executive director. In devoting more time to grantees, program officers monitor fewer grantees. Grantmakers can handle the additional workload by adding program officers, reducing the number of grantees, or moving to multiyear grants.

To play a role in organization improvement, program officers should be knowledgeable about management and skilled at teaching and influencing others. Many program officers are knowledgeable about a program area, but lack training or experience in management topics. Nevertheless, many people with experience working in organizations believe that they can offer sound advice about management. There are undoubtedly program officers without any special training or experience who have been invaluable to grantees. At the same time, it is all too easy for well-intentioned program officers to dispense simplistic advice, or steer organizations to adopt "best practices" that are not relevant or important. Many funders playing a more active role in capacity building have concluded that some or all of their program officers need different skills and experience. Others have decided to try a combination of program officers, some with program expertise and others with management expertise, who work together to assess applicants and grantees.

A second problem is how to obtain candid information about organization issues from grantees. Many have concluded that program officers will rarely enjoy a completely candid relationship with grantees. Program officers have considerable power over funding for grantees, a fact that cannot be erased by a philosophy of "partnership" or the best of intentions. Grantees have good reason to be cautious. Stories abound of grantmakers who learned of organization issues through capacity building work and decided to eliminate or reduce further program grants. Thus, grantees remain cautious about revealing internal issues, despite pleas for candor.

To reduce the potential for misunderstandings and inappropriate advice based on partial information, some funders refuse to offer advice on how to solve problems. Instead, they raise only general issues with grantees, such as the need to diversify funding, develop a stronger board, or improve financial reporting, without suggesting how to do it. To obtain further assistance, grantees are often encouraged to seek assistance from consultants who do not report back to the grantmaker. Complete confidentiality offers the possibility of greater candor from the grantee and increases the likelihood that important issues will be addressed.

Whether or not grantees use outside assistance, their progress in addressing issues is monitored by program officers. Grantmakers report that this type of general pressure can be very effective at motivating an executive director to address organizational issues that might otherwise be neglected.

Challenge of external pressure. External pressure or incentives can increase participation in capacity building, and may be the only effective technique to induce grantees to address difficult issues, such as financial stability and outcome measures. Relying on external pressure can be tricky. Several sponsors cited evidence that forcing a grantee to "get help" does not work. When pressure or incentives are used to entice grantees to seek assistance, then an educational process has to convince leaders that there is a problem, and that it needs to be addressed. The challenge is to convert external motivation to internal motivation through a better understanding of issues and solutions, so that the changes are sustained over time. Once again, learning is the key.

FIGURE 2. Internal Motivation Grows as Knowledge Increases

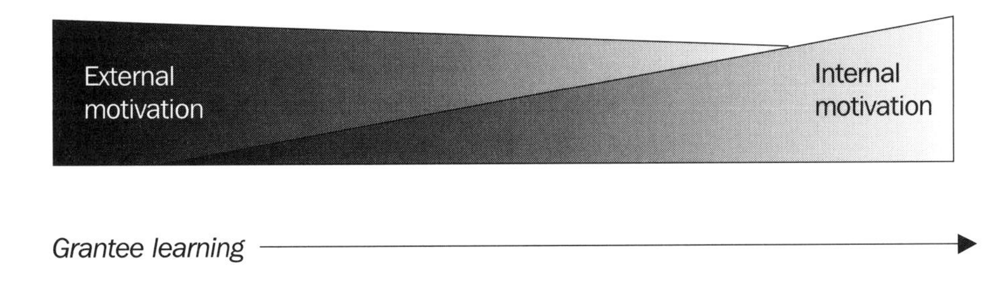

Five Steps to Designing a High-Impact Capacity Building Program

Section II reviewed three approaches to capacity building—Modified Capacity Grants, Development Partners, and Structured Programs—and used nine specific programs to illustrate these approaches. All nine set out to improve upon conventional Capacity Grants, the most common approach to capacity building. In each case, sponsors believe that organization change is a complex undertaking and that simply offering a little management advice to grantees rarely leads to lasting improvement. While these programs offer important insights, they are not offered as a template. Instead, grantmakers need to reach their own conclusions about the complexity of change, the role of consultants, and myriad other issues. Only then can they design a program that meets their goals and is consistent with their values and beliefs.

The following discussion presents five steps to help grantmakers design a program that meets their objectives: 1) grantmakers should consider their perspective on organization change and effective consulting; 2) they should consider whether a central goal should be improving program quality or financial stability, and how to support effective consulting; 3) from these considerations, grantmakers can determine whether a Capacity Grant, Development Partner, or Structured Program is appropriate; 4) grantmakers further define important components of the program; and 5) evaluation plans are developed.

These steps are useful for both grantmakers designing an in-house program, as well as sponsors that collaborate with a number of grantmakers. For first-timers, this discussion will bring some clarity to the large number of choices available. For grantmakers already engaged in capacity building, this review is an opportunity to revisit assumptions and perhaps improve the impact of ongoing programs.

Step 1. Review Your Beliefs and Practices

The choice of a capacity building approach reflects each grantmaker's conclusions about several critical issues—what makes for effective consulting; collaborating with other grantmakers; giving up direct control over resource decisions; and the length of capacity building relationships with grantees. Thus, it is useful for grantmakers to first revisit and clarify their own beliefs about these issues. The improved understanding and consensus that emerges from such an examination will provide a solid foundation for undertaking the work of capacity building.

What is effective consulting? Outside consultants are central to most capacity building programs, and funders need to clarify their assumptions about how organizations change and how consultants can help. The following questions will stimulate an important discussion among the grantmaker's staff:

- What management issues do grantees typically face? What are the underlying causes?
- How long does it take for significant change to occur? For cultural change?
- To what extent are grantees aware of underlying management issues? Are they ready to address them?
- How sophisticated are grantees? Do they accurately diagnose important issues?
- How can grantees develop projects or work plans that will address important issues?
- How can projects be adjusted so that emerging issues are addressed?

These questions can reveal important differences of perspective. Some grantmakers view organizational change as a relatively simple, straightforward process, while others view change as complex.

Change is Simple	Change is Complex
Diagnosis	
Grantees know what they need.	Grantees often do not know what they need. Outside assistance can help them better understand their issues and develop a plan to address them.
Improvement depends on learning and implementing technical systems and skills.	Improvement depends on grantee readiness and internal leadership, and often requires cultural change.

Change is Simple	Change is Complex
Defining Useful Projects	
Grantees will be candid with program officers. Program officers can tell whether a grantee is ready to address important issues.	Grantees are rarely candid with program officers and may be less than completely candid even with a capacity building program officer.
Flexibility	
Consultants can't be trusted and may try to reduce the scope of work or increase the cost. Grantees should be held accountable to the project plan.	The person responsible for deciding which projects to fund needs considerable information about the organization and its issues, both to approve a project and to decide whether a change is warranted.

Collaborating with other grantmakers. Collaboration between grantmakers offers several important advantages. Capacity building can become unwieldy if every funder who provides even minor support to a grantee decides to become directly involved in capacity building. Grantees would be inundated with funder meetings and conflicting suggestions. It is more productive for funders within a community to collaborate—both to simplify the grantee's efforts and to increase their own influence. Funders can collaborate by supporting an existing MSO or Structured Program, setting up an MSO, or launching a Structured Program and encouraging others to participate. For those who want to provide capacity building entirely on their own, the options are either Capacity Grants or funder-sponsored Structured Programs.

Control over resource decisions. Grantmakers who choose the Development Partner approach are willing to relinquish direct control over the allocation of capacity building support, allowing outside consultants to decide what level of support is appropriate for each grantee as well as which issues to address. Because this approach requires a high degree of trust in the capabilities of consultants, grantmakers either turn to an existing MSO with whom they worked, such as CRE, or create one of their own, such as SHATIL. Similarly, grantmakers that fund the work of NAS, BFF, and Matrix also give up control to sponsors. While there is some opportunity for grantmakers to help shape a Structured Program, implementation is handled by the sponsor.

By turning over control of capacity decisions to a partner, the work of program officers is largely unchanged and staff size does not increase. Extra work, however, is required to plan with the partner and reach a common understanding of the capacity building process, roles, and responsibilities, and to review progress.

Grantmakers not comfortable with sharing control over resource decisions can either hire a capacity program officer, leaving such decisions in-house, or sponsor an in-house Structured Program. Because capacity program officers typically provide confidentiality to grantees, there is an adjustment for regular program officers, and careful management of the relationship with the capacity program officer is required. A funder-sponsored Structured Program requires drastic changes, but allows the grantmaker to retain complete control over the capacity building work. The grantmaker designs the steps, selects grantees, becomes deeply involved in the diagnosis and planning, and remains closely involved in the capacity building work over several years. Again, a different type of program officer, with significant management or consulting experience, may be required.

A grantmaker that is *comfortable* with less direct control may nevertheless decide on a funder sponsored Structured Program. One explanation might be that a high-quality MSO is not available, or that the funder brings special expertise and can add value to the capacity building work by being directly involved.

Length of capacity building relationship. An important issue is the number of years of capacity building support the funder is willing to provide. Many have found that some changes take time, such as those in culture and leadership, and that coaching and support services should be available for several years. Grantmakers should also consider whether program grants should be extended to match the length of capacity building support.

The following diagram compares each of the nine programs according to the degree of funder control and the length of the capacity building relationship, illustrating the range of approaches. Five of the highlighted programs have long-term relationships with grantees and have ceded control to a partner or intermediary.

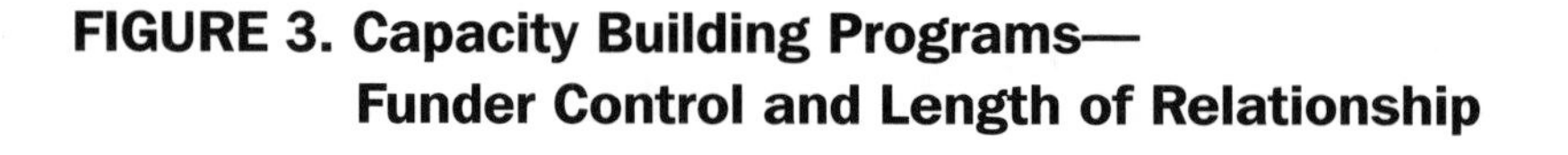

**FIGURE 3. Capacity Building Programs—
Funder Control and Length of Relationship**

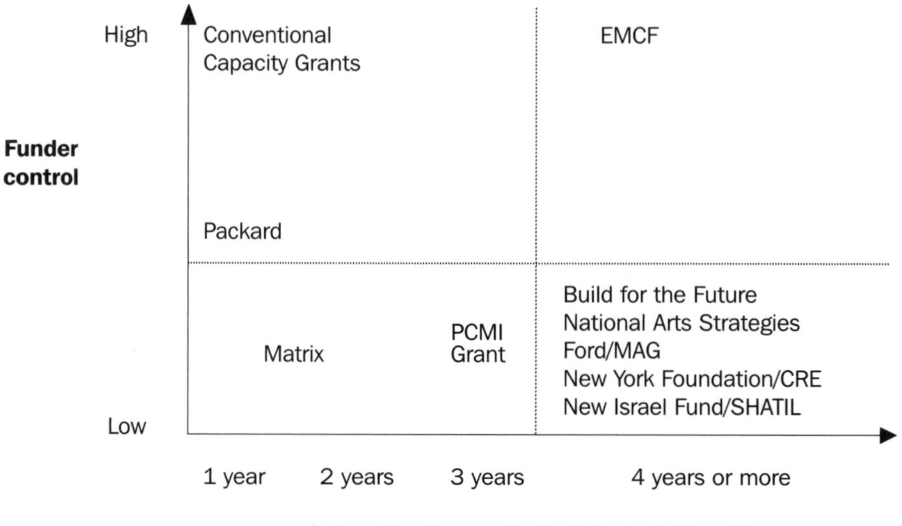

Step 2. Consider Improvement Goals

Grantmakers need to consider two issues that would favor a Development Partner or Structured Program approach over Capacity Grants.

Consider a Goal of Improving Program Quality

The first question for grantmakers to consider is whether it is important in their program area to focus on improving program quality. While much capacity building work is intended to improve program quality, it is not possible to demonstrate such improvement without some system for measuring program outcomes. If sponsors are specifically interested in program quality, a very different type of capacity building is called for that not only involves designing programs based on relevant research when available, but also includes the implementation of an outcome measurement system. Sponsors have found that grantees rarely ask for such assistance with outcome measures.

If most programs are known to be effective, then investing in a system to monitor outcomes would not be a high priority. The evidence unfortunately tells a different story: ". . . the recent history of philanthropic giving in several important areas of social policy can be characterized as having placed a major emphasis on outcomes assessment—and having concluded that the dominant result of those assessments, is that the intended outcomes were *not* achieved."[1] A leading textbook on evaluations describes how evaluators, ". . . most of whom are convinced that social programs might improve the human condition, have been disappointed by finding out that many do not produce marked improvements and some are not effective. We have learned that designing effective programs and properly implementing them is very difficult. To many, it has not been an uplifting experience to have been the bearer of bad news."[2]

Given the dismal record of evaluation findings, a strong case can be made for investing in program improvements for many social services. Program quality can be improved by designing programs based on prior research and using internal data and short-term outcomes to make improvements. Research may even reveal operational benchmarks that can tell managers whether they are on the right track and provide guidance to make adjustments if needed. Capacity building support can be instrumental in helping grantees learn about program research, install outcome measurement systems, and learn how to monitor progress and use data for problem solving.

Both Matrix and EMCF have learned that very few organizations collect information on program outcomes, and those that do are often using weak measures. Because few nonprofits have high-quality client identification and participation systems in place, let alone outcome measures, EMCF selects grantees based on "apparent effectiveness" rather than demonstrated impact, and a central component of the capacity building work with each grantee is to implement a high-quality evaluation system. Implementing such a system can be expensive, both in terms of the outside expertise required and time required of nonprofit leaders and staff. It is the sizable investment that leads many funders to jump off the outcomes bandwagon, preferring to invest directly in program. EMCF is one of the few grantmakers that has decided that a sound measurement system is an integral part of "good management" and therefore expects the costs for such a system to be built into each grantee's business plan. EMCF makes very substantial grants to support the implementation of these business plans.

Selecting grantees based on quality. An alternative for grantmakers is to select only proven programs for capacity building support. Thus, capacity building resources can help to stabilize and grow national programs such as Boys & Girls Clubs or Big Brothers/Big Sisters where research has shown a significant impact on youth development. The problem for local and regional funders is how to help the many local programs that are not based on proven models.

Quality improvement requires program expertise. EMCF's unique focus on outcomes undoubtedly arises from their considerable expertise in a primary program area—youth development—and familiarity with evaluation issues, methods, and outcomes research in that field. They work closely with grantees to develop a theory of change and measurement systems. Considerable time is required to help grantees that have little, if any, experience with sophisticated outcomes research.

If a grantmaker does not bring such program expertise but wants grantees to implement outcome measures, then outside help is needed. Unfortunately, few nonprofit consultants have deep expertise in outcomes. Many have general knowledge about logic models, and can help nonprofits to develop general measures that will answer basic questions. What is often lacking, however, is familiarity with the body of research in a particular program area.

An important dilemma for the field is how to bring national expertise and research to bear on improving the quality of local programs. One solution is to create a learning community of like programs.[3] If there is a critical mass of nonprofits dealing with the same program issues in a local community, or even region, a program expert can be brought in for a day, perhaps several times over the course of a year or two, to help grantees refine their programs. Each nonprofit presents its model as well as measurement systems, and receives valuable ideas for improvement. It can be particularly useful to bring in not only a program expert (often an academic), but also nonprofit leaders who have improved their program using outcome measures. Leaders can describe the importance of improvement work to their organization and help participants anticipate the challenges that lie ahead. Sessions are also an opportunity to help local consultants develop a deeper understanding of outcome measurement in the program area. By participating in the session, local consultants are better positioned to provide assistance to local organizations.

Consider a Goal of Improving Financial Stability

Some funders have been surprised that after years of capacity building projects that meet their goals, grantees are no more stable than when they started. One explanation is that these grantees might be at an early stage of development and inherently unstable. Capacity building helps them to cope with challenges but may not lead to stability, even over several years. Grantmakers have also cited examples of more developed organizations in which the benefits of capacity building end up in program growth, with no improvement in financial stability.[4] Capacity building work often improves the ability of board and staff to raise money, but additional revenues can go into program expansion rather than building maintenance or working capital. Achieving financial stability requires more than just money; it requires a change to the organization's culture—specifically, attitudes toward investing for the longer term. Yet it is rare to find a client that actually asks for such assistance. Instead, it asks for help raising more money.

While independent consultants and Development Partners find it difficult to convince clients of the need to set funds aside, Structured Programs can make it a requirement for participation. Both NAS and BFF have been able to entice grantees to change their spending decisions so as to improve financial stability.

Step 3. Choose an Appropriate Approach

In deciding on an approach, grantmakers may well face trade-offs between minimizing disruption, compatibility with existing values, and the effectiveness of the approach. A prolonged discussion among the grantmaker's staff and board about beliefs and practices, their improvement goals for grantees, and the importance of consulting can lead to significant learning. Initial reactions that a particular approach is a non-starter may dissolve as the advantages and disadvantages are more thoroughly discussed. As grantmakers design, learn, and implement their own capacity building program, some actually change long-held beliefs about these issues. Be that as it may, the next step in developing a high-impact program is choosing an approach that is compatible with the grantmaker's views.

The following chart summarizes differences in approach, compatibility of grantmaker beliefs, and the degree of change for each approach to capacity building.

FIGURE 4. Factors Affecting Choice of Capacity Building Approach

	Capacity Building Approaches				
	Conventional Capacity Grants	**Modified Capacity Grants** Packard, PCMI	**Development Partners** CRE, SHATIL, MAG	**Structured Programs (intermediary)** NAS, BFF, Matrix	**Structured Programs (funder)** EMCF
Compatibility of grantmaker beliefs					
Change is simple	Yes	No	No	No	No
Funder control over the allocation of funds	Yes	Yes	No	No	Yes
Long capacity building relationship	No	No	Yes	Yes	Yes
Collaboration with other funders	No	No	Yes	Yes	No
Reliance on third-party consulting	Yes	Yes	Yes	Yes	—
Goal of program quality or financial stability	Difficult	Difficult	Difficult	Yes	Yes
Degree of change in grantmaking practices	None	Low	Low	Low	High

As is evident, significant differences exist among these approaches and grantmakers should carefully consider these when deciding which, if any, to adopt. Development Partners and Structured Programs devote more attention to consulting, and create conditions that improve the quality of consulting. They also provide consultants with important feedback about long-term impact.

In addition, grantmakers must decide whether improving program quality or insuring financial stability are important goals for their capacity building work. If they are, a different approach to capacity building may be required that forces grantees to address these issues. Structured Programs may well be more effective than other approaches at achieving performance improvements as they entice grantees to join and then *require* grantees to deal with issues they might otherwise avoid. Sponsors rather than grantees control the agenda. Both EMCF and Matrix force grantees to improve program quality, while BFF and NAS grantees address financial stability.

Finally, with the exception of conventional Capacity Grants, each of the capacity building approaches requires grantmakers to consider an important change to their current practices, such as giving up direct control over the allocation of capacity building support, or changing the role of program officers. Grantmakers may find that some practices conflict with important values, while others require a significant adjustment to the responsibilities of the staff.

Step 4. Select Program Components

Having decided on a general capacity building approach, grantmakers must further define the program by deciding the type of impact, the target population and purpose, the total budget for capacity building, the selection process, and the delivery method.

1. Type of Impact

Grantmakers should set a realistic goal for the impact they hope to achieve with grantees, acknowledging that any approach is unlikely to be 100 percent successful. A program's impact can be defined as the percentage of grantees supported that make measurable progress over the longer term. Depending on the design of the capacity building program, grantmakers can expect that as few as 20 percent of grantees will see significant change, or as many as 90 percent.

In choosing the type of impact, grantmakers face trade-offs between the number of grantees to help, the needs of grantees, the delivery method, and the total budget. Grantmakers can begin with a target number of grantees to be helped and decide how best to help them within a limited budget; or begin with a total budget and determine how much is required to have a high rate of success. Each grantmaker makes assumptions about the likely impact of its program, and decides whether it is cost effective. For example, a small Capacity Grant of $5,000 may be a worthwhile investment if half of the grantees are able to increase their funding by 50 percent. Similarly, a Structured Program that invests $200,000 per grantee might be a good investment if 90 percent achieve specific improvement goals.

2. Target Population and Purpose

The evidence suggests that organizations of all sizes and stages of development can benefit from management assistance, but that challenges and success rates are likely to differ. Grantmakers may choose to limit assistance to a special population of nonprofits, and develop selection criteria accordingly. By limiting the pool of applicants, the program can be targeted to help nonprofits at a similar stage of development or with similar needs. Each of the following purposes defines a special population of nonprofits:

Help good organizations get better. Help organizations with substantial capabilities and a record of success to expand and have a greater impact.

Help programs with demonstrated effectiveness. Limit assistance to nonprofits with proven models. One way is to support programs that are part of a national model backed by evaluation research (such as Boys & Girls Clubs).

Help innovative programs. Select organizations that have innovative programs.

Reach hard-to-help organizations. The goal is to entice organizations to address capacity issues that are not already motivated to do so. By using educational programs, required assessments, and perhaps financial incentives, grantees can become motivated to address issues on their own or to seek assistance.

Sector, size. Programs often target support to nonprofits from a specific sector. Programs may restrict organizations to a minimum or maximum budget size.

National grantees. Grantmakers with grantees outside of one geographic region face a more complicated set of issues in delivering services for several reasons. Program officers are less likely to know the grantees; there are limited opportunities for site visits; many MSOs (potential partners) are regional, rather than national; and workshops may not be economical if grantees are not located in the same region. Some of the options available to a national grantmaker include:

Capacity Grants. National grantmakers run the risk that the quality of local consultants is not high, and have little ability to control for quality.

Compile a national database of high-quality consultants. While difficult and time-consuming initially, this approach allows a national grantmaker to have confidence that grants for on-site consulting will be used effectively. National or regional training of local consultants can also ensure a common philosophy and approach, and lead to common learning as projects develop. MAG identified such a national list for Ford grantees.

Partner with national MSOs. National MSOs, such as NAS and MAG already exist for particular sectors. There are many others, such as the Environmental Support Center, that provide support to specific program areas.

3. Total Budget for Capacity Building

In deciding how many organizations to help, grantmakers have to consider the total cost per grantee. While management support is the primary cost of many programs, other programs provide grants that range from modest to substantial. NAS, BFF, and EMCF offer substantial grants as part of their Structured Programs. In addition, the budget should include the costs of administering and evaluating the program.

Management support is budgeted as either the cost of Capacity Grants, a general contract to purchase a pool of hours from a Development Partner, or the consulting costs of a Structured Program. Management support can be expensive when provided by outside consultants at market rates, which vary from $500 to $2,000 per day for most nonprofit consultants. The rate is often lower for in-house consultants, and can be substantially higher for consultants from larger private sector firms. An alternative is to provide assistance using organizational change workshops, which are significantly less expensive than individual management assistance.

In addition to providing management assistance, some programs provide for some or all of the capacity needs of grantees. *Small Support Grants* cover initial investments that help capacity building work move forward. Common needs include database software, computer systems, or administrative support. More substantial and ongoing needs, such as renovations, technology, infrastructure, or administrative staff, can be covered by *General Support Grants*.

4. Selection Process

The most important feature of the selection process is the amount and quality of information used to inform decisions. In the nine programs described earlier, the time required to evaluate applicants ranges from several hours to 200 hours. The chances of getting an accurate picture of the applicant increases as grantmakers progress from written applications to interviews to a get-acquainted period.

Written applications. Written applications require the least time to review, but often provide little information about issues such as organizational readiness to change, leadership capabilities, and culture. An exception is the application for PCMI OD grants, which does try to capture such information. PCMI uses an expert panel to evaluate the applications, and focuses primarily on issues of readiness. These applications are time-consuming for grantees, as they require considerably more information than just the project description and budget.

Interviews and site visits. Most of the programs described in this book relied on interviews with applicants, often over the phone. Some made site visits. Whether site visits lead to better selection depends on a number of details, such as who is interviewed, how interviews are conducted, and what questions are asked to get an accurate picture of the organization's situation.

Get-acquainted period. Grantmakers can give grantees an initial assignment and evaluate their readiness to tackle capacity building work based on their actual progress. Those grantees that invest time and effort are better bets for further assistance.

5. Consulting Support

Grantmakers choose between four methods to provide management support to grantees:

- Grantees choose their own consultant.
- Grantees choose from a list of consultants.
- Grantees seek assistance from a Development Partner.
- Grantees are selected for a Structured Program, and consultants are assigned (perhaps with some choice).

For many grantmakers, the greatest challenge of capacity building will be finding a way to assure consultant quality. One option is to locate a suitable partner or intermediary that uses a developmental approach. The Hayden Foundation worked with the Nonprofit Finance Fund to develop a Structured Program for Boys & Girls Clubs. NAS and Matrix have already developed Structured Programs, which grantmakers can support. Partners and intermediaries are either local or national.

Some grantmakers, however, do not have a suitable partner or intermediary, and rely on the pool of local independent consultants, who often do not use a developmental approach, and may not be very effective at promoting long-term change. Nevertheless, one option is to simply provide

Capacity Grants to grantees, let them hire local consultants, and hope that something useful happens. To increase the likelihood of high-impact projects, grantmakers can provide grantees with a list of high-quality consultants. While it may sound simple, ensuring high-quality consulting can be a significant undertaking involving several steps:

- Select a pool of consultants for referrals; provide training to these consultants on a developmental approach.
- Provide adequate time for consultants to diagnose underlying issues and readiness and begin to establish a relationship with the client. Consider two-part projects.
- Encourage consultants to decline projects if grantees are not ready and to challenge clients. Guarantee consultants a minimum number of days and refer consultants to other grantees if a project is cancelled or delayed.
- Evaluate the long-term progress of grantees; incorporate this information into ongoing training for consultants.

In undertaking such steps, grantmakers in effect take responsibility for developing and overseeing a group of consultants. Managing consultants is not a responsibility that many grantmakers really want to undertake, or are equipped to handle.

The final option is to bring in consultants from outside the region. While the cost might be prohibitive for on-site consulting, workshops are substantially less expensive and involve fewer consulting days. Workshops typically are multisession, taking place over a year or more. An outside consultant can design and deliver perhaps six sessions over a 12-month period, and follow up by phone with participants between sessions. Workshops can be organized by management area, such as board development, diversifying the funding base, or implementing an outcome measurement system. In the end, however, each community benefits from developing a base of high-quality consultants trained in developmental consulting techniques. An outside consultant can also use workshops as a vehicle for developing local consultants.

Step 5. Incorporate Evaluation Plans

Given the great variation of program designs and goals, type of grantees, number of grantees, and length of assistance, it is difficult to generalize about how to design an appropriate evaluation study. This book, however, has highlighted a number of issues that affect capacity building success and should be reflected in capacity building evaluations.

1. Evaluations that Improve Practice

It is important to decide at the outset whether evaluations are intended to answer questions about outcomes of capacity building or the impact of capacity building. To explain outcomes, a study would explore what happened to grantees receiving assistance, which capabilities changed, and whether performance improved. It would seek to understand the factors leading to more successful and less successful outcomes.

Impact studies go further, and ask whether the changes observed were due to the consulting assistance. By isolating improvements that can be attributed to capacity building, it is possible to compare the costs and benefits of capacity building, and perhaps build a convincing case that such investments are worthwhile. Impact studies offer the promise of "proof" that capacity building works.

Thus far, impact studies of capacity building have not been conducted. Impact studies require a control group of grantees that did not receive assistance, and it may be quite difficult to find an appropriate control group for many programs. Such studies are also more expensive. It may also be premature to conduct an impact study, which should only be conducted when a program has been reliably implemented for a number of years, and is based on a well-developed theory of change. It is often appropriate to first conduct a monitoring study or an outcomes study that helps program sponsors and consultants to improve the quality of their work with clients. Only after sponsors conclude that important lessons and improvements have been incorporated, and that the services are being reliably delivered, does it make sense to test whether assistance "works."

While outcome studies cannot prove that capacity building works, they can lead to better results. An outcome study need only include grantees that participated in capacity building and examine variation in outcomes within this group. If there is sufficient variation, a study can reveal factors under the control of sponsors, consultants, and nonprofit leaders that affect the capacity building progress of grantees. Findings can be used by sponsors to improve the design of the program and by consultants to improve their work with grantees.

As yet, the outcome studies that have been conducted have focused more on short-term changes or project success than long-term changes in nonprofit capabilities or performance. Because consultants are often uncertain about determinants of long-term performance or whether improvements that they observe during project work are sustained over time, a great deal can be learned from outcome studies that seek to explain long-term capacity and performance.

2. Evaluations Informed by Theory

At one level, evaluations are easy to describe: decide what questions to ask and collect data to answer those questions. Evaluations, however, do not always yield interesting or insightful findings that lead to improved practice and better results. Good evaluations, like the programs themselves, are based on a well-grounded theory about how to achieve organization improvement. The distinguishing feature of a useful evaluation is that it asks *good* questions, based on insights about cause and effect. Evaluations of capacity building incorporate two theories of change: a theory of consulting impact, and a theory of nonprofit performance.

Theory of consulting impact. Evaluations of capacity building often fail to develop a theory that describes critical factors expected to affect the progress of capacity building work. This book offers considerable guidance about critical factors, particularly in Chapter 2 and Chapter 6. Research suggests that the difference between more and less successful consulting interventions is often not the specific consulting technique (such as particular strategic planning techniques), but a range of other factors, such as the following:

> **Initial conditions in the grantee organization and environment.** Initial conditions are likely to influence the success of capacity building work. Factors such as: the motivation of the grantee for seeking assistance; the extent of support within the organization for the improvement work; actions already taken;

the type of organization, size and stage of development; the tenure, education, and experience of the executive director; the funding environment, diversity of funding, and uncertainty of funding; the financial stability of the organization.

External factors that facilitate or inhibit the improvement process. As the project unfolds, external factors can make it difficult to show improved performance: change in funder priorities, political climate, economic conditions, client needs, or competition from other agencies. Funding for capacity needs and additional assistance can help an organization move forward.

Internal conditions during assistance. A number of internal factors can affect project success, such as: the nature of the relationship between the consultant and client; whether the client reveals issues and accepts feedback from the consultant; whether organization leaders are available and active in leading the change effort.

Consultant factors. Consultants can affect the outcome in a number of ways: the experience and skills they bring to the work; their consulting approach; their skill at building a relationship and sharing knowledge with the client.

Capacity building program design. Some factors are under the control of the sponsor, such as: the number of consulting days of support available; the length of the consulting relationship; other financial support for capacity needs; the confidentiality of the consulting relationship; flexibility given to consultants to address important issues; and pressure from program officers.

Theory of nonprofit performance. Consultants and their clients make choices about which issues to address in a project, whether to address financial reporting, board development, or human resource practices. For a given set of consultants or a specific capacity building program, there is often a well-developed theory about where to help first, what capabilities are most important to performance, and how organizations learn. These ideas should be reflected in the evaluation design. Evaluations provide an opportunity to look at a larger number of consulting cases, together with long-term results, and *test* whether the assumptions driving project design and consulting approach are valid. Consultants can learn a great deal from an outcome evaluation that tests their theory of nonprofit performance.

3. Focus on Long-Term Outcomes

Some capacity building evaluations focus on whether participants are satisfied with the consulting intervention. While such evaluations offer lessons about why some projects never get off the ground or factors that lead to client satisfaction, they reveal little about capacity building. Much more can be learned if in addition to project success, data is collected on actual changes in management capabilities and performance that occur during the project. More importantly, the lessons of capacity building can only be revealed if management capabilities and performance are examined several years later. The potential for learning increases as the outcomes under scrutiny shift from short-term project success (Step 1) to long-term change in performance (Step 5).

FIGURE 5. Choice of Capacity Building Outcomes for Evaluation

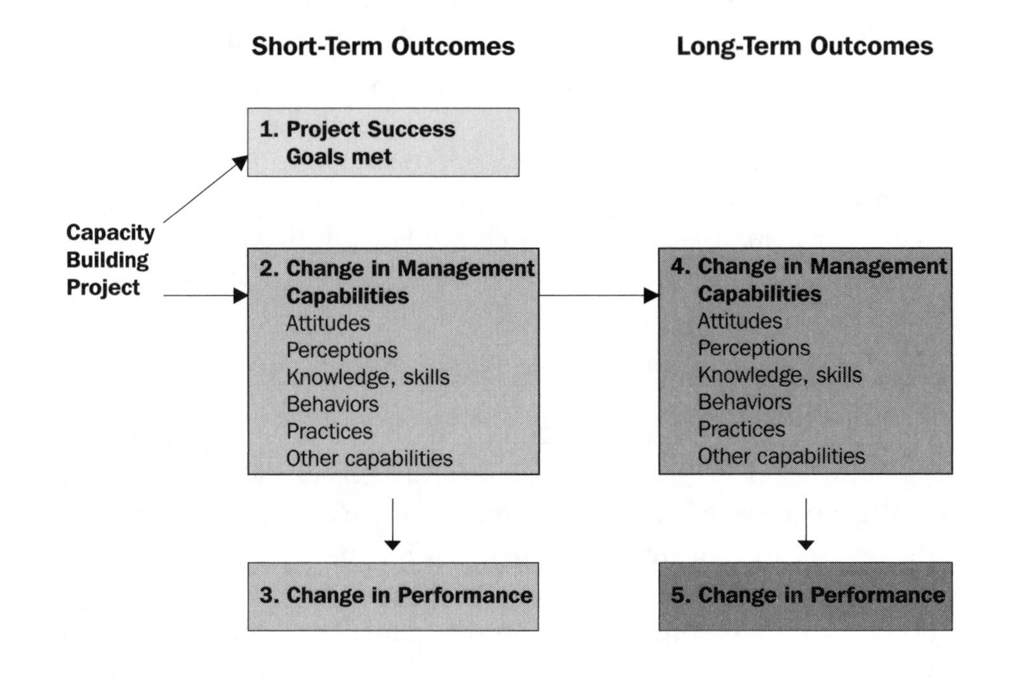

FIGURE 6. Five Steps to Designing a High-Impact Capacity Building Program

1

Review Your Beliefs and Practices
What is effective consulting?
Control over resource decisions
Length of capacity building relationship
Collaborating with other grantmakers

2

Consider Goals and Delivery Method
Consider a goal of improving program quality
Consider a goal of improving financial stability

3

Choose an Appropriate Approach

4

Select Program Components
Type of impact
Target population and purpose
- Sector, size
- National grantees

Total budget for capacity building
Selection process
Consulting support

5

Incorporate Evaluation Plans
Evaluations that improve practice
Evaluations informed by theory
Focus on long-term outcomes

Notes

1. Walker and Grossman, 1999.
2. Rossi et al., 1999, p. 398.
3. Discussions with Jean Grossman.
4. Correspondence with consultant Thomas Harris.

CHAPTER 8

Improving Impact: Conclusions for the Field

"I may be wrong and you may be right. But by an effort, together, we may discover the truth." —Karl Popper

While capacity building support has helped to transform any number of nonprofits, it has not been uniformly effective. This book has been written as a guide for those wishing to improve the impact of their capacity building assistance. Interviews with experienced grantmakers, intermediaries, and consultants, a detailed review of nine alternative approaches to capacity building, and a review of relevant research provide the basis for conclusions about effective capacity building approaches and effective consulting practices. A number of important conclusions about capacity building flow from this analysis and are presented below. This section also highlights several important debates and issues about capacity building that the field needs to consider carefully.

Consulting Is Not the Same as Capacity Building

Nonprofit consulting is based on a model of consulting adopted from the private sector and is not well-suited to the goal of long-term change. While such consulting can be effective in the short-term, it often fails to produce long-term improvement in nonprofit performance. Rather, a different consulting approach is called for, one that the author terms a developmental approach. The greatest challenge for grantmakers will be identifying partners or consultants whose approach is well suited to the grantmaker's objectives.

Capacity Building Is Not for Everyone

Grantmakers may decide not to undertake capacity building for two reasons. First, there is the question of high-quality consulting, already discussed. Second, capacity building often requires foundation staff and board to reconsider long-standing practices and beliefs. For many, capacity building means that program officers no longer control capacity grant decisions, and are not privy to the details of consultants' work with grantees. Others make an increased commitment to multiyear program grants and funding for overhead. Many decide to collaborate with a Development Partner, or intermediary for a Structured Program. For grantmakers who want to retain control over all funding decisions and do not trust consultants, there are fewer options for capacity building.

Capacity Building Requires Strong Nonprofit Leaders

It is important for grantmakers to realize that lasting organization change cannot come from outside expertise. Grantmakers can help to initiate change with outside resources, but internal leadership is needed to make it stick. Some capacity building programs recognize the importance of developing the leadership skills of clients and incorporate it into their consulting approach. Additional efforts to improve nonprofit leadership can only help the goal of capacity building.

A more general problem, with serious implications for capacity building, is leadership turnover. Several programs described in this book and a number of evaluation studies have found that a change of leadership can delay or bring to a halt any capacity building work. Consultants often find that they are starting over when a new leader comes on board. Not only is turnover a serious obstacle for capacity building, several programs report that high levels of turnover are common. Leadership turnover is an issue for the field to address, as the underlying causes may be systemic.

Consultants Need to Learn a New Approach

Training and development opportunities are needed to help nonprofit consultants adopt the practices of developmental consulting and the requisite skills. Specifically, they need to develop knowledge and skills that are not common among consultants: how to provide feedback; when and how to challenge clients; how to build a coaching relationship; techniques to build consensus for change; managing cultural change; anticipating resistance to change; when to play different consulting roles; how to jointly diagnose issues; and designing projects that maximize learning.

Not surprisingly, consultants who are considered successful and have strong client recommendations may not be interested in a new approach. The best audience for such training are experienced consultants who are frustrated that clients sometimes lack commitment to change, do not follow through on plans, and have achieved little improvement.

Consultant development will not happen without some investment. Either each community will need to figure out how to develop high- quality consulting, or funders can pool their resources to design a program, with evaluation, that can be replicated at low cost in any community. Long-term follow-up would reveal important lessons about how consultants adopt new approaches and the impact of specific techniques with clients.

Capacity Building Need Not Be Expensive

The majority of capacity building programs described earlier suggest that costs may not be out of reach of local and regional grantmakers. All three

Development Partners offered ongoing support to grantees at a modest cost of around $10,000 to $15,000 per grantee per year. Matrix offered a low-cost model for less than $20,000 per grantee over 15 months. The PCMI and the CBI programs both provided a combination of more intensive and less intensive services to about 100 grantees on a limited budget. The change workshop developed by MAG is particularly interesting, as it promises high impact at an exceptionally low cost per grantee.

Grantmakers Must Choose a Purpose

It is well known that nonprofits serve a dual purpose, to strengthen civil society and to deliver programs and services. Smaller organizations often involve the community in issues important to their lives, fulfill an advocacy role for the community represented, represent emerging issues, and fill gaps in service delivery. Larger organizations tend to provide the bulk of services, often acting as a delivery vehicle for government-sponsored programs. In providing capacity building support, grantmakers choose the size and type of grantee, and design the support with a primary purpose in mind: to improve the delivery of services or to develop civil society. This choice affects the design of the program, the type of services it provides, the duration of support, and the likely rate of success.

Purpose A: Improve the Delivery of Services

Some funders conclude that it is important to improve the stability of those nonprofits that deliver the most services. Grantmakers define a budget breakpoint, such as $500,000 and above, or target $2 million and above. Nonprofits with budgets of less than $500,000 constitute 73 percent of all nonprofits [of reporting 501(c)(3)s], but account for only 3 percent of total expenditures.[1] At the other extreme, nonprofits with budgets of more than $5 million account for 6 percent of all nonprofits, but account for 87 percent of expenditures. In between are medium-size organizations, with budgets between $500,000 and $5 million, which constitute 20 percent of all nonprofits, and account for 10 percent of expenditures. While the data differ according to the program area, the basic pattern that a large percentage of services are provided by larger organizations holds true and raises an important question about where capacity building resources should be focused.

A related issue is which organizations benefit the most from capacity building assistance. Independently, a number of capacity builders have found that organizations with budgets of at least $250,000 to $300,000 are better able to benefit from assistance. One reason is that there needs to be some level of funding stability so that the executive director can stop focusing on this week's payroll and think about the future. Also, it is difficult for an executive director alone to undertake new initiatives or complete additional administrative work without additional support, such as an assistant director or a secretary.

It appears that organizations with budgets of at least $250,000 have both a significant need for capacity building, and sufficient capabilities in place to benefit from assistance. Some grantmakers conclude that larger grantees can afford to hire consultants if they need assistance, and reserve their capacity building resources for organizations that cannot otherwise afford outside assistance.

Many observers are convinced that large organizations need to improve their management practices, but are not asking for help. Large, established organizations, often fixtures in their communities, may be slow to adjust to changing community needs or financial downturns. An important challenge for the field is how to entice larger organizations to undertake capacity building work.

A different challenge confronts multiservice organizations that provide a large percentage of social services in poor communities and are largely funded by government contracts. With budgets of $10 million or more, these organizations are starved of overhead, and have underinvested in administrative staff, technology, facilities, salaries, and working capital. They desperately need capacity building support that includes a large component of general support, along with management assistance, just to improve stability.

Purpose B: Develop Civil Society

A number of funders, such as the New York Foundation and the New Israel Fund, are committed to supporting newly formed and emerging organizations devoted to social justice and alleviating poverty. The goal is to help their grantees become stable, so that they can continue to deliver services and play a role in community organizing.

Many of these grantees, however, are inherently unstable because of their stage of development. Emerging organizations, with a budget of around $200,000 and under, may have only one or two full-time staff, few formal procedures, and uncertain funding that depends heavily on the personal contacts of the founder or executive director. Such nonprofits struggle each year to find new funding, as they have few ongoing or renewable sources. Emerging organizations are inherently unstable if they depend heavily on one person. For many organizations, real stability is not possible until the budget allows for more full-time staff, so that if one person gets sick or leaves the organization can continue. While some organizations with a budget around $200,000 may become stable, many will never be stable until there is a larger and diversified funding base, and enough funding to hire staff at competitive salaries. For some, a sense of stability may not be possible unless they get to a higher threshold, of perhaps $500,000.

It may not be realistic to expect all emerging organizations to become stable, even with capacity building support. In the short term, funders can expect management assistance to help emerging organizations cope. They can learn to write grants, to prepare budgets, and track their finances, to think through mission, prepare program descriptions, and improve program design in order to attract more funding. In the longer term, management assistance gives these organizations a chance to succeed. Consultants working with emerging organizations describe their assistance as helping these groups to put their best foot forward in the struggle to attract funding. They do not believe, however, that each and every one will succeed.

The New Israel Fund is committed to helping newly formed and emerging organizations, but also is realistic about what capacity building can accomplish. According to Brenda Bodenheimer Zlatin, former associate director of NIF:

> From the beginning, it was clear to the New Israel Fund that it could not provide ongoing support to every grantee. Rather than ignoring the issue of long-term sustainability, the Fund decided to be frank about it and to develop a strategy that would give beneficiary organizations the best possible chance

of becoming independent of New Israel Fund support. It soon became obvious that the goal of sustainability could not be achieved without an intensive investment in capacity building.

While some grantee organizations have not proved to be sustainable, the New Israel Fund does not look at its work in terms of the capabilities or growth of any individual grantee. Instead, the Fund is concerned with the collective impact of its grants on its priority issues and on the community. The New Israel Fund has helped to create an active public interest sector in Israel and its grantees have played a major role in accomplishing this. While some grantees have not survived, New Israel Fund support has helped most organizations achieve important, concrete goals both as service providers and as policy advocates.[2]

Capacity Building Should Not Ignore Program Quality

Michael Bailin, president of the Edna McConnell Clark Foundation, believes that funders should only invest in high-quality organizations that have proven products or that are willing to demonstrate that their programs are producing specific outcomes. "Capacity building is irrelevant without taking into account program quality. It's a waste of money. We ought not beef up, strengthen, or improve programs without first knowing if they are effective and implemented well."[3] Currently, many funders consider program quality but are satisfied with general information about activity levels, popularity, community support or a sense that a program is "well-managed." Bailin argues that these factors, while important, fall far short of demonstrating program quality. "Funders often think they have looked at program quality and can feel certain they really believe that grantee programs are effective. But ask them what have they done to *assure* that they are effective."

While it is difficult to disagree with the notion that grantmakers should put their limited resources into programs that have high-quality programs, there are practical problems with this strategy. How can nonprofits assure grantmakers that their programs are effective?

Demonstrating effectiveness requires tracking long-term outcomes of participants and comparing it to a control group. It would clearly be an enormous expense, and a poor use of resources, to conduct such research for every nonprofit program. Instead, every nonprofit can base its program design on available research, implement outcome measurement that provides short- and intermediate-term feedback, and make program improvements based on such feedback. "With these steps, nonprofits can at least plausibly make the case that the program is likely to have a positive impact," says Bailin.

A viable capacity building strategy would be to help nonprofits access relevant research and expertise in program design, and implement an outcome measurement system. Further investments in capacity building can be reserved for those nonprofits that are able to describe the research upon which their programs are based, and explain intermediate outcome measures that show whether they are on the right path. They should also describe what data they have collected, and how they have made program improvements using that information. While modest compared to a full-blown evaluation against a control group, this would be a great step forward for most nonprofits, and bring program quality more squarely into decisions about allocating capacity building resources.

Management Standards Can Be Dangerous

Interviews revealed that some grantmakers are turning to "management standards" to guide their capacity building work. Some have defined standards for good practices and developed formal tools to assess an organization's practices. Scores are calculated for each management area and overall management capacity. The assessment can reveal an organization's weaknesses and areas needing capacity building work. Proponents of standards believe that best practices are well understood and guaranteed to lead to improved performance; that a correct diagnosis will lead organizations to change; that organizations can be diagnosed without interviews; and that written feedback will generate commitment to action.

Others in the field are strongly opposed to using standards as the basis for capacity building work, viewing them as not only ineffective, but dangerous, for a number of reasons. First, a diagnosis can point out management weaknesses that are not obstacles to better performance. It is easy for leaders to be distracted by improvements that amount to "housekeeping," such as when standards emphasize formalization. According to Fran Barrett, executive director of CRE, "The intangibles of organizational leadership, internal communications, and organization culture—while difficult to assess and to affect—are often far greater determinants of organization effectiveness than the degree of adherence to formal management practices, such as the drafting of a strategic plan or the revision of a comprehensive personnel practices manual."[4]

Second, the complexity of organizations cannot be easily captured in a survey instrument, so the diagnosis will sometimes miss the mark. Readiness, leadership, and culture are more difficult to assess in a survey than in face-to-face discussions. Finally, survey findings rarely produce strong commitment to take action.

Despite the weaknesses, standards have a certain appeal for some grantmakers. By administering a formal tool, grantmakers can be directly involved in the assessment of capabilities, and don't have to rely on consultants and clients to come up with a subjective assessment. Even better, grantmakers themselves need not become experts in management; they simply trust the tool. Without such a tool, grantmakers would have to rely on the judgment and skills of consultants and grantees to make a correct diagnosis and develop useful work plans.

Capacity Building Requires Evaluation

There is a woeful lack of research on important questions about the long-term impact of capacity building. Few independent studies have been conducted. A large number of studies have been sponsored by grantmakers, but most fail to address the question of long-term impact. Stronger methodologies and larger sample studies are needed to unravel the complex set of factors that affect long-term change and performance improvement. Two types of longitudinal research are needed to better understand capacity building. Large sample quantitative research can suggest which factors explain impact, while qualitative research can explain the process of change and why these factors are important.

The field will benefit greatly from research on a variety of capacity building programs that clarify the rate of success, the extent of change and impact on long-term performance. Research can help sponsors understand trade-offs between cost and impact: does intensive consulting have a greater impact than less intensive consulting; what is the minimal level of support required to produce meaningful change; what is the impact of funding overhead? Research can also help consultants to learn which management areas and consulting work has the greatest impact, and the conditions under which consulting can be most effective.

Valyrie Laedlein, director of research, planning, and evaluation at CRE, describes the impact of their current evaluation project: "At CRE, we could never have anticipated the impact that undertaking an evaluation has had on our perspective and our practice of capacity building, even before the first batch of data has been collected. The process of designing the evaluation—which has required us to develop our evaluation questions, examine the elements of our approach to be tested, and undertake genuine reflection about our work and intended results—has catalyzed a number of fundamental changes in how we go about our work."

It is difficult to ignore the plight of many executive directors as they struggle with unstable funding streams, largely untrained staffs, and broken copiers to help at-risk youth, promote culture, or assist recent immigrants. Yet if capacity building support is based on sympathy or vague notions about the benefits of good management, it will become simply another fad that does not lead to the improvement of the sector. In other words, grantmakers should support capacity building not because it is a nice thing to do for grantees, but a necessary expense that improves the impact of dollars invested in programs. If the largely invisible costs of *not* investing in organizations were calculated, capacity building investments would promise a high rate of return.

The programs described in this book should reassure grantmakers that capacity building assistance can have a profound impact on nonprofit management and performance, and that a range of approaches at varying costs are possible. With a carefully thought-out program, grantmakers of any size can have an impact. For many, this means starting small, evaluating impact, and making adjustments until the program makes a significant contribution to the health of nonprofit organizations and the communities that they serve.

Notes

1. Lampkin, 2002, p. 131.
2. Interview with Brenda Bodenheimer Zlatin, December 19, 2002.
3. Interview with Michael Bailin, December, 6, 2002.
4. Correspondence with Fran Barrett, January 15, 2003.

APPENDIX A

Evaluation of Community Resource Exchange's Capacity Building

Research Purpose

Community Resource Exchange (CRE) has embarked on an ambitious research project designed to improve its capacity building work with community-based organizations (CBOs) in New York City. CRE provides management assistance that helps CBOs improve their own performance, often evidenced by greater stability, expanded programs and services, and improved program quality. Ultimately, CRE's work helps CBOs to increase services and catalyze change in poor communities.

CRE hopes to learn more about why some clients achieve greater improvement than others. The research reflects two important realities of CRE's work: consulting work with clients often occurs through projects of relatively short duration, while the outcome of this work—

organization stability, growth, and quality—may not be evident until much later. As a result, for consultants immersed in client work, it is not always clear which types of projects, consulting approaches, or client conditions lead to the greatest improvement in nonprofit performance.

The challenge for CRE is to focus on the long-term development needs of clients within the constraints of a relatively short-term relationship. There are several reasons why assistance often takes the form of short-term projects, lasting from three to 12 months, even though CRE's goals are long term. First, clients often ask for assistance with an immediate need or limited issue. Second, third-party funders are often focused on short-term outcomes and provide funding for discrete short-term projects. Also, limited projects can provide a useful vehicle to bring about specific changes within a relatively short time frame.

This research reflects a number of assumptions, derived from both CRE experience and from organization research, about the nature of consulting and organization change:

- Most projects meet their defined goals and are judged as successful by clients. Short-term success, however, does not guarantee that organization changes will endure or that performance will improve.
- There is considerable variation in outcomes between clients. External factors can affect an organization's progress. Equally important, internal factors such as leadership and client readiness affect progress.
- Even when the other factors are favorable, organization change is often difficult and improvement efforts do not always work.
- Client outcomes are greatly affected by how a project is conducted, such as the consultant's approach, and the degree of candor and trust between the consultant and client.
- Some variation in outcomes may be due to choices made by consultants. The project design, the type of issues addressed, or the number of days devoted to a project are choices that consultants influence.
- There is often great variation in the tactics used by individual consultants with individual clients. Consulting interventions do

not follow a standard design, even for similar organization issues. A variety of tactics and project designs can be effective for a given client.

- Variation in outcomes may also be due to consultant characteristics, such as experience, training, or ethnic match with the client.

In their daily work, CRE consultants believe that they will be able to help each and every client to improve their capabilities and performance. This research, however, recognizes the reality that such aspirations are not always met and seeks to understand why. Some characteristics of projects and consultants can be influenced by CRE, such as the number of consulting days, consulting experience and skills, project design, choice of issues to address, and how consultants allocate their time on a project. In addition, with a better understanding of how organization context and current organization capabilities also affect long-term change, CRE can respond more effectively to individual clients.

Research findings can also help grantmakers to create favorable conditions for organization improvement, whether it is more intensive consulting assistance, or more funding for administrative overhead.

FIGURE 1. Factors that Affect Project Outcomes and Long-Term Performance

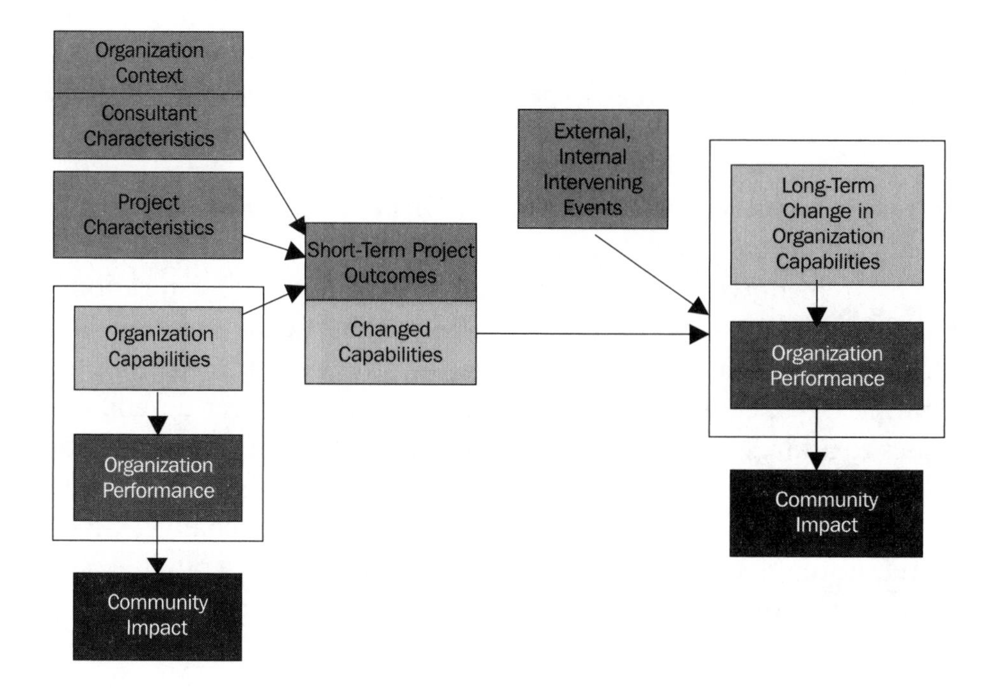

Specific Research Questions

The central research questions concern which factors explain long-term improvement in organization capabilities and corresponding improvements in organization performance.

- Under what conditions are consulting projects more successful in the short term?
- Under what conditions do projects lead to long-term change in capabilities? Under what conditions do successful short-term projects *not* lead to long-term change in capabilities?
- Which consultant characteristics are related to more successful projects? To long-term change in capabilities?

- Which aspects of the consulting approach—the nature of the client relationship, extent of client collaboration, extent of client learning—are related to long-term change in capabilities?
- What effect do project characteristics, such as the number of consulting days, have on long-term change in capabilities?
- Which external and internal conditions or events promote or undermine long-term change in capabilities?

Two final research questions are of general interest to the field of nonprofit management, and are important to effective consulting. With a better understanding of which capabilities are linked to high performance, consultants can offer better advice and construct more effective projects.

- Which organization characteristics (such as systems, leadership, or culture) are associated with high levels of organization performance?
- Which organization characteristics are associated with changes in organization performance over time?

In addition to evaluating factors that cause improvements in performance, CRE would like to *document* the performance and characteristics of their nonprofit clients. CRE believes that the field will benefit from greater knowledge of the actual practices and capabilities of both typical nonprofits and high-performing nonprofits.

- Describe patterns of effective nonprofit management. Describe management patterns by sector and by sources of funding.
- Describe patterns of development—how capabilities change as organizations increase in age and size.
- Document whether performance improves after assistance from CRE. Document the level of performance of clients before work begins and several years after the work is completed.

Population of Interest

CRE works with community-based organizations in New York City. By studying a sample of clients, the knowledge gained will apply to its work with future clients, assuming that future clients have similar characteristics and face similar issues. In addition to improving its own consulting practice, CRE would like to add to the general knowledge about effective consulting and nonprofit management.

Findings about characteristics of high-performing nonprofits may well apply to nonprofits in other communities. The description of CRE's sample will help capacity builders in other communities to evaluate whether their nonprofits are similar to CRE's clients. It is likely that organizations similar to CRE clients represent a sizable portion of nonprofits in every region of the country.

Another feature of this sample is that CRE works primarily with organizations that are motivated to seek help. It is not clear whether the findings can be generalized to other nonprofits in New York City that either are not motivated to seek assistance or that obtain assistance from other sources.

Impact of CRE Assistance

The primary research questions are designed to help CRE improve its work with clients. Another important question, not central to the current study, is whether CRE's work with clients has an *impact* on client performance. In other words, is the improvement observed for some clients attributable to CRE's consulting work or due to other factors? Would pressures to improve have led these clients to develop the same level of capabilities, even without outside assistance? Evidence of impact would help to make a strong case for investing additional resources in this type of capacity building work.

This research is not designed to test the presumption that CRE has a significant impact on clients, largely because of the additional complexity involved in such research. To test the impact of consulting work would require comparing a sample of clients that received assistance to a *sample of comparable nonprofits* that did not receive assistance. The greatest challenge would be to locate nonprofits that were equally motivated to improve, but did not have access to assistance. The control group would have to be sizable, perhaps as large, or larger than the client group. Another challenge is that nonprofits not receiving assistance have little incentive to participate in research. One possibility is to select nonprofits from another geographic area, not eligible for CRE assistance, although they would have to be carefully matched on other characteristics.

Another question that is not addressed in the current research is whether CRE is more effective than other consulting groups or approaches. Adding a sizable sample of nonprofits that received assistance from other consultants would allow an analysis of the relative impact of consulting approaches.

Research Hypotheses

This research explores two complex topics: organization performance and organization change. Two models have been developed that underlie this research, the Nonprofit Performance Model (NPM) and the Consulting Impact Model (CIM). The constructs of each model and selected hypotheses are described in some detail at the end of this Appendix.

Choice of Research Approach

An important decision is whether a study should use quantitative or qualitative research techniques. Using qualitative techniques, researchers would investigate a small sample of consulting cases, conducting field interviews to understand why the project succeeded or failed, and what changed in the organization as a result of the consulting work. Case studies provide a more detailed, in-depth explanation of outcomes that takes into account the organization's context and idiosyncrasies, as well as a holistic understanding of the organization dynamics. The major drawback is that the sample size is too small to generalize these findings to other consulting cases.

Quantitative methods require respondents to fit their opinions and experiences into predetermined response categories. Researchers can compare these standardized measures and aggregate the data for analysis. The primary benefit of quantitative studies, when carefully designed and executed, is that the findings can be generalized to the larger population. In addition, sophisticated analysis (multivariate) can reveal patterns in the data that would not necessarily be obvious to researchers engaged in a qualitative study. In addition, a quantitative study can repeat measurements before and after an intervention (such as consulting) and identify factors that affect organization change.

A major limitation of quantitative research is construct validity. Survey research relies on individual self-reports of their knowledge, attitudes, or behaviors. It can be difficult to construct questions that adequately capture the construct of interest and can be answered reliably by informants. A number of techniques have been developed to improve the validity of questions.

A second limitation is that quantitative research does not establish causality. Large sample studies reveal associations between organization factors (independent variables) and dependent variables such as organization performance, but do not offer evidence of cause and effect. Researchers can take steps to strengthen the argument that a particular factor *leads* to better performance. First, constructs are based on prior research. Second, specific hypotheses are developed before data is collected that explain why a relationship should exist.

A stronger argument can be made that capabilities changed *because of* consulting interventions by using a longitudinal study, which has pre- and post-measurements of capabilities. Also, researchers use triangulation or multiple research techniques to more fully understand a complex subject. Quantitative findings are strengthened if important constructs are investigated using qualitative, field-based research. The goal is to explain associations arising from the quantitative study, which are sometimes surprising and difficult to interpret.

Research Design

The research questions posed by CRE call for findings that can be generalized to the larger population of potential clients. A large sample size is required in order to generalize results, and it would be far too expensive to conduct qualitative field research on 500 or more consulting cases. Given the complexity of organization change, the large number of factors that can affect organization performance, and the time lag that sometimes occurs between interventions and performance improvement, CRE decided to conduct a large sample longitudinal study of nonprofit management and improvement.

The research design includes the following features, illustrated in Figure 1.

- The goal is to collect comprehensive data over a period of about three years on at least 500 consulting cases. CRE currently serves 300 clients per year and expects to obtain data on at least 200 clients each year.
- Client information will be collected before consulting work begins (Time 0), at the end of the project work, about three to twelve months later (Time 1), and two years after the project is completed (Time 2).
- In addition to the client's perspective, consultants will provide their perspective on the client project at Time 0 and Time 1.
- Constructs described in the Consulting Impact Model are measured primarily at Time 0 and Time 1.
- The organization capabilities described in the Nonprofit Performance Model will be measured for each client at Time 0 and again at Time 2. An evaluation of Time 0 data can reveal which nonprofit capabilities are associated with performance. Time 2 data can reveal which factors are associated with changes in capabilities and performance.

FIGURE 2. Client and Consultant Surveys at Time 0, 1, and 2

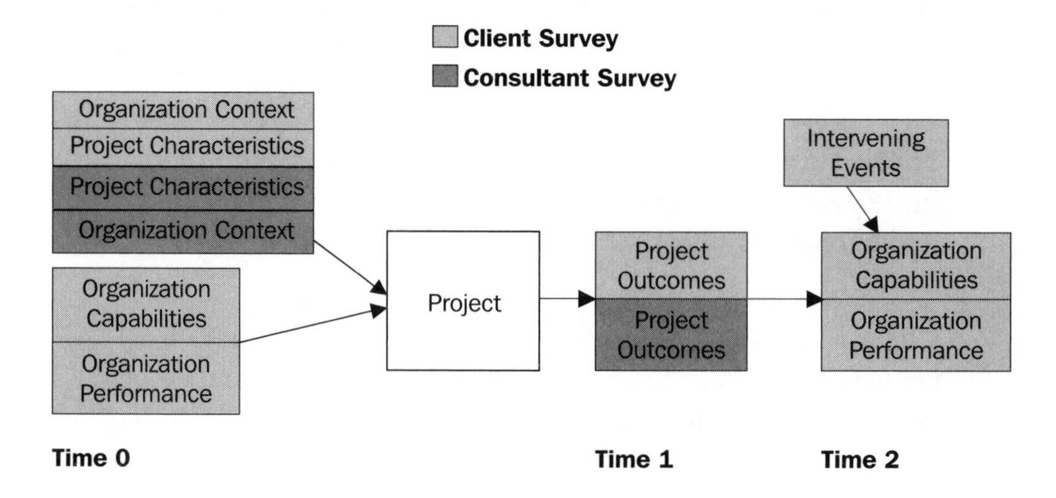

Research Challenges

While a large sample quantitative study offers important advantages, this study presents a number of methodological challenges.

Sample Size

It is important to note that there has not been a comprehensive quantitative study of determinants of nonprofit performance. Most empirical studies have focused on one aspect of management, such as the board of directors or strategic planning, but have not included a broad range of organization constructs. An important reason is the large number of variables that are hypothesized to impact nonprofit performance. There are trade-offs between the number of variables being analyzed, the number of cases in the sample, and the strength of the conclusions that can be drawn. With a large number of variables to consider, a larger sample size is needed to draw strong conclusions.

Researchers have found it difficult to get thousands of nonprofits to complete a comprehensive survey for such an analysis. CRE will be able to require clients to complete a survey at the outset of a consulting project and expects a high response rate for recently completed projects. Even though CRE expects to develop a database of 500 cases or more within a few years, this sample size is still too small to use all of the variables described in the Nonprofit Performance Model. A variety of statistical techniques will be used to reduce the number of independent variables.

Even so, an increase in the total number of cases (beyond 500 to 1000 or more) would greatly improve the ability to detect patterns in the data. In addition to CRE clients, cases from other consulting groups could be included if the same survey instrument is used. CRE plans to make the survey available to others.

Outcome Indicators

The primary research questions posed by CRE call for the measurement of project success and nonprofit performance. Both outcomes present significant challenges.

Project success. One way to evaluate project success is to compare the specific project goals agreed upon by the client and consultant with the actual changes achieved. It would be difficult, however, to develop a predetermined set of specific project goals that might apply to any project. Unfortunately, short-term outcomes for consulting clients are highly individualized and not easily compared across projects.

The achievement of project goals may not, however, be the most useful indicator of project success. Asking whether a project addressed important issues and whether deep changes occurred during the course of the project, are better intermediate-term indicators than simply asking whether the original goals were met. It would nevertheless be interesting to compare the client's perception of successful projects with actual long-term outcomes. For this purpose, clients are asked at Time 1 whether goals for the project were met, and whether they are satisfied with the impact of the project.

Hypotheses are tested using several indicators of project success:

- Goals for the project were met;
- Client is satisfied with the impact of the project on the organization;
- Evidence of changed capabilities at the end of the project;
- Evidence of improved outcomes during the project—increased funding, more or higher quality programs.

Nonprofit performance. While it is difficult to identify appropriate measures of nonprofit performance that are general enough to apply to a wide range of organization types and sizes, several indicators have been widely used in research on nonprofits. The most basic indicator of "success" is whether an organization survives. In tracking organizations over time, survival is an appropriate indicator to use at a later time period. Past research has found that survival is strongly associated with organization size, age, and diversity of funding.

A second general indicator of success is organization stability. Successful organizations are able to keep staff turnover to acceptable levels; have low levels of unwanted turnover; and have high levels of staff morale.

A third general indicator is financial stability. Organizations that have acceptable levels of working capital and net assets compared to their overall budgets are able to survive fluctuations in cash flow. Organizations with substantial debts or few assets have little leeway to deal with a shortfall in revenues; while those with a more diversified funding base are more stable.

A fourth indicator is whether a program is growing. A decline in either the overall budget or the number of clients served can indicate an organization in trouble. Growth, while not required for success, can nevertheless indicate that an organization is healthy and able to attract resources, if growth is accompanied by adequate financial stability. Some nonprofits engage in unhealthy growth, overlooking the need for management systems, increasing debt, or failing to maintain adequate levels of working capital.

A fifth indicator is whether programs are of high quality. Unfortunately, few nonprofits track substantial outcome data that would enable either the staff or outsiders to judge the program's quality. Even if they did, such measures would not be comparable across programs, and would have to be converted to a general assessment of low, moderate, or high quality. One option is to ask each client's opinion of program quality or their opinion of the program's reputation for quality programs. Such responses can be quite biased and are not a good substitute for objective data on program outcomes or impact. A second option is to ask for evidence that an organization is taking steps to improve program quality. Two process questions are included in this study—whether the nonprofit has implemented outcome measures; and whether research is used to inform the program design. A final indicator of quality is the extent of resources devoted to each client or unit of service. While it is not possible to compare the intensity of client services across nonprofits, a change in intensity from Time 0 to Time 2 might indicate that the organization is addressing the quality of services.

CRE has decided to obtain an independent measure of program quality from a panel of community experts to supplement information obtained directly from the client. The panel will be asked to evaluate the relative effectiveness of all nonprofits under study, by providing a general assessment of the quality of programs as well as an overall assessment of each organization's performance. While such judgments provide another view of performance, they are also quite subjective. Steps can be taken to improve reliability by posing very specific issues for evaluators to consider in forming their opinion.

Unfortunately, there is no single general indicator that reveals whether a nonprofit provides effective programs, has an impact on the community, and is soundly managed so that it can continue providing services for the foreseeable future. Given the inherent weaknesses of the measures already described, it is unclear how finely the study will be able to distinguish between levels of performance. At the very least, it is expected that these measures will be able to distinguish between healthy, stable organizations and those that are headed for trouble. As described, the following indicators are captured in this study:

1. **Organization survival**
2. **Organization stability:**

    Turnover of executive director

    Staff turnover

    Staff morale

3. **Financial stability:**

    Working capital

    Net assets

    Funding diversity

    Funding uncertainty

4. **Organization growth:**

    Increase in annual expenditures

    Number of clients served

Number of staff
Increased intensity of program services

5. **Program quality:**

Reputation for program quality—outside panel
Use of outcomes measures
Use of research for program design
Increased intensity of program services

Respondent Knowledge

Perhaps the greatest challenge of this study is developing a reliable instrument to assess each client's capabilities. Organization capabilities can be assessed by a knowledgeable insider or by an outsider. Insiders have much greater knowledge of the organization, but it may be difficult to compare ratings across organizations, particularly if the executive director has limited experience working in other organizations. While a trained outsider would provide a more consistent assessment across organizations, it would be difficult for an outsider to complete a comprehensive assessment for a large number of organizations. This research relies on a single respondent in the client organization, typically the executive director, to assess the organization.

Assessing the change in capabilities presents another challenge. A changed score may indicate that the executive director believes that the capability actually changed or may indicate that the executive director's perception of the capability has changed. For example, it is not unusual during change efforts that people recalibrate their understanding of an organization construct, such as the clarity of goals; or change their basic understanding of the concept. Both can lead a respondent to report a lower value even though they may feel that the capability has improved. For this reason, respondents will be asked for a retrospective assessment of "improvement" for some capabilities to complement their pre- and post-assessments.

Construct Validity

Questions were carefully designed to improve internal validity. Surveys were developed with assistance from a survey designer from P/PV, a leading evaluation firm, and from the Survey Research Center at Princeton

University. Questions were designed to be meaningful to nonprofit managers who may have little if any training in management. In addition, some questions were tailored to differences in the respondent's type and size of organization. As much as possible, questions were designed to elicit factual information related to the construct, and specific behaviors rather than attitudes.

To improve the candor of respondents, the surveys contain information about confidentiality in the introduction, and reminders about confidentiality are placed with particularly sensitive questions. For research purposes, data is reported in the aggregate, not on individual clients, and the database does not contain information that identifies clients. For consulting purposes, consultants are provided with a report about each client's responses at Time 0. More sensitive responses at Time 1 about how the project was perceived by the client are not shared directly with the consultant, although each consultant will obtain an annual report with aggregate information from his or her clients.

Questions were tested extensively and revised over more than a year. First, the major concepts and hypotheses of the Consulting Impact Model and the Nonprofit Performance Model were reviewed with CRE managers and consultants from January 2002 through January 2003. CRE consultants played a critical role in testing all questions for content and wording.

Six rounds of client testing took place from September 2002 until January 2003. The Time 0, Time 1, and Time 2 surveys underwent extensive revisions to improve clarity and provide appropriate choices that reflected the full range of experiences of CRE clients. Several longtime clients were asked to complete a Time 2 survey and then discuss the organization's history with researchers to determine whether the survey responses captured significant organization changes that had occurred. Executive Directors were able to complete the longest survey, client Time 0, in 30 to 40 minutes.

Response Rates

Time 0 surveys are completed before work begins on a project, and CRE expects a high response rate (close to 100 percent). Time 1 surveys, completed at the end of a project, will require some follow up from CRE staff, but should also have a high response rate. Time 2 is a more significant problem, as this survey is sent out two years after the completion of a project.

Various strategies have been suggested to increase the completion rate at Time 1 and Time 2. First, CRE will employ an administrator to track and follow up on Time 1 and 2 surveys. At Time 2, CRE may offer an incentive for clients to complete the survey. Several options have been suggested:

- Each organization completing a follow-up survey can receive a report comparing their responses to a summary of responses from the total sample.
- On a monthly basis, clients that have completed a follow-up survey can be invited to attend small group discussion/training on an important subject. Groups can be scheduled at a time convenient to executive directors and held in different locations.
- If funding is available, a financial incentive can be offered to complete the Time 2 survey. If CRE offers $50 to each nonprofit, it will cost $10,000 each year for 200 surveys, or a total of $25,000 to acquire 500 completed Time 2 surveys.

Data Collection and Analysis

This study has been designed in partnership by CRE and the author, who will each participate in analyzing and disseminating the findings to the philanthropic community. The first round of analysis will involve describing the first 300 Time 0 cases and Time 1 project completion data, in late 2004. Multivariate analysis will wait until there are 500 Time 0 and Time 1 cases in the database, probably by late 2006. Mulitivariate analysis using Time 2 data will wait until there are 500 completed cases, probably in mid-2008.

FIGURE 3. Projected Data Collection and Analysis

	5/03	11/03	5/04	11/04	5/05	11/05	5/06	11/06	5/07	11/07	5/08	11/08	5/09	11/09
Eligible New Projects	0	100	200	300	400	500	600	700	800	900	1000	1100	1200	1300
Complete T0 (90%)		90	180	270	360	450	**540**	630	720	810	900	990	1080	1170
End of project		45	135	225	315	405	495	585	675	765	855	945	1035	1125
Complete T1 (90%)		41	122	203	284	365	446	**527**	608	689	770	851	932	1013
24 months later						41	122	203	284	365	446	527	608	689
Complete T2 (80%)						32	97	162	227	292	356	421	486	**551**
Describe data, preliminary analysis				Early TO, T1 data					Early T2 data					T0, T1, T2 data
Multivariate analysis of data								T0, T1 data						T0, T1, T2 data
Write up findings					Early T0, T1 data				ST result	Early T2 data				LT result

Nonprofit Performance Model—Constructs and Hypotheses

In order to improve consulting, it is important to understand which organization characteristics or capabilities lead to high performance. Consulting projects that address critical elements are more likely to improve performance. To explore these issues, this research defined a Nonprofit Performance Model that includes a wide range of constructs expected to affect nonprofit performance. These constructs were identified based on prior research on organization effectiveness, research on nonprofit performance, and opinions of experienced nonprofit consultants. Prior research highlights the importance of organization culture—specific attitudes and behaviors that underlie effective management practices. It also suggests that specific organization capabilities are contingent on factors such as environment, organization size, and strategy. The following diagram provides an overview of constructs hypothesized as important to nonprofit performance.

FIGURE 4. Nonprofit Performance Model

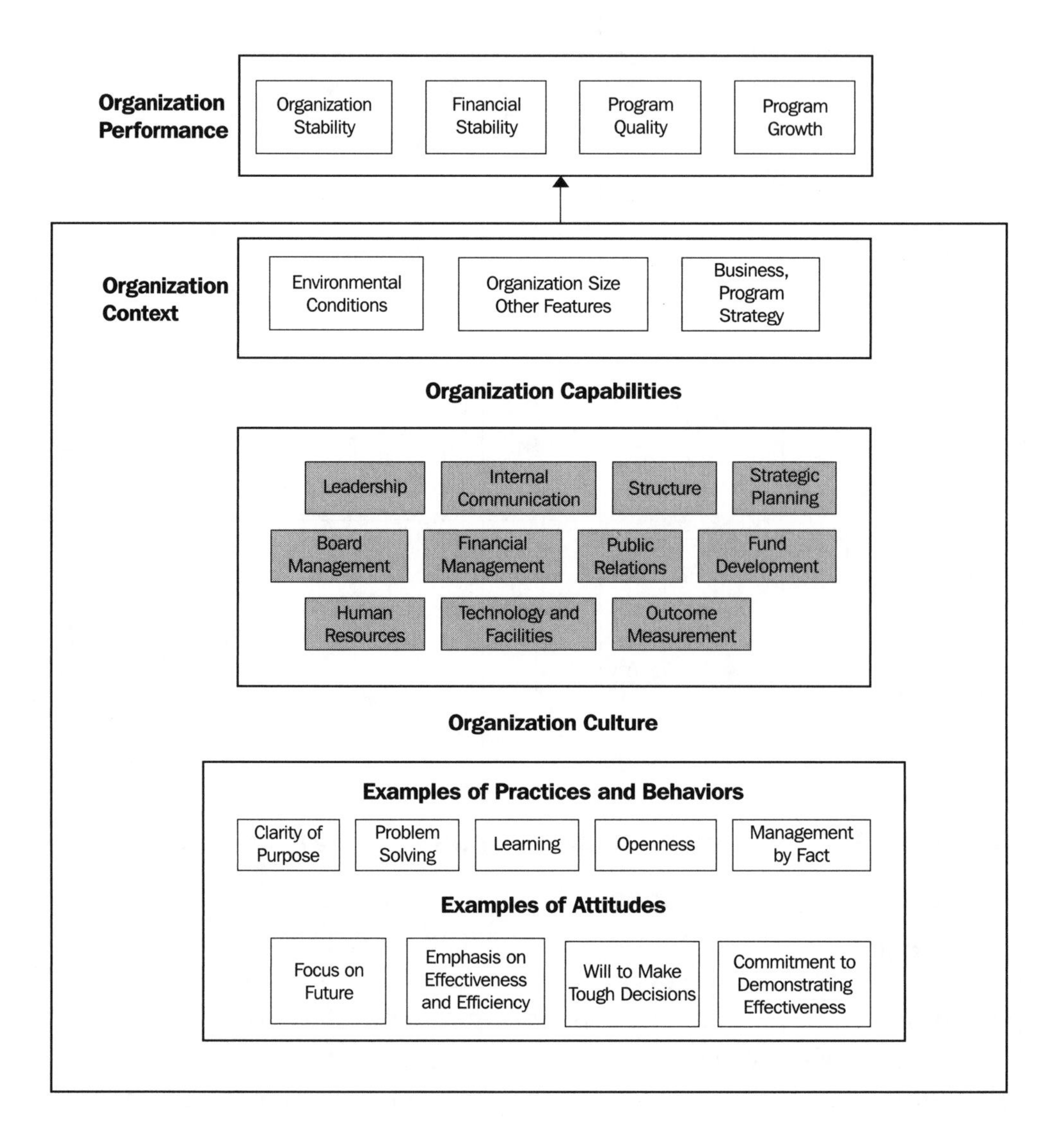

The following chart identifies all constructs included in the Nonprofit Performance Model. For each construct, hypotheses were developed that describe the expected relationship with performance. A limited number of hypotheses are described below. Finally, indicators were developed for each construct, and survey questions were designed to capture important aspects of organizations' capabilities. To obtain the complete set of surveys used for this research, readers can contact CRE.

Model of Nonprofit Performance

Summary of Key Constructs and Indicators

Organization Context and Performance

Activities: Select from nine major program areas

Type of organization: faith-based; affiliated

Geography: citywide, borough, or neighborhood

Education of ED:

- Tenure of ED: New leaders with extensive experience in organizations are more effective leaders of change.
- Sex of ED: (document)

Client age: Clients that are significantly older than the consultant will not establish as much trust and candor.

Client experience in organizations: Clients with significant organization experience are more effective leaders of change.

Nonprofit age: Young nonprofits are more likely to be unstable or fail than older nonprofits.

Size: Small nonprofits are less stable; less likely to survive.

Indicators: size of expenditures; number of full-time staff; number of part-time staff; number of volunteers.

Level of services: number of "units" of service provided.

Funding: Nonprofits with a diversified funding base are more successful.

Indicator: percentage of revenues from each major source.

Discretionary funds: Nonprofits with a high percentage of discretionary funds are more successful.

Working capital: Nonprofits with low levels of working capital are less likely to survive.

Indicator: ratio of current assets to current liabilities.

Funding uncertainty: Nonprofits with a high level of uncertainty around major sources of funding are less successful (stable).

Past stability: Nonprofits that have recently experienced a cash flow problem are less likely to be stable.

History of expenditures: Nonprofits that have experienced rapid decline in the recent past will be less financially stable.

Nonprofits that have experienced rapid growth will be motivated to address internal management issues, leading to greater success.

Capacity building support: Nonprofits that have access to capacity building support are more successful.

Availability of funding.

Communication/ Clarity of Purpose

Nonprofits are more successful when the mission is widely understood.

Nonprofits are more successful when the mission is revisited periodically.

Indicators:

- Mission understood
- Mission revisited
- Goals understood
- Priorities are clear
- Priorities are used

Board Management

Nonprofits are more successful when the board takes time to examine its own effectiveness and takes steps to improve it.

Nonprofits are more successful when the board includes community representatives who are able to represent the community's interests.

Nonprofits are more successful when the board adds value to the organization's work, by adding a valuable perspective on program matters, on organizational issues, or effective oversight of the organization's financial health.

Nonprofits are more successful when the board is able to recruit and retain new members.

Indicators:

- Proactive management
- Board improvement, reflection
- Relation with ED
- Evaluate ED
- Community representation
- Community interests
- Board contributions

- Board recruitment
- Size of board: control variable
- New members

Strategic Planning

Nonprofits are more successful when information is used to develop the organization's activities, such as outcome data, client feedback, community needs, funder interests, and research on similar programs.

Nonprofits are more successful when plans are developed with participation from the board, staff, clients, and external stakeholders.

Indicators:

- Have a plan
- Last updated
- Use of information
- Participation in planning

Financial Management

Organizations with an appropriate level of financial management systems (appropriate to their size and complexity) are more successful.

Indicators:

- Consolidated budget
- Adequate financial accounting system
- Internal controls
- Audit
- Long-term financial plan
- Use financial information for decisions
- Understand financial information

Structure

Larger organizations are more successful if the executive director has some dedicated support positions; if managers do not micromanage direct reports.

Indicators:

- Levels of hierarchy
- ED span of control

- Support Positions
  - Fund development
  - Financial management
  - Public relations
  - Technology
  - Human resource management
  - Facilities management
- Autonomy of direct reports
- Autonomy provided by other managers
- Productive relationship between ED and staff

Strategy

Organizations are more successful if they pursue proactive strategies, such as increasing earned income or service fees; eliminating programs that are ineffective or no longer a priority; seeking to improve effectiveness through better implementation.

Organizations that have weak financial stability or external threats are more successful if they take proactive steps to cut back programs or staff.

Indicators:

- Diversification of services
- Collaboration with other nonprofits
- Increase donations
- Increase other funding
- Change priorities
- Improve implementation
- Cutbacks
- Improve financial reserves
- Improve program quality
- Increase program capacity
- Attitude toward stability; growth; improvement
- Have a for-profit venture
- Merged with other organization
- Adapted to funder interests
- Expanded to an additional site

Fund Development

Organizations that have an appropriate level of fund development systems and skills are more successful.

Indicators:

- Proactive management of funder relationship
- Multiyear plan
- Management of FR activities
- System to identify gaps
- Staff skills
- Board contribution to FR
- Research funding opportunities
- Track donors
- Approached new type of donors

Public Relations

Organizations that communicate proactively with important groups are more successful.

Indicators:

- Communicate with funders
- Communicate with community
- PR strategies identified
- External views of program quality
- Barriers to PR

Technology/Facilities

Organizations that have adequate facilities and technology are more successful.

Indicators:

- Facilities adequate
- Computer information systems adequate
- Sufficient technical support
- Size of capital investment in facilities

Outcome Measurement

Organizations that identify and collect outcome data are more likely to have higher quality programs.

Indicators:

- Identified outcomes
- Collect outcomes data
- Collect client satisfaction data
- Developed standards
- Should collect more data?
- Constraints on use of outcomes

Human Resources

Organizations in which staff understands what is expected of them are more successful.

Organizations in which managers are accountable for staff development are more successful.

Organizations that devote time to staff development are more successful.

Organizations that have trouble attracting and retaining staff because of salaries and benefits are less successful.

Organizations that are able to retain staff are more successful.

Organizations that evaluate job performance of staff are more successful.

Organizations that terminate staff due to poor performance are more successful.

Organizations that have written personnel policies and apply them are more successful.

Indicators:

- Expectations clear
- Accountable for staff development
- Invest in management development
- Proactive staff development
- Staff is effective—managers; program delivery; support functions
- Salary sufficient
  to attract candidates
  to retain staff

- Merit compensation
- Retention is problem
- Employee evaluations conducted
- Forced turnover
- Personnel policies are written

Leadership

Organizations with effective leaders are more successful.

Leaders that make difficult decisions; have ambitious goals; demonstrate commitment; reflect on effectiveness; invite feedback; and change their practices are more effective.

Indicators:

- Managers make difficult decisions
- Managers have ambitious goals
- Managers demonstrate commitment
- Managers reflect on effectiveness
- Managers invite feedback
- Managers change practices
- Eliminate program because of weak impact

Culture

Organizations that promote open discussions are more successful.

Organizations that engage in effective problem solving are more successful.

Organizations with effective internal communication are more successful.

Organizations that have clear priorities and monitor goals are more successful.

Indicators:

- Openness:
  Encourage disagreement
  Disagreements become personal
  Staff resists feedback
  Acceptable to disagree with managers
  Staff avoids risks
- Problem solving:
  Disagreements left unresolved
  Staff solves problems

Program delivery improved
Discuss how to improve
Make same mistakes
Try to eliminate work
Collect and use information

- Morale:
  Staff is overworked
  Intense work effort
  Frustration with working conditions
  Staff gets recognition
- Communication:
  Staff complain about not being informed
  Benefit from better communication
  Knowledge of financial information
  Leaders share information
  Staff have information to do work
- Adaptability:
  Managers discuss external trends
- Quality:
  Compare programs to others
- Opportunities for staff development
- Reputation for management
- Reputation depends on single person
- Procedures are defined
- Leaders cooperate
- Attitude toward documenting outcomes
- Attitude toward growth versus financial stability
- Monitor Goals:
  Staff participates in assessing progress
  Leader participates in discussion of progress

Consulting Impact Model—Constructs and Hypotheses

The Consulting Impact Model (CIM) is the second model that provides the groundwork for this research. It describes factors that are expected to affect the success of a consulting project and the likelihood of long-term organization change. While CRE has a well-defined point of view about factors that explain organization change, the purpose of the model is to test many of these assumptions. The hypotheses described represent both widely accepted views and issues that are debated within CRE or the broader consulting field. Key concepts in CIM include: presenting issues; project focus; client readiness; client relationship; consulting approach; client leadership; barriers to change; and consultant skills.

Presenting Issues

When clients approach CRE, they have often identified a "presenting issue" to be addressed. Some presenting issues deal with safe topics that clients are comfortable addressing, but that may only be symptoms of more important issues. In other cases, safe issues are the most important issues facing the organization, and addressing them will improve performance.

Which presenting issues are most common?

How often do presenting issues change during the course of a project?

Are some presenting issues more likely to lead to lasting change?

Project Focus

The extent of performance improvement depends on what issues are actually addressed during the course of a project. Some project issues are more likely to lead to improved performance because they deal with fundamental capabilities, such as leadership. It is not unusual for consultants to help clients redefine issues during an initial diagnosis; or for consultants to help the client redefine issues once a project is under way, as the consultant learns more about the organization. It is important to learn what issues are actually addressed during a project, not simply which issues were identified when the project was started. Whether a project met its goals (as originally defined) is often less important than whether a project addressed important issues.

Projects also vary in the extent of organization change that occurs during the course of the project. For example, a project may only get as far as developing a new plan, or may include steps to implement the plan. When projects go beyond new knowledge and skills and help staff to apply those skills, there is greater learning and greater likelihood of continued improvement. Organizations continue to learn and improve even after a project is completed, particularly if there has been a change in perception, attitudes, the use of new knowledge and skills, or the implementation of new systems and procedures. Some projects not only change practices but also achieve specific outcomes that help to reinforce the importance of new practices and lead to further improvements.

Fundamental changes: Changes that are more likely to result in improved long-term performance include:

- Improved board leadership
- Improved leadership of executive director and managers
- Improved working relationships among staff members
- Improved processes for budgeting, tracking, or managing finances
- Improved methods or processes for managing or evaluating program
- Improved processes or systems for human resources administration
- Improved processes for managing fundraising
- Changed thinking about organizational issues or problems
- Increased funding or higher quality programs
- New executive director or manager hired
- New administrative positions established
- Merger with another organization agreed upon, or implemented

- Cutbacks of administration or overhead; cutbacks of programs or services (if needed)
- Improved morale

Preliminary changes: Changes that are less likely to result in improved long-term performance include:

- Documentation or revision of policies and procedures
- Improved board participation (only)
- Projects that only result in new plans
- New knowledge and skills *without* improved methods or processes
- Projects that result in the implementation of new systems *without* any changes in skills or perceptions

Client Readiness

Client readiness means that key leaders and staff are ready to tackle important organization issues. While all CRE clients are "ready" to some extent simply because they asked for assistance, many are not prepared to tackle important issues that emerge during the diagnosis with consultants.

> **Client readiness:** Projects in which the client is ready to tackle difficult issues are more likely to lead to long-term change in capabilities and improved long-term performance.

There are a number of factors that explain *why* a client is ready. Low readiness is indicated if a client asks for assistance because a funder required or suggested it, or because they want to follow good management practices. High readiness is indicated if the project is motivated by an internal crisis or problems; external conditions; or a strong desire to make organizational improvements.

Strategic planning, for example, can be a significant event that leads to fundamental change, or an exercise that leads to few changes and no improvement in performance. Research suggests that low readiness is a key explanation for weak outcomes.

> **Strategic planning:** Strategic planning initiated because of funder pressure is less likely to lead to a change in capabilities or improved long-term performance.

Client Relationship

In capacity building work, developing a strong client relationship is critical to performance improvement, for several reasons. First, a relationship of trust makes it easier for the client to reveal potentially embarrassing issues and for the consultant to offer feedback, making it possible for the client and consultant to focus on important, rather than symptomatic issues.

Second, the executive director is critical to organization improvement work, and consultants can "coach" the executive director on diagnosing organization issues or building support for change. While not the primary focus of the consulting project, such issues are important for continued performance improvement.

> **Client relationship:** A strong relationship of candor and trust results in improved long-term performance.

A number of factors affect the quality of the client relationship.

> **Prior relationship:** A strong client relationship is more likely when the organization has worked with CRE previously, and had a positive experience.

> **Initial expectations:** A strong client relationship is more likely when clients seek out CRE because they know of CRE's reputation, or have heard recommendations from other clients.

> **Face time with client:** A strong client relationship is more likely when the consultant spends more time dealing directly with the client.

> **Consultant's financial incentives:** Consultants are more likely to forcefully challenge a client's views if the client is not paying directly for the services.

Funder confidentiality: Clients are less likely to be candid with the consultant if the consultant shares potentially embarrassing information with the funder.

To build a strong relationship depends on establishing a high level of trust with the client. The following consultant behaviors are more likely to result in a strong client relationship:

- Shows genuine concern about the client's mission
- Understands the client's service area
- Respects the client's community
- Works well with people from diverse backgrounds
- Non-judgmental
- Approachable
- Presents ideas in a supportive, collaborative manner

Consulting Approach

Consultants use different approaches in their work with clients. Some use an "expert" approach in which the consultant diagnoses the organization's issues and proposes a solution; others use a "developmental" approach designed to build client commitment to the work. While CRE advocates using a developmental approach with clients, there may be instances where a consultant deviates from this approach. If there is sufficient variation within the CRE staff, the data may reveal which aspects of the consulting approach are most important. Greater insights about approach will require including a range of consultants with a variety of approaches in the database.

With a developmental approach, an important goal is to ensure that the client organization is committed to taking on the work required to address the issues identified. To do so requires a strong client relationship; significant time spent with the client; substantial coaching of the executive director or other key managers; the development of skills and knowledge and implementation steps.

Client collaboration: Clients that strongly agree with the selection of issues to address and the design of the project work plan are more likely to have a successful project and improve long-term performance.

Time for coaching: Clients that spend a greater percentage of project time in direct contact with the consultant are more likely to improve capabilities and long-term performance.

Developmental approach: Projects are more likely to improve capabilities and long-term performance, when the consultant:

- Tailors the project to the needs and characteristics of the organization
- Is flexible and able to rethink approach when needed
- Helps the client learn to diagnose their own issues
- Helps the client come up with their own solutions to problems
- Helps the client to practice using new systems, structures and/or skills
- Is able to raise tough issues for discussion
- Helps the client understand how to support and sustain change

Client Leadership

While outside consultants can assist an organization, improvement depends on strong, involved leadership within the organization.

Client leadership: Projects in which organization leaders are available and involved lead to improved capabilities and long-term performance.

Driving force: Projects are more successful if there are key players driving the project—either the board, the executive director, managers, or staff. Projects with multiple groups driving the project are more likely to be successful.

There are several reasons why leaders are not able to play this role during a project.

Absent leadership: Client leadership will be weak during a project if key players are absent because of illness or emergency.

Weak leadership: Projects will be less successful if leaders are unwilling to confront important issues; unwilling to make the project a priority; assign the wrong person to work with consultants; unwilling to make difficult decisions; or not candid with consultants about the organization's challenges.

Barriers to Change

Projects with otherwise committed clients and skilled consultants might nevertheless be ineffective for a number of reasons.

External barriers: Projects are less likely to be successful or lead to improved long-term performance if there is:

- Loss of organization's funding
- Significant increase in organization's funding that diverts the client's attention
- Lack of external support for changes
- Unfavorable political climate

Internal barriers: Projects are less likely to be successful or lead to improved long-term performance if there is:

- Resistance from staff
- Resistance from board
- Internal conflicts about changes
- Change in leadership

- Lack of experience leading improvement effort
- Proposed work no longer needed/desired
- Lack of financial resources to purchase equipment
- Lack of financial resources to hire staff
- Insufficient time for management and staff to address issues adequately
- Insufficient time from the consultant
- Ineffective consulting

Even if a project is successful at completing its goals, a number of factors can interfere with the organization's ability to fully implement improvements.

> **Barriers to further progress:** Projects are less likely to lead to improved long-term performance if:

- Lack of financial resources
- Organization as a whole doesn't value improvement efforts
- Leaders don't recognize the need for further change
- Leaders are unwilling to confront important issues
- Leaders are ineffective at leading organization change and/or building internal support
- Leaders are unwilling to change their own practices

Consultant Knowledge, Skills, Experience, and Compatibility

In addition to the consultant's approach to client work, the success of a project and long-term improvement are affected by the consultants overall knowledge and experience, and may be affected by ethnic and language compatibility with the client.

> **Consultant experience:** Projects are more likely to be successful and lead to improved long-term performance if the consultant has:

- At least five years of experience with CRE
- A high level of expertise in change management
- A high level of expertise in the subject area of the project
- Advanced training in management topics

Consultant knowledge and skills: Projects are more likely to be successful and lead to improved long-term performance if the consultant:

- Brings knowledge about management and organizational issues
- Uses knowledge of local conditions and key players
- Suggests helpful program ideas and/or organizational strategies
- Brings clarity to a complex situation
- Helps the client see the big picture

Consultant compatibility: Projects are more likely to be successful if the consultant:

- Belongs to the same ethnic group as the client
- Speaks the language preferred by the client
- Is not significantly younger than the client

Consulting Impact Model

Summary of Key Constructs and Indicators

Prior to the Project

Organization Context and Performance

(same as in Nonprofit Performance Model)

External Conditions that Impact Nonprofit Success

- Change in funder priorities
- Change in political climate
- Reductions in funding due to governmental fiscal constraints
- Change in economy
- Change in demographics of clients
- Change in client needs
- Change in funder reporting requirements
- Delays in collecting payments on government or other contracts
- Competition from other agencies

Presenting Issue

- Fundraising
- Board development
- Planning (mission, strategy, or program)
- Evaluation
- Human resources, including search for new staff
- Financial management
- Public relations, marketing
- Internal relationship, conflicts, team building
- Organization design, restructuring
- Technology

Motivation for Project

- Response to internal problems or crisis

- Response to external conditions
- Response to funder's suggestion
- Desire to make organizational improvements
- Desire to follow good practices
- Project is critical to organization's success
- Additional work is needed to meet goals
- Funder requirement

Client Relationship

- Reason for selecting CRE
- Worked with CRE in the past
- Worked with consultant in the past
- Length of relationship with CRE
- Number of CRE projects in past five years

Client Commitment, Leadership

- Client agrees with issues to address
- Client agrees with design of project work plan
- Importance of board, executive director, management team, or staff to the success of this project
- Key players from board, executive director, management team, or staff are supportive of the project
- Key players have a realistic view of what will be required of them to implement this project
- The organization's leaders are capable of successfully implementing this project
- The executive director needs to make changes in his/her leadership
- The board leaders need to make changes in their leadership
- The executive director is candid about his/her own contributions to the organization's problems
- The board leadership is candid about its own contributions to the organization's problems
- The organization needs to make substantial improvements over the long term to reach its goals

- The organization will be able to survive only if substantial improvements are made
- The executive director is committed to pursuing needed improvements over the long term

Racial Match

- Executive director is same ethnic group as consultant
- Client population is same ethnic group as consultant

Following the Project

Project Outcome

- Goals were met; satisfied with impact of project
- Project completion, delay, change in scope

Project Impact

- Which organization capabilities changed? Which changes had the greatest impact?
  Board functioning
  Change in staff members' perspective
  Expanded knowledge and skills
  Improved processes or systems
  Staff functioning
  Improvements to program
  Funding
  Mission
  New or changed plans
  New executive director or manager hired or search initiated
  New administrative positions established
  Merger
  Cutbacks
- Project addressed critical issue
- Project identified other important issues

External Events that Affect Project Success

- Loss of funding
- Significant increase in funding
- Absence of key players (i.e., illness)
- Unfavorable political climate

Internal Events that Affect Project Success

- Support from key organization players
- Leadership support during project
  Willing to confront important issues
  Willing to make project a priority
  Assigned to right person
  Willing to make difficult decisions
- Commitment of executive director to project; active support
- Change in leadership
- Experience leading improvement effort
- Financial resources for equipment/ staff
- Staff time to address issues is adequate
- Consultant time is adequate
- Effective consulting

Consultant / Client Relationship

- Client reaction to consultant—rapport, knowledge, skills, work habits
- Consulting approach
- Language impediment
- Level of client confidentiality
- Degree of client candor
- Client view—prior relationship with CRE
- Consultant view of client relationship

Consulting Time

- Total days; paid days; prior to work plan approval; work plan implementation
- Direct contact with client; prep time; at client site
- Duration of project

Sources of Project Funding

- Level of funder involvement

Consultant Support from CRE Staff, Resources

Consultant Obstacles

- Mismatch of client needs and consultant experience
- Consulting delays
- Lack of expertise in program area
- Limitations imposed by funder
- Insufficient time for assessment
- Insufficient time for coaching client
- Insufficient time for client to use systems, skills
- Insufficient access to CRE staff
- Lack of coordination among CRE consultants

Impediments to Further Improvement

- Lack of financial resources
- Organization doesn't value improvements
- Leaders don't recognize the need for further change
- Leaders unwilling to confront important issues
- Leaders ineffective at leading change
- Leaders unwilling to change own practices
- Lack of consensus among leaders

APPENDIX B

Cited Works and Recommended Readings

Baldridge National Quality Program, Criteria for Performance Excellence, www.quality.hist.gov.

Berger, Renee A. and Liz Vasile, *Strategic Planning: A Review of Grantee Practices* (David & Lucile Packard Foundation, April 2002).

Berman, Paul and Milbrey Wallin McLaughlin, *Federal Programs Supporting Educational Change: Volume 1: A Model of Educational Change* (Rand Corporation. Prepared for the U.S. Office of Education, Department of Health, Education and Welfare R-1589/1-HEW, September 1974).

Bolman, Lee G. and Terence E. Deal, *Reframing Organizations: Artistry, Choice and Leadership* (San Francisco: Jossey-Bass Publishers, 1997).

CSC Index, (1994) State of reengineering report (North America and Europe).

Cameron, Kim S. and Robert E. Quinn, *Diagnosing and Changing Organizational Culture: Based on the Competing Values Framework* (Addison Wesley Series on Organization Development, 1999).

Daft, Richard L., *Organization Theory and Design, 7th edition* (Mason: South-Western College Publishing, 2001).

David and Lucile Packard Foundation, *Lessons Learned from 15+ Years of Grantmaking to Support the Organizational Effectiveness of Grantees* (Adopted from comments made at Pacific Northwest Grantmakers Forum, March 2000).

David and Lucile Packard Foundation, *Organizational Effectiveness and Philanthropy Program Guidelines.*

Edna McConnell Clark Foundation 2001 Annual Report, May 30, 2002.

Edna McConnell Clark Foundation, Due Diligence, http://www.emcf.org/programs/youth/ifb/duediligence.htm.

Edna McConnell Clark Foundation, Mainstreaming Evaluation, http://www.emcf.org/pdf/eval_mainstreamingevaluation.pdf.

Fletcher, Kathleen, *A Study of the Long-Term Effectiveness of Technical Assistance Grants in Fund Raising* (Nonprofit Sector Research Fund Working Paper Series, The Aspen Institute, Spring 1994).

Forbes, Daniel, "Measuring the Unmeasurable: Empirical Studies of Nonprofit Organization Effectiveness from 1977–1997," *Nonprofit & Voluntary Sector Quarterly*, Vol. 27, No. 2, June 1998, pp. 183–202.

Foundation Center, *Foundation Giving Trends: Update on Funding Priorities,* 2003 edition.

Harlem Children's Zone: A Case Study in Learning to Grow with Purpose, www.Bridgespangroup.org.

Herman, Robert D. and David O. Renz, "Nonprofit Organizational Effectiveness: Contrasts Between Especially Effective and Less Effective Organizations," *Nonprofit Management & Leadership*, Vol. 9, No. 1, Fall 1998, pp. 23–38.

Holland, Thomas, "Self-Assessment by Nonprofit Boards," *Nonprofit Management & Leadership*, Vol. 2, No. 1, Fall 1991, pp. 25–35.

Jackson, Douglas and Thomas Holland, "Measuring the Effectiveness of Nonprofit Boards," *Nonprofit and Voluntary Sector Quarterly,* Vol. 27, No. 2, June 1998, pp. 159–182.

Lampkin, Linda and Thomas Pollak, *The New Nonprofit Almanac and Desk Reference* (Washington, DC: The Urban Institute, March 2002).

Lippitt, Gordon L., Petter Langseth and Jack Mossop, *Implementing Organizational Change: A Practical Guide to Managing Change Efforts* (San Francisco: Jossey-Bass Publishing, 1985).

Marble, Melinda, *The Capacity Building Initiative: A Fifth-Year Snapshot*, A report to the Ford Foundation's Peace and Social Justice Program, September 22, 2000.

Nohria, N. and S. Ghoshal, *The Differentiated Network: Organising Multinational Organisations for Value Creation* (San Francisco: Jossey-Bass Publishing, 1997).

Nonprofit Finance Fund, Youth Servers Facility Study, www.nonprofitfinancefund.org.

Nonprofit Finance Fund, Building for the Future℠, Review of Program Effectiveness, January 2000–June 2002.

Nutt, P.C., "Selecting Tactics to Implement Strategic Plans," *Strategic Management Journal*, Vol. 10, 1989, pp.145–161.

Pettigrew, Andrew, T.J.S. Brignall, Janet Harvey, and David Webb, *The Determinants of Organizational Performance: A Review of the Literature* (Coventry: Warwick Business School, March 1999).

Philadelphia Cultural Management Initiative, Guideline revisions for 2002, www.artshelp.org.

Philadelphia Cultural Management Initiative, Program Guidelines 2001–2002, www.artshelp.org.

Phillips, Jack, *The Consultant's Scorecard: Tracking Results and Bottom-Line Impact of Consulting Projects* (New York: McGraw-Hill, 1999).

Quinn, Robert E., *Beyond Rational Management: Mastering the Paradoxes and Competing Demands of High Performance* (San Francisco: Jossey-Bass Publishing, 1988).

Rossi, Peter H., Howard E. Freeman, and Mark W. Lipsey, *Evaluation, A Systematic Approach, Sixth Edition* (Thousand Oaks: Sage Publications, 1999).

Salamon, Lester M., *America's Nonprofit Sector: A Primer, 2nd Edition* (New York: The Foundation Center, 1999).

Schaffer, Robert H., *High Impact Consulting: How Clients and Consultants Can Leverage Rapid Results into Long-Term Gains* (San Francisco: Jossey-Bass Publishers, 1997).

Stone, Melissa, Barbara Bigelow, and William Crittenden, "Research on Strategic Management in Nonprofit Organizations: Synthesis, Analysis and Future Directions," *Administration & Society*, Vol. 31, No. 3, July 1999, pp. 378–425.

Technical Assistance & Progressive Organizations for Social Change in Communities of Color, A report to the Saguaro Grantmaking Board (New York: The Funding Exchange, 1999).

Wahl, E., M. Cahill, and N. Fruchter, *Building Capacity: A Review of Technical Assistance Strategies* (New York: Institute for Education and Social Policy, New York University, 1988).

Walker, Gary and Jean Baldwin Grossman, *Philanthropy and Outcomes: Dilemmas in the Quest for Accountability* (New York: Public/Private Ventures, April 1999).

Weick, Karl E., "Drop Your Tools: An Allegory for Organizational Studies," *Administrative Service Quarterly,* Vol. 41, June 1996, pp. 301–313.

Weisbord, Marvin R., "Towards a New Practice Theory of OD: Notes on Snapshooting and Moviemaking," *Research in Organization Change and Development*, Vol. 12, 1988, pp. 59–96.

Selected Readings on Consulting

Block, Peter, *Flawless Consulting: A Guide to Getting Your Expertise Used* (San Francisco: Jossey-Bass Publishers, 1981).

Kibbe, Barbara and Fred Setterberg, *Succeeding with Consultants: Self Assessment for the Changing Nonprofit* (NY: Foundation Center,1992).

Lukas, Carol, *Consulting with Nonprofits: A Practitioner's Guide* (Saint Paul: Amherst H. Wilder Foundation, 1998).

Schaffer, Robert H., *High Impact Consulting: How Clients and Consultants Can Leverage Rapid Results into Long-Term Gains* (San Francisco: Jossey-Bass Publishers, 1997).

Schaffer, Robert H., "Where Consulting Goes Awry," *Across the Board*, October 1997, pp. 31–35.

Schein, Edgar H., *Process Consultation Volume II: Lessons for Managers and Consultants* (Reading: Addison-Wesley Publishing Company, 1987).

Schein, Edgar H., *Process Consultation Revisited: Building the Helping Relationship* (Reading: Addison-Wesley Publishing Company, 1999).

Selected Readings on Capacity Building

Blair, Jill, Steven LaFrance, Melinda Moore, and Fay Twersky, *Organizational Capacity Grants Initiative Year 2 Evaluation Report* (BTW Consultants, Inc., 2000).

Castle, Mary Ann, Lorinda R. Arella, Joanna Stuart, and Ellen Schnepel, *The Capacity Project, Final Report* (U.S. Department of Health and Human Services, Office of Minority Health, October 2002).

Culver, D. M. and L. G. Pathy, *The Study for Charitable Excellence: A Status Report on Capacity Building* (Montreal: Foundation for Charitable Excellence, 2000).

De Vita, Carol J., Cory Fleming, and Eric Twombly, *Building Capacity in Nonprofit Organizations* (Washington DC: Urban Institute Press, 2001).

Fletcher, Kathleen, *A Study of the Long-Term Effectiveness of Technical Assistance Grants in Fund Raising* (Nonprofit Sector Research Fund Working Paper Series, The Aspen Institute, Spring 1994).

Galaskiewicz, Joseph and Wolfgang Bielefeld, *Nonprofits in an Age of Uncertainty: A Study of Organizational Change* (New York: Aldine de Gruyter, 1998).

Gulati, Gita and Kathleen Cerveny, *General Operating Support, A View from the Field: Case Studies and Reflections on Nine Grantmaking Programs* (Seattle: Grantmakers in the Arts, November 1999).

Marble, Melinda, Christine Green, and Greg Propper, *The Capacity Building Initiative: A Fifth-Year Snapshot*, Ford Foundation's Peace and Social Justice Program (New York: Ford Foundation, 2000).

Roberts Enterprise Development Fund (REDF), "The box set" complete evaluation study, www.redf.org.

Ryan, William, *When Projects Flounder: Coming to the Rescue When Good Grants Go Astray* (New York: The Ford Foundation, 2002).

Savaya, Riki and Mark Waysman, *Evaluation of the SHATIL Support Project for Nonprofit Organizations*, Center for Evaluation of Human Services (Rishon Lezion, Israel, 1996).

Contact Information

Community Impact Consulting
Rudeen Monte, Director
1-800-352-6286
cic@wenet.net

Community Resource Exchange
Fran Barrett, Executive Director
(212) 894-3394
www.crenyc.org

David and Lucile Packard Foundation
(650) 948-7658
www.packfound.org

Edna McConnell Clark Foundation
Michael Bailin, President
Nancy Roob, Vice President Youth Development/Institution & Field Building
(212) 551-9100
www.emcf.org

Ford Foundation
Alan Jenkins, Director, Peace and Social Justice Program
(212) 573-5000
www.fordfound.org

Management Assistance Group
Susan Gross, Executive Director
(202) 659-1963
www.managementassistance.org

National Arts Strategies
Russell Willis Taylor, President
(410) 223-1900
www.artstrategies.org

New Israel Fund
Dorit Karlim, Associate Director
Rachel Liel, Director Shatil, New Israel Fund
www.nif.org.il

New York Foundation
Madeline Lee, Executive Director
(212) 594-8009
www.nyf.org

Nonprofit Finance Fund
Clara Miller, President
(212) 868-6710
www.nonprofitfinancefund.org

The Pew Charitable Trusts
Barbara Lippman, Program Associate
(215) 575-9050
www.pewtrusts.com

Philadelphia Cultural Management Initiative
Martin Cohen, Director
(215) 496-9596
www.artshelp.org

ABOUT THE AUTHOR

Dr. Blumenthal's work in the nonprofit sector has included research, teaching, and consulting. She has a Ph.D. in Management from the University of Michigan and has been a Visiting Lecturer at Princeton University since 1999, teaching management of government and nonprofit organizations at the Woodrow Wilson School of Public and International Affairs.

She has advised a number of foundations on the design and implementation of capacity building programs, and has recently worked with Community Resource Exchange in New York City to design an evaluation of its own capacity building work with grantees. Currently, she is conducting research on consulting and delivering workshops for nonprofit consultants designed to help them improve their effectiveness at capacity building. A related article, "Improving the Impact of Nonprofit Consulting," appeared in the *Journal for Nonprofit Management,* Volume 5, Number 1, in the Summer of 2001.

Dr. Blumenthal is an independent management consultant with extensive domestic and international experience in the commercial sector as well, having worked on large-scale change programs at global firms such as Royal Dutch Shell, Ameritech, Moore Corporation, DaimlerChrysler, and Cap Gemini. Leadership development has been central to many consulting projects, often using an action learning workshop format to help senior executives develop their leadership capabilities. In addition, Dr. Blumenthal has conducted research on mergers and acquisitions and worked with clients on merger implementation.

INDEX